Essays and Studies 2021

Series Editor: Ceri Sullivan

The English Association

The English Association is a membership body for individuals and organisations passionate about the English language and its literatures. Our membership includes teachers, students, authors, and readers, and is made up of people and institutions from around the world.

Our aim is to further the knowledge, understanding and enjoyment of English studies, and to foster good practice in their teaching and learning at all levels, by

- encouraging the study of English language and literature in the community at large
- working toward a fuller recognition of English as core to education
- fostering discussion about methods of teaching English at all levels
- supporting conferences, lectures, and publications
- responding to national consultations and policy decisions about the subject

More information about the Association is on our website: http://bit.ly/join-the-EA

Publications

The Year's Work in English Studies – published annually, *The Year's Work in English Studies* is a qualitative narrative bibliographical review of scholarly work that year about the English language or literatures in English, from Old English to contemporary criticism.

The Year's Work in Critical and Cultural Theory – a companion volume in the field of critical and cultural theory, recording significant debates in a broad field of research in the humanities and social sciences.

Essays and Studies – published since 1910, *Essays and Studies* is an annual collection of essays on topical issues in English, edited by a different distinguished academic each year. The volumes cover a range of subjects and authors, from medieval to modern.

English – published quarterly, *English* is a forum for people who think hard and passionately about literature and who want to communicate those thoughts to a wide audience. It includes scholarly essays and reviews on all periods of literary history, and new work by contemporary poets.

English 4 to 11 – published three times a year, this magazine contains material produced by, and for, the classroom leader. It is a reader-friendly magazine, backed by sound pedagogy, offering ideas for developing classroom practice.

The Use of English – published three times per year, this journal's articles and reviews are designed to encourage teachers to further their own interest and expertise in the subject.

Newsletter – produced three times per year, the Newsletter contains topical articles, news items, and interviews about English studies, and updates about The English Association's activities.

Benefits of Membership

Unity and voice – members join others with a wealth of experience, knowledge, and passion for English, to foster the discussion of teaching methods and respond to national issues.

Resources – members can access high quality resources on the Association's website, and in its volumes, journals, magazines, and newsletters.

Networking – members can network with colleagues and leading practitioners, including joining national special interest groups and their local Regional Group. Members also are given reduced rates for the Association's conferences and other events.

Essays and Studies 2021

The Literature of Hell

Edited by
Margaret Kean

for the English Association

D. S. BREWER

ESSAYS AND STUDIES 2021
IS VOLUME SEVENTY-FOUR IN THE NEW SERIES
OF ESSAYS AND STUDIES COLLECTED ON BEHALF OF
THE ENGLISH ASSOCIATION
ISSN 0071-1357

First published 2021
D. S. Brewer, Cambridge

D. S. Brewer is an imprint of Boydell & Brewer Ltd
PO Box 9, Woodbridge, Suffolk IP12 3DF, UK
and of Boydell & Brewer Inc.
668 Mt Hope Avenue, Rochester, NY 14620–2731, USA
website: www.boydellandbrewer.com

ISBN 978-1-84384-609-3

A CIP catalogue record for this book is available
from the British Library

The publisher has no responsibility for the continued existence or accuracy of URLs
for external or third-party internet websites referred to in this book, and does not
guarantee that any content on such websites is, or will remain, accurate or appropriate

This publication is printed on acid-free paper

Printed and bound in Great Britain by TJ Books Limited, Padstow, Cornwall

Contents

Part III   Mind the Gap: Telling the Tale

Illustrations

The editor, contributors and publisher are grateful to all the institutions and persons listed for permission to reproduce the materials in which they hold copyright. Every effort has been made to trace the copyright holders; apologies are offered for any omission, and the publisher will be pleased to add any necessary acknowledgement in subsequent editions.

Acknowledgements

The editor would like to thank the contributors for their resilience and good cheer across 2020, and the general editor for her remarkable forbearance and support in what was a difficult year for all. Thanks also to Daniel Carey, Gareth Evans, Maoliosa Kelly and Noël Sugimura for their kind assistance, and to George Manning for his help with the copy-editing.

Notes on Contributors and Interviewees

David Almond is a contemporary children's author. His novel *Skellig* was the Whitbread Children's Book of the Year and winner of the Carnegie Medal in 1998. In 2010 he received the Hans Christian Anderson Award. His reworking of the Orpheus myth as *A Song for Ella Grey* was published in 2014 and won the Guardian Children's Fiction Award, 2015.

Helen Appleton is an Associate Member of the Faculty of English, University of Oxford. She works on early medieval English literature, especially the relationships between Christianity, culture, and the land. Recent publications include pieces on architectural imagery in Middle English and Latin lyric, on boundary marking in *Beowulf,* and on the northern world of the Anglo-Saxon *mappa mundi (Anglo-Saxon England 47,* 2018). She is the co-editor, with Louise Nelstrop, of *Art and Mysticism: Interfaces in the Medieval and Modern Periods* (London, 2018).

Jeya Ayadurai is a historian by training and the Managing Director of *Journeys Pte Ltd,* Singapore. His company runs a number of major heritage sites in Singapore, including the Changi War Museum. 'Hell's Museum' at Haw Par Villa is his latest venture.

Lisa Dwan is an Irish-born actor who has won international acclaim for her dramatisation of Samuel Beckett's late works. She first performed *Not I* in 2005. In 2013, she produced and began a lengthy tour of her greatly admired solo show, *The Beckett Trilogy* (consisting of *Not I; Footfalls;* and *Rockaby). No's Knife,* Dwan's own selection and adaptation for the stage of Beckett's prose fragments, *Texts for Nothing,* premiered at the Old Vic in London in 2016.

Rachel Falconer is Professor of Modern English Literature at the University of Lausanne. Her publications include *Orpheus Dis(re)membered: Milton and the Myth of the Poet-Hero* (London, 1996), *Hell in Contemporary Literature* (Edinburgh, 2005), and *The Crossover Novel: Contemporary Children's Fiction and Its Adult Readership* (Abingdon & New York, 2009). She is currently working on a book entitled *Seamus Heaney, Virgil and the Good of Poetry* (Edinburgh, forthcoming).

Charlotte Jones is a Leverhulme Early Career Fellow at Queen Mary, University of London, and the author of *Realism, Form, and Representation in the Edwardian Novel* (Oxford, 2021). She has published on modernism and neo-Hegelian philosophy, realist visual cultures in mid-nineteenth century Europe, biopolitics, and the *Bildungsroman*. Her current research project relates to anarchist politics and the modern novel.

Margaret Kean is the Dame Helen Gardner Fellow and Tutor in English at St Hilda's College, University of Oxford. She has published on the works of John Milton, including *John Milton's "Paradise Lost: a sourcebook"* (London, 2005), and on early modern theatre. Her research interests include literary journeys to hell and the reception of the epic. She is the author of *Philip Pullman: Writers and their Works* (Liverpool, 2022).

Jonathan R. Olson is Associate Professor of English at Grand Canyon University. He was a Leverhulme Early Career Fellow at the University of Liverpool and held a Mellon Visiting Research Fellowship at the University of Warwick's Centre for the Study of the Renaissance and at the Newberry Library. His research focuses on early modern English literature, book history, and cinema, and he has held bibliographical fellowships at the Beinecke, Clark, Houghton, and Huntington libraries. He co-edited, with Angelica Duran and Islam Issa, *Milton in Translation* (Oxford, 2017), and contributed to *Global Milton and Visual Art* (Lanham, 2021).

Laura Seymour is a Lecturer in Seventeenth-Century Literature at Birkbeck College, University of London, and holds a stipendiary lectureship in English at St Anne's College, University of Oxford. She specialises in disability, cognition, and performance in early modern literature. She has published articles and book chapters on Shakespeare and cognition, Andrew Marvell, and hell in Renaissance plays. Her book, *Refusing to Behave in Early Modern Literature* (Edinburgh, 2022), examines refusals to behave according to social norms in early modern English and Spanish literature. Her current research project analyses representations of neurodiversity in early modern Scottish and English texts.

Hannah Silverblank is a Visiting Assistant Professor in the Department of Classics at Haverford College, where she teaches courses in Greek, Latin, Comparative Literature, and Religion. She is interested in nonhuman sociologies and the power-sensitivity of linguistic and conceptual categories. Her most recent research focuses on occulture, disability studies, and classical reception. She has recently published, in collaboration with Marchella Ward, 'Why does Classical Reception need Disability Studies?' (*Classical Receptions Journal*, 12, 2020).

Introduction

MARGARET KEAN

All you who enter here, abandon hope![1]

The literature of hell is certainly voluminous. Narratives of a descent into the underworld, of the sights to be seen there, and the punishments meted out, have always had a strong hold on the creative imagination. Hell has appeared over millennia in the stories mankind tells. It functions as a religious belief, as a disciplinary threat to enforce social conformity, as a metaphor for man's inhumanity to man, as a barbed satiric riposte, and as a source of entertainment, whether to produce thrills and spills or ludic transgressions.

In religious terms, hell can be identified as the supreme place of retribution for wrongdoing, where the judgement imposed on deceased individuals by a superior authority is unalterable. In both the Christian and Islamic traditions, the torments in hell will endure for all eternity. This is the place to send enemies: those who oppress the faithful or the vulnerable, those who cold-heartedly exploit people or natural resources for their own material gain, those identified as the accurst. Yet universal agreement is not to be found on what constitutes either an afterlife or a hell. The Hebrew Bible gives little detail of an afterworld, for instance, and Buddhist thought makes the punishments in hell purgative, part of Samsara (the cycle of death and rebirth).[2]

There is no one vision of hell and no single thread of representation. The fundamental motifs for a journey made by a living being to the land of the dead and for a post-mortem judgement day (a river crossing, or the image of a precariously narrow bridge which spans the divide between the worlds of the living and the dead, the scales of justice where the merit of an individual's life will be weighed, a lake of fire) come to us from the ancient religions and myths of Mesopotamia and Persia. These ideas are passed forward through a number of routes (for instance, through trade

---

[1]   Dante Alighieri and Alastair Gray, *Hell. Dante's Divine Trilogy, Part I: Decorated & Englished in Prosaic Verse by Alastair Gray* (Edinburgh, 2018), p. 12.
[2]   Alan E. Bernstein, *The Formation of Hell: Death and Retribution in the Ancient and Early Christian Worlds* (Ithaca, 2017), pp. 3–18, 131–202.

or imperial expansion or by means of pedagogical systems), but retain their
valency due to the powerful nature of the imagined geography and its focal-
ised markers. Such stories embed deeply in cultural memory because their
speculative qualities are opened out by means of recognisable spatial and
temporal features: the gateway to hell can be discovered in the landscape
as a cave mouth at the far end of a peninsula in Greece, or in the sterile
environs of a volcanic region, or at a barred tunnel mouth in the centre
of Newcastle.[3] Doctrinal and ideological hegemonies (such as a foundation myth for imperial Rome, or the eschatology endorsed by medieval
Catholicism) influence how such stories are interpreted, but hell is hard to
control. This is because it has always been a shared narrative world. Thus,
for instance, the explosion of medieval first-person accounts of the vision
of hell seem to the modern reader to be early examples of fan fiction just as
much as they are acts of medieval piety.[4] Later renderings of a story from
hell compete for priority simply by their act of telling, their occupancy
of the immediate moment, and the direct attention of a living audience.
Acoustic interference occurs at each telling, and this means that even a
dominant imaginary function can be contravened or made obsolete.

   Despite the plurality of approaches, descriptions of hell are consistent
in wanting to allow the reader to experience the immediacy of the state of
hell, whilst also taking time to reflect on its meaning and its aesthetic structures. The inhabitants of hell no longer have any opportunity to change
their outcomes, but the living can still alter their own behaviours. The *katabatic* descent, where the journey down presumes the possibility of return,
is often presented as a trajectory by which a hero will be given knowledge
to take back to his own life. The reading experience, however, suggests that
it is the testing nature of the journey through hell, not any one encounter
or moment of prophecy, which is important. For instance, while reading
Dante's *Inferno*, the reader cannot see the whole pattern mapped out in
detail, all at once (by contrast, say, to the viewer of Michelangelo's *Last
Judgement*). Instead, she joins the pilgrim to venture, step-by-step, from
one encounter with hell's inhabitants to the next, until the gravitational

[3]   A sea cave near Taenarum on the Mani Peninsula of Greece is said to have
been where Hercules entered Hades and vanquished its monstrous gatekeeper,
Cerberus. Lake Avernus, from where Aeneas is said to have accessed the underworld in Virgil's *Aeneid,* is a volcanic crater. David Almond locates Hades at the
dark mouth of a culvert in post-industrial Newcastle in his novel *A Song for Ella
Grey* (London, 2014).
[4]   Eileen Gardiner, *Medieval Visions of Heaven and Hell: a Sourcebook* (New York,
1993).

pull reverses, and the slow descent into the dismal reaches of icy Cocytus becomes the climb which leads up to the light of the stars in a Southern hemisphere. The pilgrim has come to recognise what sin is, and to reject it, through an unfolding process of measured steps.

Hell as a zone of being which necessarily lies beyond mortal knowledge is best understood sensibly: its afterlife torments must be made to feel real to the living audience, especially if the intention is to warn against actions in this life which would result in the auditor's soul being consigned to hell for all eternity. It is easy to fixate on the physical (and imaginative) cruelty of a system which imposes such penalties on others. However, this is to ignore the psychology of sin. In the case of Dante's *contrapasso* (where souls suffer punishments which either fit, or are opposite to, their crimes), the penalty imposed is to be understood both as a reprisal for past actions and as a delineation of the psychic state of existence caused by those actions. The physical contortions of the damned in Dante reflect their mental distortions, as the wilful impenitents experience what it is to remain in sin and to know the wretchedness of enduring an eternity of self-willed alienation from their Creator. Hell is then best understood in religious terms both as a place of physical sufferance and as a separation from God. This allows for better comprehension of the two distinct types of pain associated with damnation: *poena damni* (the pain of loss or self-alienation) and *poena sensus* (torments of sense). John Donne movingly articulates the pain of loss, which weighs on the damned no less than their sensible pains of torture, in a sermon preached before the Earl of Carlisle on Mark 16:16, 'He that believeth not, shall be damned':

> ... when we shall have given to those words, by which hell is expressed in the Scriptures, the heaviest significations, that either the nature of those words can admit, or as they are types and representations of hell, as *fire*, and *brimstone*, and *weeping*, and *gnashing*, and *darknesse*, and the *worme*, [...] when all is done, the hell of hels, the torment of torments is the everlasting absence of God, and the everlasting impossibility of returning to his presence; *Horrendum est*, sayes the Apostle, It is a fearefull thing, to fall into the hands of the living God; but to fall out of the hands of the living God, is a horror beyond our expression, beyond our imagination. [...] That that God should loose and frustrate all his owne purposes and practises upon me, and leave me, and cast me away, as though I had cost him nothing, that this God at last, should let this soule goe away, as a smoake, as a vapour, as a bubble, and that then this soule cannot be a smoake, nor a vapour, nor a bubble, but must lie in darknesse, as long as the Lord of light is light it selfe, and never a sparke of that light reach to my soule; What Tophet is not Paradise, what Brimstone is not Amber,

what gnashing is not a comfort, what gnawing of the worme is not a tick-
ling, what torment is not a marriage bed to this damnation, to be secluded
eternally, eternally, eternally from the sight of God?[5]

The darkness suffered by the damned soul is both physical and metaphysical, and the terror which is here expressed in terms of eternal self-
isolation also shows why so many secular authors have been willing to
repurpose hell motifs in their explorations of the modern psyche.[6]

***

One common point of inquiry for the essays in this new volume has been
to explore how hell makes us feel. The various critical responses reflect contemporary interests in narratology, reception history, performance studies,
cognitive science, and the nature of embodied existence. Cross-period literary analysis has been complemented by the findings of a museum director,
actor, and fiction writer who curate and create hellscapes in the present day.
Their insights reveal remarkable continuities with the scholarly essays, and
hearing from these practitioners sharpens our insights into the rhetorical and
physiological techniques which allow the reader or audience to 'feel' their
way to hell (and back). The volume starts in fear and trembling, with the
eschatological preaching which contains some of the earliest hell texts in the
English language. It ends the story of hell (for now) with young adult fiction,
in which a paean to the natural world and all the beauties of mortal existence
is sung by Orpheus from the depths of Hades.

Part I of the collection explores the mapping of hell onto a lived landscape as a conscious anticipatory interface between this world and the
next. Helen Appleton takes up Old English homilies for Rogationtide, a
period of penitence in preparation for the celebration of the feast of the
Ascension, when the risen Christ returned to heaven to assume his role as

---

[5]   George R. Potter and Evelyn M. Simpson (eds.), *The Sermons of John Donne*, vol.
5 (Berkeley & Los Angeles, 1959), pp. 265–7. Tophet or Topheth, in the Valley of
Hinnon, is said to be where Canaanite idolaters burnt their children alive as a sacrifice
to their god Moloch.

[6]   David L. Pike, *Passage Through Hell: Modernist Descents, Medieval Underworlds*
(Ithaca, 1997) offers particular insight into how modernism figured hell; Rachel
Falconer focusses on the latter half of the twentieth century in *Hell in Contemporary
Literature: Western Descent Narratives since 1945* (Edinburgh, 2005) and her work is
particularly significant for the ways in which it relates ideas from psychoanalysis to the
descent narrative; Evans Lansing Smith, *The Myth of the Descent to the Underworld
in Postmodern Literature* (Lewiston, N. Y., 2003) has taken the argument forward to
explore the syncretic approach taken by contemporary authors in their appropriation
of infernal motifs.

Judge at the end of time. These homilies were preached outdoors, during a parish's springtime peregrination across their local landscape. Certain sites were earmarked for stops in the procession, with the preacher exhorting his congregation to appease God's righteous anger against a sinful people. The homilies on these springtime feast days explicitly link good husbandry of crops to the need for immediate moral reform. Fear of the Lord will bring His blessing to the land, and will allow the faithful to avoid the pains of hell at Judgement Day. It is a strong message, embedded in the memory both through vivid imagery and by the localised nature of the event. The abstract eschatological teachings have been brought close to home and provided with markers within the physical landscape that will restimulate the fearful memory and encouragement towards better behaviour whenever parishioners pass that site throughout the year. Turning from rural communities in the eleventh century to the politics of the industrial city, Charlotte Jones alters the standard demarcations for the hellish East End of *fin de siècle* London. She compares the literature about the underground cultural movements which existed there, particularly those demonised by the popular press as anarchist, with the way in which such clubs actually operated and inhabited space. The transient and underground nature of the political clubs left few traces, other than the evidence collated by a hostile press and police force. The anarchists' radical ideology of inclusivity challenged the establishment so deeply that, in this evidence, a condemnatory rhetoric of damnation was used to contain the threat from their revolutionary politics. This framework of containment was taken up in the literature of the period, and Jones's work reveals the social regulation that is embedded within the literary descriptors of infernal spaces and demonic activities found in popular melodramatic plotlines. Part I ends with an interview with Jeya Ayadurai, who has been instrumental in the recent establishment of the world's first Hell's Museum, at Haw Par Villa, a major tourist attraction in Singapore. The best-known attraction at Haw Par Villa is a mid-twentieth-century series of dioramas, which combine eschatological fears with entertainment thrills as they take the visitor on a tour of gruesomely graphic depictions of the punishments meted out to wrong-doers by the judges in each of the Ten Buddhist Courts of Hell. Pinterest and travellers' blogs show widespread curiosity about the horrors to be seen: there is great enthusiasm for the opportunity to take a selfie at the gates of hell, but little engagement with the philosophical thought that underpinned the foundation of the sculpture park. The new Hell's Museum is intended to reframe the visitor's encounter with the dioramas, and offer comparative interpretative information on Buddhist, Daoist, and Confucian philosophical views about the afterlife.

The next part of the volume deals with sensory hells and questions of embodiment. The attenuated substance which is the shade of Tantalus in the afterlife remains subject to instinct and the habitual need of a living body for nourishment, trapped in a never-ending cycle of involuntarily desire in what it knows is a remediless situation. Laura Seymour argues that early modern literary hells regard the 'baneful' taste of the foods offered to the damned as suggestive of what the state of perdition might mean for sensory perception. She shows how the imaginative challenge to conceive of the torments of taste suffered by the damned draws on wider theological and philosophical questions regarding personhood in the afterlife. She then relates the early modern debate over the retention within the soul of sensitive memory to current scientific findings from the study of the interaction between mind and body, in the field of psychophysiology. Seymour identifies fresh imaginative and philosophical qualities in the early modern staging of material hells but it is nonetheless the case that, in this period, hell's inhabitants can be mocked and left to their fate as reprobates. Later attempts by individuals to express their own experience of sensory and psychic disturbance function differently. Memoirs that tackle questions of mental health are particularly likely to apply a narrative of descent in a temporally undefined plane, although if such a frame implies an expected 'return' it must in and of itself prove restrictive and problematic. The surrealist writer and artist Leonora Carrington's attempts to narrate her experiences of psychosis are the subject of Hannah Silverblank's essay. Carrington's incarceration in a mental institution during the 1940s meant that judgements were imposed upon her in a clinical setting. Her private means of resistance was to undertake a mental quest through infernal spaces in search of transformative knowledge. The occult tools which Carrington employs to support this non-formal investigation of her psyche reject the tyrannies of the rational world and its attendants in favour of the therapeutic potential of symbolist and hermetic ordering of thought. Silverblank compares the narrative structure and tone of two very differently constructed prose works by Carrington: an early memoir, *Down Below*, and a late comic novel, *The Hearing Trumpet*, where the 92-year-old toothless and bearded heroine's *katabasis* is a downward tumble into a cauldron of infernal vegetable soup. As the essay explains, Carrington's mapping of traumatic experiences is a form of feminist Surrealism. Finally, the actor, Lisa Dwan, shares her experience of performing Samuel Beckett's mouth-only piece, the tortuous monologue *Not I*. The voice should press in on the audience from across a divide, as a seemingly relentless and unfiltered consciousness. It is a technical challenge like no other: no prompts, no props, no cues. The actor trains to endure real-time physical discomfort within performance: she must cover her skin, be strapped into a harness and hoisted high backstage, so that only her mouth is visible to the audience. Spot-lit on an otherwise blacked-out stage, the mouth will appear to exist unsupported in mid-air and the audience's experience will be that it oscillates. The dark functions as an intensifier of sensory responses, and both actor and audience share in the extended intensity of the piece, and experience how it plays directly on the nerves.

The final part of the volume has the subtitle 'Mind the Gap: Telling the Tale'. It focusses on the use of structural narrative safeguards for the descent into the unknown, and the upheavals which may occur, regardless. The ancient models of *katabasis* and *neykia* (the calling-up of the spirits of the dead) are well established as the two main principles of literary engagement with the afterworld and its inhabitants. These models differentiate the types of boundary markers which may be consciously traversed (as in Virgil, discussed above) or vigilantly respected (as in Homer, when Odysseus pours a libation of blood into a trench and calls the dead to speak to him from the far side of that division). Rachel Falconer examines how Seamus Heaney reconfigures his long-standing interest in *katabasis* to construct a measured response to the shocking acts of atrocity and violence that marked the start of the twenty-first century. His immediate response to the 2001 terrorist attacks in the USA was to translate one of Horace's *Odes*, in which the speaker is shocked at hearing Jupiter, the god of thunder, drive his chariot across what had been a clear sky. This occasional piece is refashioned for inclusion in Heaney's 2006 volume, *District and Circle*, where Heaney also publishes a five-sonnet sequence, 'District and Circle', expanded from two existing sonnets as a response to the bombing of the London Underground in 2005. The convulsions and consequences of contemporary violence are used structurally within Heaney's volume to disrupt the poet's established conceptual frames (extant poems are rewritten, literary echoes are reassessed, Heaney's love of Virgilian and Dantean reflective models is countered by the admission, via his translation of Horace's ode, of the random, destructive energies which shape our lives). The honesty in such recalibration of personal memories and poetic relationships is part of the mature poet's examination of conscience, and it highlights the ethical challenge required to encounter violence without resorting to recrimination or retaliation. The companion essay is from Jonathan Olson, who also explores the threat of arbitrary destructive forces. He begins with Odysseus's *nekyia* (Odyssey XI) but challenges conventional criticism to argue instead that the encounter with the dead should be read as an episode controlled by the wider structural reliances on repetition and cyclical movements that exist within the *Odyssey*. The adventurer Odysseus is less threatened by the shades who rise at his calling than he is by the swelling power of the whirlpool that rises <u>unbidden</u> from the depths. The neutral and neutralising power source that is the whirlpool is capable of pulling human beings out of their element and down into unfathomable dark. Such a spin cycle threatens annihilation to the individual and closure to all narrative impulse for progression. The fight by the living to retain a personal narrative, an evolving literary heritage, and an unfolding storyline finds its nemesis in the overdetermined cyclonic convulsions of a circular motion that does not project forward but instead goes nowhere but down. Olson identifies this as the binary stimulus which produces the literature of hell (the critical tradition's division of the boundary models of *katabasis* and *nekyia* being a minor eddy which has failed to recognise a deeper predatory current), and he follows the lost-without-trace narrative of the whirlpool from Homer to Virgil, on to the 'closure' of the story of Ulysses in Dante's hell, the fiction of Edgar Allan Poe, science fiction, and, finally, the metaphors used in the science of black holes. To conclude the volume, the novelist David Almond discusses both his personal rejection of religious orthodoxies and his long-standing commitment to the Orpheus myth. His young adult novel, *A Song for Ella Grey* (2014), was stimulated by a dream where Almond saw Orpheus 'roaming the Durham coalfields in search of entrance to Hades'.[7] The cadences and locations of Northumberland revitalise the myth, passing the story forward to a new generation who will associate it first with the landscapes of Northern England rather than placing it in a Mediterranean setting ('Orpheus sang and played. Northumberland was Greece').[8] Almond describes his writing process in terms which mirror a *katabatic* undertaking. What matters for Almond is that the song goes forward: in this case, a tale of love, and life, and active resistance to untimely loss that encourages readers to face their future with courage, determination, and a strong belief in this life, if not the next.

Works Cited

Alighieri, Dante, and Alastair Gray, *Hell. Dante's Divine Trilogy, Part I: Decorated & Englished in Prosaic Verse* (Edinburgh, 2018)

Almond, David, *A Song for Ella Grey* (London, 2014)

Almond, David, 'Diary MSS', *Seven Stories Archive, Newcastle*

---

[7]   David Almond, Personal Diary: entry 31 December 2012, *Seven Stories Archive, Newcastle*.

[8]   David Almond, *A Song for Ella Grey* (London, 2014), p. 157.

Bernstein, Alan E., *The Formation of Hell: Death and Retribution Among Christians, Jews, and Muslims in the Early Middle Ages* (Ithaca, 2017)

Clark, Raymond, *Catabasis: Vergil and the Wisdom-Tradition* (Amsterdam, 1979)

Falconer, Rachel, *Hell in Contemporary Literature: Western Descent Narratives since 1945* (Edinburgh, 2005)

Gardiner, Eileen, *Medieval Visions of Heaven and Hell: a Sourcebook* (New York, 1993)

Potter, George R., and Evelyn M.Simpson, eds, *The Sermons of John Donne*, 10 vols (Berkeley & Los Angeles, 1953–62)

Pike, David L., *Passage Through Hell: Modernist Descents, Medieval Underworlds* (Ithaca, 1997)

Smith, Evans Lansing, *The Myth of the Descent to the Underworld in Postmodern Literature* (Lewiston, NY, 2003)

PART I

Cum Timor et Tremore:
Landscapes for Hell

Folk Horror: Hell and the Land in Old English Homilies for Rogationtide

HELEN APPLETON

The threat of Hell, as Old English Rogationtide homilies frequently remind us, is ever-present. But what is Hell like? How does it work? What does it contain? And perhaps most importantly for the Christian creators of these texts, how does one encourage one's audience not to discover the answers to these questions from personal experience? We imagine the centuries from which these homilies date, the tenth to the twelfth, as an 'age of faith'. Yet, while Christianity was undoubtedly deeply woven into the fabric of life and dominated the activities of intellectual and cultural elites from the conversion to the Norman Conquest, what piety actually meant for the general population in this period often surprises a modern audience. Although the lives of 'the common people' are difficult to recover as they left few documentary traces, we can be fairly certain from the works of reformers such as Ælfric of Eynsham that most did not go to church as often as Canon Law suggested they should, nor did they always behave themselves appropriately once they got there.[1] Those tasked with preaching to the laity at the points in the liturgical year when large congregations were guaranteed had to make the most of the opportunity. For a modern English church the popular preaching occasions would be Christmas and Easter, but in the early medieval period peak attendance came at Easter and on the Rogation Days. The predominantly anonymous authors of Old English Rogationtide homilies aim to induce a reverential fear of God in their audiences, with stress placed on the need to appease God's righteous anger through penance. Everything is explained for the unlearned in clear terms and with memorable imagery. Homilists prompt their audiences to imagine the eternal spiritual landscapes of Heaven and Hell as inextricably

---

[1]   In *Lives of the Saints* XIII, lines 75–86, Ælfric complains about noisy drunkards in church. Walter W. Skeat, ed., *Ælfric's Lives of the Saints*, EETS o.s. 76, 82, 2 vols (Oxford, 1881–5), vol. 1, p. 288. For a discussion of when the laity in tenth-century England were ideally supposed to attend church, and when they were realistically expected actually to turn up, see Sarah Hamilton, *Church and People in the Medieval West, 900–1200* (London, 2013), pp. 163–77. On bad behaviour in church, see John Blair, *The Church in Anglo-Saxon Society* (Oxford, 2005), p. 458.

linked to their transient, earthly home; abstract promises of salvation are connected to appealingly concrete rewards. In keeping with the springtime setting of Rogation and its associated processions, preachers exploited the importance of agricultural prosperity to the laity to communicate and embed Christian principles. As the homilist of a late-eleventh-century text from Worcester, found on folios 97*v–102v in MS Oxford, Bodleian Library, Hatton 114, explains, at Rogationtide: 'we sceolon biddan ure eorðlicra wæstma genihtsumnysse and us sylfum gesundfulnysse and þæt gyt mare is ure synna forgyfennesse' ('we should pray for the abundance of our earthy fruits and our own health, and that yet more for the forgiveness of our sins').[2]

This essay focusses on representations of Hell in the surviving corpus of Old English Rogationtide homilies. It first addresses the relationship between piety and agricultural prosperity in early medieval England and offers some background on the nature of Rogation practice in this period. The focus then shifts to the relationship between the physical and metaphysical landscape at Rogationtide. I argue that Rogation practice is presented as a type of Judgement Day to the unlearned audience of these homilies in order to engender a horror of damnation that encourages good behaviour. Rogation is a liturgical event designed to prepare the population for closeness to God at the celebration of the Ascension by cleansing them of their sins, but it also has an obviously agricultural flavour that comes across in these texts, where piety is repeatedly linked to fruitfulness, and sin to crop failure, drought, and disease. Traditionally, Rogation occurs biannually in the liturgical calendar: the *litaniae maiores* and *litaniae minores*. In later medieval calendars, the major litany is 25 April, while the three Rogation Days before the Ascension, always a Monday, Tuesday, and Wednesday, are the minor litanies. In early medieval England this sense of priority was reversed.[3] As Joyce Hill has shown in her study of Rogation in this earlier period, the three days before Ascension are commonly designated *litaniae maiores* in England and were evidently the more important.[4] The date of the Ascension is dictated by Easter, a moveable feast. This means that the three Rogation Days do not take place at a fixed point in the calendar

---

[2]   Joyce Bazire and James E. Cross, eds, *Eleven Old English Rogationtide Homilies* (London, 1989), p. 109 (Homily 8, lines 3–4). All translations are my own, unless otherwise stated. On the manuscript, see N. R. Ker, *Catalogue of Manuscripts Containing Anglo-Saxon* (Oxford, 1957), §331.

[3]   Joyce Hill, 'The *Litaniae maiores* and *minores* in Rome, Francia and Anglo-Saxon England: Terminology, Texts and Traditions', *Early Medieval Europe* 9 (2000), 211–46, p. 224.

[4]   See Hill, '*Litaniae maiores* and *minores*'.

year, but they are always a late spring event in England. As people observed blossoming trees, growing crops, and young livestock, they naturally considered what that year's growing season and subsequent harvest would be like. Rogation's vernal setting therefore provided an ideal opportunity for homilists to remind their audience that the earth's bounty was God's to distribute and would be dependent on the population's piety.

The three Rogation Days, in which outdoor processions were a key feature, probably owe something to the Christianisation of fertility rites, such as the Roman *ambarvalia*. However, the conventional story of Rogation's establishment is that around the year 470, Mamertus, Bishop of Vienne in Gaul, used fasting and penitential processions to deliver the population from earthquakes and fires, thereby popularising the practice.[5] Although Rogation was performed across Christian Europe, it seems to have been more popular, and popular from an earlier point, in England than almost anywhere else. Max Förster highlights that Rogation was not customary in Germany or Italy until about 800 (around the time it was established in Rome), but was already well established in England in the early eighth century.[6] In the account of the conversion in his *Historia Ecclesiastica*, completed in 731, the Northumbrian scholar Bede (672 or 673–735) places a Rogation antiphon into the mouth of St Augustine when he first enters Canterbury. The image is anachronistic but shows Bede expected his audience to recognise the blessing of the land at Rogation as relating to Augustine's claim on a portion of Kent, and by extension the souls of the English, for the church.[7] From later centuries we find numerous references to Rogation as a temporal marker in law codes, legal documents, the *Anglo-Saxon Chronicle*, and scientific texts.[8] Finally, as well as Latin sermons, a large corpus of around twenty-

---

[5]   Rogation extended to the whole of Gaul by the first Council of Orleans in 511; it was introduced in Rome by Pope Leo III, probably in 801. D. de Bruyne, 'L'origine des processions de la Chandeleur et des Rogations à propos d'un sermon inédit', *Revue bénédictine* 34 (1922), 14–26, pp. 17–18.

[6]   Max Förster, *Zur Geschichte des Reliquienkultus in Altengland* (Munich, 1943), pp. 3–4.

[7]   As Bertram Colgrave and Roger Mynors note, the antiphon is from the Gallican liturgy. Rogation was not performed in Rome at this time, so, if the account were correct, Augustine would have brought the antiphon with him from Gaul; however, as Augustine did not pass through Gaul at a time when he could have heard it, it seems probable this detail is later embellishment. Bede, *Bede's Ecclesiastical History of the English People*, ed. and trans. Bertram Colgrave and R. A. B. Mynors (Oxford, 1969), p. 76, n. 1; Ian Wood, 'The Mission of Augustine of Canterbury to the English', *Speculum* 69 (1994), 1–17, pp. 3–4.

[8]   *Dictionary of Old English Web Corpus* [accessed 20 August 2020].

five distinct vernacular homilies for Rogation survives in manuscripts from
both West Saxon and Mercian/Anglian areas that range in date from the tenth
century to the twelfth.[9] This unusually large body of preaching material for a
single liturgical event means that it is possible to gain a clear understanding of
how Rogation was intended to be understood by the laity in tenth-, eleventh-,
and twelfth-century England. Rogationtide is penitential, so, as with Lenten
homilies, Heaven, Hell, and Judgement are frequent topics. But the way in
which these metaphysical subjects are presented by Rogation homilists is dis-
tinctive. At Rogationtide, the fate of an individual's soul is directly related to
their behaviour in the liturgical processions, intimately connecting this world
and the next. Rogation has an evidently transactional tenor, with participants
involved in a quasi-mercantile spiritual economy. Piety is exchanged for reward,
as is stated in Vercelli Homily XII (for Rogation Tuesday): 'Mid þam egesan
we us geceapiað heofenlicu þing' ('with that fear we buy for ourselves heavenly
things').[10] Appropriate, often reverential, fear of God ensures worldly blessings,
the agricultural prosperity for which Rogation also pleads. Rogation homilists
are often evidently pragmatic, using immediate, earthly concerns to appeal to
the laity and encourage behaviours that also bring about spiritual salvation.

Piety and the Land

Rogation homilies are not alone in explicitly connecting the spiritual state of
the population to the fruitfulness of their land. It is a very common trope in
early medieval English literatures. From mankind's first disobedience, sin has
tainted the soil. God punishes Adam for eating the forbidden fruit by stating
'maledicta terra in opere tuo' ('cursed is the earth in thy work', Genesis 3:17),
connecting original sin to a withdrawal of the earth's bounty. The more
grievous the crime, the harsher the land becomes: evil stains and pollutes
the ground. In an evocative mixture of the literal and metaphorical, Cain's
shedding of Abel's blood onto the earth in the act of murder is represented
as an enduring cause of sterility. The Old English poem *Genesis A*, preserved
in the tenth-century MS Oxford, Bodleian Library, Junius 11, depicts God
addressing Cain after Abel's murder:

---

[9]   Ker, *Catalogue*, p. 529; Bazire and Cross, eds, *Eleven Rogationtide Homilies*,
pp. xvii–xx. As some general penitential homilies are attached to Rogation in some
manuscripts, but not in others, the tally is approximate.
[10]   MS Vercelli, Biblioteca Capitolare CXVII, c. 975; Ker *Catalogue*, §394. Donald
Scragg, ed., *The Vercelli Homilies*, EETS o.s. 300 (Oxford, 1992), pp. 229–30, lines
58–9.

Ne seleð þe wæstmas eorðe

wlitige to woruldnytte,   ac heo wældreore swealh
halge of handum þinum;   forþon heo þe hroðra oftihð,
glæmes grene folde.[11]

(The earth does not give fruits to you, fair for your worldly needs, but she swallowed the slaughter-gore, holy from your hands; therefore she withholds comforts from you, the gleam of the green earth.)

Here, murder, as an evil concealed under the soil, has rendered the ground totally barren. The *Prose Solomon and Saturn*, a wisdom text which presents esoteric information drawn from a long tradition of monastic trivia dialogues, also refers to the effects of Abel's murder on the land. It makes clear that the effects of such iniquity are enduring, and that the present population suffers for the sins of its ancestors:

Saga me for hwam stanas ne synt berende.
Ic þe secge, for ðon þe Abeles blod gefeoll ofer stan þa hyne Cham hys
    broðer ofsloh
myd annes esoles cyngbane.[12]

(Say to me why stones are not fruitful – I say to you, because Abel's blood fell over a stone when Cham, his brother, killed him with an ass's jawbone.)

The metaphysical stains of Abel's literal blood persist. However, this same text later offers a solution to this problem, as curses can be lifted:

Saga me for hwilcum þingum þeos eorðe awyrged wære, oððe æft
    gebletsod.
Ic þe secge, þurh Adam heo wæs awirged and þurh Abeles blod and æft
    heo wæs gebletsod þurh Noe and þurh Abraham and þurh fulluhte.[13]

(Say to me for which things this earth was cursed, or afterwards blessed – I say to you, through Adam it was cursed and through Abel's blood, and after it was blessed through Noah and through Abraham and through baptism.)

---

[11] A. N. Doane, ed., *Genesis A: A New Edition* (Madison, 1978), p. 127, lines 1015b–18a.
[12] J. E. Cross and Thomas D. Hill, eds, *The Prose Solomon and Saturn and Adrian and Ritheus* (Toronto, 1982), p. 30, §36.
[13] Cross and Hill, eds, *Prose Solomon and Saturn*, p. 32, §45.

There is sin in the soil, but piety is a way to cleanse the land. Time and again in Old English and Anglo-Latin texts, as in the broader Christian tradition, virtuous individuals such as saints can act to bring creation closer to its prelapsarian state. Ordinary people too can play their part.

The controversial Northumbrian Bishop Wilfrid (c. 633–709 or 710) is said to have ended a famine afflicting the South Saxons by baptising them. The incident is narrated by the scholar Alcuin (c. 735–804) in his poem on York:

> Illius australis studio Saxonia Christum
> credidit et claro perfusa est lumine vitae.
> Nec solum populos animae de morte maligna
> illos antistes doctrinis eruit almis,
> sed nece de praesente simul salvavit eosdem.
> ...
> Ipsa namque die, qua gens susceperat illa
> doctrinis imbuta sacris baptismatis undam,
> descendit pluvia telluribus aura serena,
> et terris rediit specimen viridantibus arvis:
> florigero campi montesque ornantur amictu.
> Frugifer agricolis laetantibus inditur annus ...

> (By his efforts the South Saxons came to believe in Christ and were suffused in the shining light of life. Not only did that bishop by his holy teaching save those people from the hideous death of the soul, but he preserved them too from doom on this earth. ... The very day on which that people, imbued with holy teaching, received the waters of baptism, a breeze settled with a calm shower on the earth, the fields grew green, and beauty returned to the land: the plains and the mountains were arrayed in a flowering mantle. To the farmers' delight the harvest was fruitful ...)[14]

The spiritual and physical salvation of the South Saxons is connected; Wilfrid's actions restore their land from a waste, bring calm after terror, and promise salvation for their souls. What these texts do not make explicit, probably because their audiences did not need to be told, is that the sinful are liable not only to endure starvation and other earthly miseries, but also to suffer the fearful torments of Hell – the hideous death of the soul to which Alcuin alludes. Alcuin and the authors of *Genesis A* and the *Prose Solomon and Saturn* were all writing for an intellectual elite. Yet, the same ideas recur again and again in Old English Rogationtide

---

[14]   Alcuin, *The Bishops, Kings, and Saints of York*, ed. and trans. Peter Godman (Oxford, 1982), pp. 50–1, lines 583–601. Translation by Godman.

homilies, texts which, unusually for this period, were primarily intended for mass consumption. The authors of Rogation homilies, when handling this theme for their audience of the unlearned, tend to be rather more explicit about damnation.

Rogation in Early Medieval England: Form, Function and Crowd Control

Rogation was very much a collective undertaking. The entire population kept a fast and processed on each assigned day from the church to set points in the landscape, where prayers and readings would take place. They then returned again to church. In later centuries these processions became fused with rites to assert boundaries, leading to the custom of 'beating the bounds', but in this period boundary walking was a separate, and more secular, event.[15] At Rogationtide the community ritually traversed the landscape to bless it whilst asking God's forgiveness for their sins, thereby hoping to ensure the health of both their land in the immediate and their souls in the hereafter. The homilies preached on the occasion reveal Rogation practice in the tenth, eleventh, and twelfth centuries, whilst earlier descriptions are to be found in texts such as the acts of the 747 Council of Clofesho and the *Old English Martyrology*.[16] The *Martyrology* describes the events of Rogationtide and its collective nature:

On ðæm ðrym dagum sceolon cuman to Godes cirican ge weras ge wif, ge ealde men ge geonge, ge þeowas ge ðeowenne, to ðingianne to Gode, forðon ðe Cristes blod wæs gelice agoten for eallum monnum. On ðæm þrym dagum Cristne men sceolon alætan heora ða woroldlican weorc on ða þriddan tid dæges, ðæt is on undern, ond forð gongen mid þara haligra reliquium oð ða nigeðan tid, þæt is þonne non. Ða dagas syndon rihtlice to fæstenne, ond þara metta to brucenne ðe menn brucað on ðæt feowertiges nihta fæsten ær eastran. ... Ðas ðry dagas syndon mannes sawle læcedom ond gastlic wyrtdrenc; forðon hi sendon to healdanne mid heortan onbryrd-

[15]   See Blair, *The Church in Anglo-Saxon Society*, pp. 487–8; Helen Gittos, *Liturgy, Architecture, and Sacred Places in Anglo-Saxon England* (Oxford, 2013), pp. 137–8. For a record of perambulations to assert boundaries in this period, see Charter S 1441 dated 896, for an estate in Gloucestershire: P. H. Sawyer, *From Roman Britain to Norman England* (London, 1978), p. 146.

[16]   An entry for Rogation in a martyrology is highly unusual. It is unmatched by any of the narrative martyrologies of the Latin tradition. See Günter Kotzor, 'The Latin Tradition of Martyrologies and the Old English Martyrology', in *Studies in Earlier Old English Prose*, ed. Paul E. Szarmach (Albany, 1986), pp. 301–34 (p. 310).

nesse, þæt is mid wependum gebedum ond mid rumedlicum ælmessum ond fulre blisse ealra mænniscra feonda, forþon ðe God us forgyfeð his erre, gif we ure monnum forgeofað.

(On those three days both men and women shall come to God's church, both old people and the young ones, both male and female servants, to ask favour with God, because Christ's blood was equally shed for all men. On those three days Christians shall leave behind their worldly occupation at the third hour of the day, that is at 'undern', and process with the relics of the saints until the ninth hour, and that is 'non'. Those days are rightly there for fasting and for the use of those foods which are used during the fast of forty days before Easter. ... These three days are the medicine of man's soul and a spiritual portion; they are therefore to be kept with compunction of the heart, that is, with weeping prayers and with generous alms and the complete benevolence of all human enemies, because God will spare us his anger, if we forgive our people.)[17]

The *Martyrology*'s composition remains a topic of discussion, but its most recent editor Christine Rauer argues that it can cautiously be dated c. 800–900. It therefore provides evidence of Rogation practice in the ninth century.[18] References to processions by all of the population, accompanied by the cross, relics, books, and singing also occur in many of the homilies, but the precise details remain obscure. Evidently the processions involved prayers at various stations in the landscape, but the locations of these stations are never mentioned and their dedication appears variable.[19] As the

---

[17]   Christine Rauer, ed. and trans., *The Old English Martyrology* (Cambridge, 2013), pp. 94–7. Translation by Rauer.

[18]   Rauer, *Martyrology*, pp. 2, 3. See also J. E. Cross, 'English Vernacular Saints' Lives before 1000 A.D.', in *Hagiographies: International History of the Latin and Vernacular Literature in the West from Its Origins to 1550*, ed. Guy Philippart (Turnhout, 1996), pp. 413–27, (p. 422).

[19]   As M. Bradford Bedingfield highlights, the ninth-century liturgical material in the Leofric Missal (MS Oxford, Bodleian Library, Bodley 579) specifies the forms for the first day of processions, with rubrics for stations representing St Laurence, St Valentine, the Milvian bridge, the cross, and 'in atrio', but in the late-eleventh-century Portiforium of Wulstan (MS Cambridge, Corpus Christi College 391) all the forms are lumped together under the rubric 'Statio at sancto Vincentium'. M. Bradford Bedingfield, *The Dramatic Liturgy of Anglo-Saxon England* (Woodbridge, 2002), p. 196. See also Nicholas Orchard, ed., *The Leofric Missal*, 2 vols (London, 2002), vol. 2, pp. 191–2; Anselm Hughes, ed., *The Portiforium of Saint Wulstan (Corpus Christi College, Cambridge Ms. 391)*, 2 vols (London, 1958–60), vol. 1, p. 62. The limited nature of references to something as localised as stations in liturgical books is, as Bedingfield notes, to be expected, and it is probable that the stations varied. Goscelin of Saint-Bertin's eleventh-century *Vita Mildrethae* makes reference to a stone visited

processions moved beyond the church and through the countryside, they imparted blessings and prompted the populace to consider how the physical world about them related to the invisible world beyond.

We know that Rogation genuinely was a time of mass church attendance, not only from the large volume of surviving preaching materials, but also from references to the scale of the crowds. Archbishop Wulfstan of York (d. 1023), with characteristic shrewdness, writes that Rogation is an ideal time to remind people about tithes: 'And riht is þæt man þisses mynegige to eastrum, oðre siðe to gangdagum, þriddan siðe to middan sumera þonne bið mæst folces gegaderod' ('And it is right that one remind them of this at Easter, another time at Rogation and a third time at midsummer, when most people are gathered').[20] Further corroboration of Rogation's scale comes from an account of the miraculous visions of Earl Leofric of Mercia (d. 1057). Leofric sees a great multitude of people in a field, who are described as being assembled 'swylce on gangdagan' ('as if on Rogation Days').[21] Leofric's analogy also relates to the setting for Rogation processions, which took place out in the fields, rather than inside the church. A priest at Rogationtide would have to control a large group of unlearned people during a spectacular occasion that ranged across the countryside; there is ample evidence that this often proved quite challenging. The sixteenth chapter in the acts of the 747 Council of Clofesho shows that even in the eighth century Rogation had a reputation for disorder:

Et item quoque secundum morem priorum nostrorum, tres dies ante Ascensionem Domini in cœlos cum jejunio usque ad horam nonam et Missarum celebratione venerantur: non admixtis vanitatibus, uti mos est plurimis, vel negligentibus, vel imperitis, id est, in ludis et equorum cursibus, et epulis majoribus; sed magis, cum timore et tremore, signo passionis Christi nostræque æternæ redemptionis, et reliquiis sanctorum Ejus coram portatis, omnis populus genu flectendo Divinam pro delictis humiliter exorat indulgentiam.[22]

---

by Rogation processions that miraculously preserved the eighth-century abbess's footprints. See D. W. Rollason, ed., *The Mildrith Legend: A Study in Early Medieval Hagiography in England* (Leicester, 1892), pp. 132–3; Hilary Powell, 'Following in the Footsteps of Christ: Text and Context in the Vita Mildrethae', *Medium Aevum* 82 (2013), 23–43.

[20]   Roger Fowler, ed., *Wulfstan's Canons of Edgar* (London, 1972), p. 13.

[21]   A. S. Napier, 'An Old English Vision of Leofric, Earl of Mercia', *Transactions of the Philological Society* 26 (1907–10), 180–8, p. 182 (line 11).

[22]   A. W. Haddan and W. Stubbs, eds, *Councils and Ecclesiastical Documents Relating to Great Britain and Ireland*, 3 vols (Oxford, 1869), vol. 3, p. 368. On the 747 Council of Clofesho and its interest in liturgy, see Catherine Cubitt, *Anglo-Saxon Church Councils c.650–c.850* (London, 1995), pp. 99–152.

(And likewise, according to the custom of our forefathers, we venerate the three days before the Ascension of our Lord into Heaven with a fast until the ninth hour and the celebration of masses: not admixed with vanities, as is the custom with many, either negligent or ignorant, that is, in games and horse races and great feats; but rather, with fear and trembling, and bearing in front the sign of Christ's passion and our eternal redemption and the relics of His saints, the whole people should, on bended knee, humbly pray for divine indulgence for their sins.)

This call to approach Rogation 'cum timore et tremore' was far from the end of such problems. Homilies dating from the tenth century to the twelfth continue to admonish their audiences for the same ills. It is easy to imagine how a late spring spectacle, with everyone processing and singing and relieved from their normal work, could become 'admixtis vanitatibus' as this text complains. Persuading the laity to process penitently and reverently, then stand respectfully at the stations for prayer and gospel readings, was evidently not easy. Fear is a powerful coercive instrument, and some of the more enterprising (or perhaps exasperated) homilists employ the threat of Hell as crowd control.

Anonymous Rogation homilies are often termed 'composite': assembled from a variety of sources into a more or less coherent whole.[23] These sources may be Latin homilies, scripture, apocrypha, or other Old English homilies, such as works by the late-tenth-century reformer Ælfric of Eynsham. Rogation is a period of penance, preparing the population for closeness to God at the Ascension. This creates what Bradford Bedingfield terms 'eschatological expectation', and hence the homilies' emphasis on Judgement, where reformed behaviour leads to Heaven, and Hell is the alternative.[24] Images of Hell are an effective preaching tool because they are both memorable and intelligible – key advantages when addressing a large, unlearned, and potentially distracted audience. For this reason, vivid eschatological apocrypha such as the *Visio Pauli*, which purports to be St Paul's account of the otherworld, frequently provide material for Rogation homilies.[25] These apocrypha were

---

[23]   For a study of this structure in relation to lamp imagery in anonymous rogation homilies, see Hildegard L. C. Tristram, 'Die "Leohtfæt"-Metapher in Den Altenglischen Anonymen Bittagspredigten', *Neuphilologische Mitteilungen* 75 (1974), 229–49; M. R. Godden, 'Old English Composite Homilies from Winchester', *Anglo-Saxon England* 4 (1975), 57–65.

[24]   Bedingfield, *Dramatic Liturgy*, p. 193.

[25]   See Milton McC. Gatch, 'Eschatology in the Anonymous Old English Homilies', *Traditio* 21 (1965), 117–65; Hildegard L. C. Tristram, 'Stock Descriptions of Heaven and Hell in Old English Prose and Poetry', *Neuphilologische Mitteilungen*

disseminated across Europe, but were especially popular in Ireland, from where they were readily transmitted across the Irish Sea. Ideas and images from these scholarly and abstruse texts filtered down to popular English vernacular preaching. As Joyce Bazire and James Cross, amongst others, have shown, Latin antecedents can be found for many of the strange infernal descriptions in Rogation homilies.[26] So prevalent, in fact, are these apocryphal otherworldly visions that in the Rogation texts of his Second Series of *Catholic Homilies* (c. 995), designed to provide a complete cycle of effective and orthodox preaching for the year, Ælfric condemns the *Visio Pauli* as spurious, yet evidently feels obligated to offer accounts of the otherworld visions of St Fursey and the monk Dryhthelm as a relatively similar alternative (Homilies XX and XXI).[27] Hell is compelling, affecting, and expected.

Homilists employ eschatology in general exhortations to right living, but also connect it directly to conduct in the processions. In an anonymous homily for Rogation Wednesday preserved in an early-twelfth-century manuscript (MS Cambridge, Corpus Christi College 303, pp. 223–6), misbehaviour at Rogation is explicitly linked to punishment in Hell.[28] This homilist, who Bazire and Cross describe as showing a 'notable lack of concern for accuracy of information', moves from the story of Elias to a discussion of Rogation via the voice of Christ issuing prohibitions on bad behaviour:[29]

---

79 (1978), 102–13; Charles D. Wright, *The Irish Tradition in Old English Literature* (Cambridge, 1993); Thomas N. Hall, 'Old English Religious Prose: Rhetorics of Salvation and Damnation', in *Readings in Medieval Texts: Interpreting Old and Middle English Literature*, ed. Elaine M. Treharne and David F. Johnson (Oxford, 2005), pp. 136–48; Brandon W. Hawk, *Preaching Apocrypha in Anglo-Saxon England* (Toronto, 2018).

26   See notes to the text in Bazire and Cross, eds, *Eleven Rogationtide Homilies*; Charles D. Wright, 'Old English Homilies and Latin Sources', in *The Old English Homily: Precedent, Practice, and Appropriation*, ed. Aaron J. Kleist (Turnhout, 2007), pp. 15–66.

27   In 2 Corinthians 12, Paul states that he cannot tell what he learnt when caught up in the third heaven. Fursey and Dryhthelm are endorsed by Bede's inclusion of both in his *Historia Ecclesiastica*. Ælfric of Eynsham, *Ælfric's Catholic Homilies: The Second Series*, ed. M. R. Godden, EETS ss. 5 (Oxford, 1979), pp. 190–203; Roberta Bassi, 'The accounts of Fursey and Dryhthelm in Bede's *Historia Ecclesiastica* and the Homilies of Ælfric', in *Art and Mysticism: Interfaces in the Medieval and Modern Periods*, ed. Helen Appleton and Louise Nelstrop (Abingdon, 2018), pp. 221–45.

28   Ker, *Catalogue*, §57.

29   Bazire and Cross, eds, *Eleven Rogationtide Homilies*, p. 57.

Þa com Cristes stefn of hefenum to eorðan and let dynian ofer ealc þæra
manna þe þas þry dagas his fæsten abræc ær þa halgan reliquias eft into þam
temple comon, and on ælc þæra manna þe an fodspor gesceod eode mid þam
halgan reliquium oððe mid linenum hrægle oððe mid wæpne oððe on horse
geride oððe huntian ongunne binnan þysum þreom dagum oððe fram mæsse
gange ær he hæfde hlam genuman æt þæs prestes handum.[30]

(Then came Christ's voice from heaven to earth and resounded over all of the
people who had broken the three days of his fast before the holy relics came
again into the temple, and on each person who went a footstep shod with the
holy relics or with linen garments or with weapons or riding on a horse or
who hunted within these three days or went from mass before he had received
bread from the priest's hands.)

There are initial reminiscences here of the fast of the Ninevites, often connected to Rogation. In this instance, however, by the end of Christ's upbraid-
ing, these are clearly complaints related to contemporary England rather than
Old Testament Mesopotamia. The audience of this homily now knows that
misbehaviour will incur God's wrath, but as this alone may not induce sufficient fear, the homilist encourages proper penance by explaining the consequences of disobedience:

And se man þe nele nu þas þry dagas mid Godes halgan reliquian bærfot
gangan, þurh þa nigon helle he sceal ær domesdæge ealswa feola siðan swa
he her fotspora gesceod eode ofer þæs prestes bebod. And æfre he sceal
steppan on byrnendum næddran and æfre he gemet deofol æfter oðrum
and þeostru æfter þeostrum; forþi þe þær syndon IX hus innan þære helle
and ælc þære huse is anra mile deop and oðre wid, and nis nan man in
bocum swa cræftig þæt mage asecgan hwæt innan þam nigo husum sy
godes oððe winsumes, swa micel swa an fugel mæg mid his læstan fiðere
windes aswingan.[31]

(And the man who will not now process barefoot with God's holy relics
on these three days, he shall go through the nine hells before Doomsday
even as many times as he went with shod footsteps here against the priest's
command. And ever he shall step on fiery serpents and ever he shall meet
with one devil after another and darkness after darkness; because there
are nine houses inside Hell and each of those houses is one mile deep and
another wide, and there is no man so learned in books that he may say what

[30]   Bazire and Cross, eds, *Eleven Rogationtide Homilies*, p. 62 (Homily 4, lines 31–7).
[31]   Bazire and Cross, eds, *Eleven Rogationtide Homilies*, pp. 62–3 (Homily 4, lines
38–45).

there is in those nine houses of the good or the pleasant, so much as a bird
may beat the wind with his littlest feather.)

This is a belt-and-braces approach from a homily composed more for drama
than coherence, but this passage does reveal key aspects of Rogationtide.
Jill Fitzgerald states 'that a quasi-Rogation might also occur within the
vast confines of Hell is crucial; it suggests that one may choose to process
earthly boundaries as a means of penance or otherworldly boundaries as
a form of interim punishment'.[32] While I disagree with Fitzgerald on the
importance of literal estate boundaries to Rogation, her point about the
equation of earthly and metaphysical space here is undoubtedly important.
Unsubtle this homily may be, but it addresses two intersecting aspects of
the use of Hell in Rogationtide homilies that I will now consider: the
overlap between the lived landscape and the metaphysical, and Rogation
as anticipating Doomsday.

The Lived Landscape and the Metaphysical

Hell, and likewise Heaven, are ineffable. We cannot truly know what either
is like whilst we remain in this world. But the problem with ineffability is
that it does not, in and of itself, make for a very effective sermon. It is difficult for a complete mystery to make the audience appropriately frightened.
Something more comprehensible is needed to convey to the laity that they
should make sacrifices in order to end up in one place rather than the other.
The pairing of specific and conceivable descriptive details with a statement
of Hell's inherent indescribability, as in the passage above, is, therefore, a
commonplace in Old English homiletic material. As Charles Wright has
shown, inexpressibility *topoi* are a marker of Irish influence; they characterise the colourful eschatological apocrypha so often drawn on by homilists.[33]
Yet, the image of the little bird's inability to beat the wind appears unique
to Old English Rogation homilies, illustrating how some homilists adapted
their dramatic source material to the specifics of Rogationtide.

A little bird, this time singing, forms part of an inexpressibility *topos* in
another Rogation homily, from folios 97v–102v of MS Bodleian, Hatton 114:

---

[32]   Jill M. Fitzgerald, 'Measuring Hell by Hand: Rogation Rituals in Christ and
Satan', *The Review of English Studies* 68 (2017), 1–22, p. 9.
[33]   Wright, *Irish Tradition*, esp. pp. 145–56.

se witega cwæþ be heofona rice and be hellewite þæt næfre nære gemet on
heofona rices wuldre swa mycel unwynsumnes, on ænigum laðe oððe on
hunger oððe on þurste oððe on cele oððe on hæte oððe on ece oððe on adle
oððe on ænigum laðe gewinne, þæt wære swa mycel swa anes lytles fugeles
sweg; swylce he cwæð, se ylca witega, þæt næfre nære on hellwitum swa mycel
wynsumnes swa anes lytles fugeles sweg.[34]

(the prophet said about the heavenly kingdom and about the torments of
Hell that never in the kingdom of Heaven's glory would be encountered
so much unpleasantness, in any evil, or in hunger, or in thirst, or in cold,
or in heat, or in pain, or in sickness, or in any hateful strife, that were so
great as the song of a little bird: such he said, the same prophet, that there
never were in the torments of Hell so much of pleasantness as the song of
a little bird.)

A variant of the same passage appears in another Rogation homily in a late-
eleventh/early-twelfth-century manuscript (MS Cambridge, Corpus Christi
College 302 (pp. 205–12)).[35] Although the images are clearly related, no
Latin source for these birds has been found.[36] What about them so attracted
the authors of three separate Rogation homilies? Perhaps it is because they
belong to the mundane and familiar. As people processed with relics and
stood in the fields listening to readings and prayers, they would no doubt
have seen and heard little birds. As these birds exemplify, depictions of
nature appear not only in descriptions of the worldly bounty for which the
homilies' audience is thanking God, but also in metaphysical passages. In the
Rogation homily found on pages 223–6 of MS Cambridge, Corpus Christi
College 303, and discussed above on page 23ff, the inexpressible delights of
heaven are 'beohtra beama' ('brighter trees') and 'hwitra blosmena' ('whiter
blossoms'); an idealised vision drawn from the springtime countryside.[37]
Fragments of the audience's world are inserted into visions of Heaven and
Hell, creating tiny anchors of tangibility amongst the abstracts, and the hom-
ilies are the more affecting for it.

[34]   Bazire and Cross, eds, *Eleven Rogationtide Homilies*, p. 113 (Homily 8, lines
125–31).
[35]   Bazire and Cross, eds, *Eleven Rogationtide Homilies*, p. 71 (Homily 5, at lines
44–9). Ker, *Catalogue*, §56.
[36]   Hildegard Tristram and Charles Wright have both pointed to the use of
bird images in inexpressibility *topoi* related to Heaven and Hell in Irish vernacular texts, but they do not parallel these examples very closely. Wright, *Irish
Tradition*, pp. 230–2.
[37]   Bazire and Cross, eds, *Eleven Rogationtide Homilies*, p. 64 (Homily 4, lines
89, 90).

It is not only the landscape of this world that bleeds into images of the next. The population too is in both places: Hell, in Rogation homilies, gets personal and familiar. The homily's nine houses of Hell which the shod must traverse are described later in the text. The specifics of the houses derive from the *Visio Pauli* tradition, but details are introduced which adapt the material to suit Rogation. Echoing the image of the shod man condemned to walk through Hell, familiar figures appear among the damned. As well as the standard negligent priests and adulterers of the *Visio Pauli* tradition, those suffering torment also include corrupt local officials. They occupy the seventh compartment of Hell, 'and ælc þæra manna þe gerefa byð and oðre men repeð and reafeð; ælc byð deofles þegen. On þam fyre hi sceolan besincan upp oð ða eagan' ('and each of those men who are Reeves and reap and plunder other men; each is the devil's thane. In that fire they shall sink up to their eyes').[38] This image of Hell has been tailored to suit its audience; the lists of the damned reflect contemporary society. Connecting Hell, and to some extent Heaven, to the lived experience and the local landscape makes the value of piety clearer to the audience in that it ties tangible earthly things, such as agricultural prosperity, to abstract spiritual concepts that are much more difficult to apprehend. In this way, the agrarian flavour of Rogation proves a useful spiritual aid, embedding lasting principles of Christian behaviour.

Rogationtide as Anticipating Doomsday

Although the lessons of Rogation are designed to stand the population in good stead for the rest of the liturgical year, it is in the immediate moment, the Feast of the Ascension, that their value becomes acute. Ascension, as Johanna Kramer has persuasively highlighted, is characterised by liminality. The population is brought close to God, but does not yet cross into the next world. As Kramer states, when the population celebrates the Ascension: 'they witness both the eternal events of Christ's Ascension and the as-of-yet undecided moment of *their own* ascension and salvation. This means that much is at stake for them in the Ascension. It represents both a risk and an opportunity'.[39] As Bedingfield points out, although Rogation

---

[38]   Bazire and Cross, eds, *Eleven Rogationtide Homilies*, p. 64 (Homily 4, lines 64–8).

[39]   Johanna Kramer, *Between Earth and Heaven: Liminality and the Ascension of Christ in Anglo-Saxon Literature* (Manchester, 2014), p. 10. Kramer's study includes a discussion of Rogation, particularly of Ascension theology in homilies by Bede and Ælfric.

and the Ascension have separate origins, 'by the time of the late Anglo-Saxon church, the relationship between the two has been recognised and enhanced to grant the Rogations an eschatological focus and allow liturgical participants to process to the threshold of Heaven along with Christ at his Ascension'.[40] But on reaching the threshold of Heaven, you reach a point of judgement – will you be admitted or rejected? The Rogation processions thereby become something akin to Doomsday. Like the celebration of the Ascension, Rogation too presents risk; the space that the congregation pass through and the way that they assemble reflect this liminality, poised between Heaven and Hell. While the processions might be spectacular, they are also essentially about reverential fear. Rogation is connected to Judgement, and the population is reminded that God is watching.

A skilfully composed homily, preserved on folios 105v–111r of MS Bodleian, Hatton 114, gradually brings the prospect of eternal punishment in Hell closer to its audience:

> Swylce eac beoð þa synfullan asceadene on þa wynstran healfe þæs Scyppendes. Þær beoð þonne gemette þa woruldstrangan kynegas and caseras and woruldwelige gitseras and unrihthæmede and struderas and werigcwedende and oferdrinceras, and ða æfestegan and ða leasan hi sylfe þær ongytað. Hwæt willað hi þonne cweþan beforan þam reþan Deman þonne hi nabbað naht to syllanne buton heora lichoman and sawle?[41]

> (So also are the sinful separated on the left-hand side of the Creator. There will then be met the powerful, temporal kings, and emperors, and rich misers, and adulterers, and robbers, and swearers, and drunkards, and the envious, and the lying perceive themselves there. What will they then say before the glorious Judge when they have nothing to offer except their body and soul?)

The diminishing scale of the sinners here, moving from people one would never expect to encounter in rural England to near neighbours, draws Hell ever closer to the self. Among the crowds listening to preaching on Rogationtide, one could identify people on the list. As the homilist asks what the sinful will say, the audience internalises the questioning: what will I say? How will I avoid Hell?

Several homilies make references to actions at Rogation being relevant to Doomsday, exploiting the way that Rogation places people on the

---

40   Bedingfield, *Dramatic Liturgy,* pp. 191–3.
41   Bazire and Cross, eds, *Eleven Rogationtide Homilies,* p. 132 (Homily 10, lines 45–51).

border between this world and the next. Homilists emphasise the presence of God in the processions, conceiving of them as a meeting with him, just as Judgement will be. For example, Vercelli Homily XII says:

> Uton bion gemyndige þæt us hafað God gehaten þæt he wile in þære gesamnunge bion þe for his naman sie gesamnod. ... he cwæð: Þær twegen oððe þry bioð gesamnode in minum naman, ic bio symle on hira midlene. We þonne syndon nu gesamnode. We gelyfað in dryhtnes naman. He is us betweonum on andweardnesse.[42]

> (Let us be mindful that God has commanded us that he will be in the assembly that is assembled in his name. ... He says: where two or three are assembled in my name, I am with them in their midst. We are then now assembling. We believe in the Lord's name. He is between us in the present time.)

The emphatic insistence on collective identity and God's presence, 'he is us betweonum', both reassures and terrifies. The audience becomes acutely aware that He, who perceives all, is here now, encouraging them to consider the condition of their souls. The homily (MS Cambridge, Corpus Christi College 303) which describes a little bird's inability to vie with the wind (see page 25ff above) is even more explicit in connecting behaviour during Rogation to God's response at the Last Judgement. In a passage urging good behaviour the homily explains that relics in the processions create a 'gastlice gemotstow' ('spiritual meeting place') around them where disputes with God can be resolved, and states:

> Gyf we þas gastlican domas gelæstað willað, þe Crist sylf on his godspelle beodað on þisse gemotstowe, þonne beoð we beforan cristes heahsetle on þam myclan dome þam soðfæstan Deman gecorene, and we þonne motan gehyran þone cwyde þe he sylf cwæð to þam þe he sette on þa swyðran healfe, 'Cumað, ge gebletsode, to mines Fæder rice þæt eow wæs gegearwod fram middaneardes fruman'.[43]

> (If we will follow those spiritual judgements, which Christ himself in his gospel commands in this meeting place, when we are before Christ's high-seat in the Great Judgement among the truth-fast chosen by the Judge, we may then hear the words that he himself says to those whom he sets on the

---

[42]   Scragg, ed., *Vercelli Homilies*, p. 229, lines 44–50.
[43]   Bazire and Cross, eds, *Eleven Rogationtide Homilies*, pp. 72–3 (Homily 5, lines 123, 130–5).

right half, 'Come, ye blessed, to my Father's kingdom that was prepared for
you from the beginning of the earth'.)

This homily offers a reassuring image of reconciliation with God at Rogation
in anticipation of a similarly positive meeting at Doomsday, but a note of
uncertainty remains: everything is governed by the conditional, 'gyf' ('if').
Another homily of the mid-eleventh-century, found on folios 228r–238r of
MS Cambridge University Library Ii. 4.6, emphasises the need for respectful
behaviour and the hazards of transgression.[44] It reads:

> Hit is swiðe unþæslic and pleolic þæt we on Godes huse idele spellunga and
> hlacerunga began, forði þe hit cymð us to mycelan hearme; buton we ær ges-
> wican ure plega and hleahter byð eall mid wope and wanunge geendod þonne
> we heonon gewitan sculon.[45]

> (It is very unseemly and perilous that we enter into God's house with both
> idle conversation and scoffing, because great harm comes to us from it; unless
> we cease beforehand our play and laughter it will all end in weeping and lam-
> entation when we must depart from here.)

The moment of departure here is both death and the more immediate exit
from the church on the Rogation Day itself. This creates a sense of urgency –
behave now, or it will be too late. Frivolity may be tempting at Rogationtide,
but it leads to the devil, and the devil, the same homily reminds us, 'us ne mæg
nan oþer rice forgyfan buton þæt ylce þæt he him sylf on wunað' ('can offer us
no other kingdom except that which he dwells in himself') wherein we will find
'ecan tintregan on hellewite þe næfre ne ateoriað ne ne ablinnað on ecnysse'
('eternal torments in the punishments of Hell that never exhaust nor cease
in eternity').[46] The echoing use of *ece* and the paired synonyms here, 'ne ateoriað ne ne ablinnað', are classic features of emphatic style in Old English prose
which reinforce for the audience the warning that a moment's foolishness can
have everlasting consequences.

The homilist of a Rogation homily preserved in two early-twelfth-
century manuscripts makes specific reference to the laity on Doomsday
as representative of their own audience.[47] In a highly unusual image, the
homilist states that the good shall present virtues to God according to their

[44]   Ker, *Catalogue*, §21.
[45]   Bazire and Cross, eds, *Eleven Rogationtide Homilies*, p. 96 (Homily 7, lines 73–6).
[46]   Bazire and Cross, eds, *Eleven Rogationtide Homilies*, p. 97 (Homily 7, lines 94–6).
[47]   MS Cambridge, Corpus Christi College 162, on pp. 422–31; and MS Bodleian,
Hatton 116, on pp. 382–95. Ker, *Catalogue*, §38 and §333.

status: martyrs, for example, will offer up their suffering. For the common people: 'Læwede men, þa ðe her on worulde rihtlice heora lif libbað, hi bærað heora ælmysdæda and hluttor lif and clæne on ansyne þæs heahstan Scyppendes; and þonne cwyð se eca Cyning to ðam godum, "Cume ge geb-letsode"' ('unlearned men, those who live their lives rightly here in this world, they bear their almsgiving and pure and clean life into the sight of the highest Creator; and then the eternal King will say to the good, "Come ye blessed"').[48] The audience of the text is momentarily given a hopeful image of their potential future, but not everyone will be counted among the blessed. This joyful depiction of God's words to the righteous is imme-diately followed by what awaits those not called to the right-hand side:

Þonne þa arleasan and þa synfullan hi bærað nearowne wæstm and sceand-fulne on ansyne þæs hehstan Scippendes; þonne cwyð se heofona Cyning, 'Fare ge fram me, awyrgede, on þa ecan susle hellegrundes'. And hi þonne ahwyrfað fram haligra manna dreame and swiðe heofigende hellewitu secað, þær is dead buton life and þystru butan leohte and hreownys butan wæstmum and sar buton frofre and yrmðu butan ende. Þær ne ongyt se fæder þone sunu ne se sunu þone fæder ne wyrðað, ne seo dohtor þa modor ne lufað ne seo modor þære dehter ne miltsað. Ac anra gehwilc hys sylfes yrmða wepað and heofað; forðan ðe hellefyr næfre ne byð adwæsced ac þa dracan and þa wyrmas þæra arleasra manna sawla slitað and hi næfre na beoð sweltende. Þær is eagena wop and toða gristbitung and þær is welera þurst and wita stow.[49]

(Then the disgraced and the sinful bear mean and shameful produce into the sight of the highest Creator; then says the King of Heaven, 'Get you from me, accursed, into the eternal torment of the abyss of Hell'. And they then turn away from the joys of holy people and grieving seek the torments of Hell, there is death without life and darkness without light and repentance without fruit and sorrow without comfort and misery without end. There the father does not recognise the son, nor the son honour the father, nor does the daughter love the mother nor the mother show kindness to the daughter, but each one weeps for their own misery; because the hellfire will never be quenched, but the dragons and the worms rend the disgraced men's souls and they never die. There is weeping of eyes and gnashing of teeth and there is thirst of the lips and a place of torment.)

---

[48]   Bazire and Cross, eds, *Eleven Rogationtide Homilies*, pp. 51–2 (Homily 3, lines 107–9).

[49]   Bazire and Cross, eds, *Eleven Rogationtide Homilies*, p. 52 (Homily 3, lines 110–20).

The use of *wæstm* here in its metaphorical meaning of 'produce' momentarily evokes a more literal image of growth and fruit. This means that those judged are both spiritual and physical farmers, and so recalls Rogation's focus on piety and the land.[50] Hell is imagined in a series of conventional oppositions; abstract, but easily intelligible. The patterned pairs are succeeded by a moving image of familial disintegration, then come commonplace but nonetheless evocative images of worms, dragons, and the gnashing of teeth. This is not an especially original homily, but it effectively informs an unlearned audience of what may await them if their *wæstm* is poor, both literally and metaphorically. As these homilies show, Rogation must be treated with fear and reverence: it is understood as both an immediate and deferred Judgement, with behaviour in Rogation assemblies dictating the fate of the soul in the last great assembly on Doomsday.

Conclusion

It is striking that, although the key focus of Rogationtide is theoretically intercessionary prayer, as reflected in its names (Rogation from Latin *rogare* 'to ask' and *litaniae* from a Greek word meaning 'supplication'), in Old English the usual term is *gangdagas* 'procession days'.[51] The emphasis for the English laity is on actions, on moving through the space. Rogation occurs both inside and outside the church, and so makes the population's land into an extension of ecclesiastical space through the dissemination of blessings. This focus on the spiritual state of the physical land highlights the metaphysical spaces that parallel it, connecting the population more closely to Heaven and Hell than at other points of the year. As the population's souls are cleansed by their penance in preparation for the Ascension, so their land is washed of the sin which has marked it, making the physical world more paradisical than infernal and bringing the hope of a good harvest. The assemblies at Rogation offer an image of Judgement, but with the processions of the (hopefully) pious and fearful following the cross, Rogation Days also reflect the popular narrative of Christ leading the righteous out of Hell and up to Heaven before his

---

[50]   On *wæstm*, see J. Bosworth and T. Northcote Toller, *An Anglo-Saxon Dictionary* (Oxford, 1898), pp. 1158–9.

[51]   Hill, 'Litaniae maiores and minores', pp. 211–12. The term *gebeddagas* ('prayer days') is also used, but with much lower frequency, and principally by Ælfric. See *Dictionary of Old English Corpus*.

resurrection; this is the Harrowing of Hell, an extrabiblical event often connected to the Ascension.[52] As Vercelli Homily XII states, 'Se egesa us gelæded fram helwarum, & he us onfehð to þam uplican rice' ('The fear leads us from the inhabitants of Hell, and it receives us into the sublime kingdom').[53] Appropriate reverence at Rogation will deliver the population from Hell.

Christ's salvation of mankind through his death and the Harrowing of Hell is related to the springtime setting of Rogation; Christ's blessing of the land and his delivery of the population from hunger reflect his greater triumph over death and Hell. The first Rogation homily quoted in this essay (MS Oxford, Bodleian Library, Hatton 114, 97*v-102v) explains that because everything is growing and blossoming it is an appropriate time to honour the Saviour, then connects the agricultural blessings of the procession to the spiritual blessing of Christ's sacrifice:

> We sculon beon Gode lof secgende, and Cristes rodetacen forðberan and his þa halige godspell and oðre halignessa, mid þam we sceolon bletsian ure þa eorðlican speda, þæt synd æceras and wudu and ure ceap and eall þa þing þe us God forgyfen hafað to brucanne þe we bileofian sceolon. Utan we nu symle þang secgan urum Scyppende his miltsa, forðon he us swyðe lufode ofer ealle oðre gesceafta þa ðe nu under heofonas hwolfe syndon. He sylfa us gescop and us geworhte þa we næron, and he us gesohte þa we forwordene wæron, and he us abohte of hellewitum and of deofles anwealde mid his ðy deorwyrðan blode, and us opene gedyde þone weg to heofonanrice.[54]

> (We should be praising God, and bearing forth Christ's cross and his holy gospel and other holy things, and we should bless our earthly successes with them, which are our fields, and woods, and our cattle, and all the things that God has given to us to use, so that we should live. Let us now always give thanks to our Creator for his mercy because he greatly loves us over all other created things which are now under the arc of the heavens. He himself created us and wrought us when we were not, and he sought us when we were become nothing, and he bought us from the torments of Hell and the devil's power with his precious blood, and he opened up for us the way to the heavenly kingdom.)

---

[52]   Kramer, *Between Earth and Heaven*, p. 111. On the Harrowing see Karl Tamburr, *The Harrowing of Hell in Medieval England* (Cambridge, 2007).

[53]   Scragg, ed., *Vercelli Homilies*, p. 230, lines 64–5.

[54]   Bazire and Cross, eds, *Eleven Rogationtide Homilies*, p. 112 (Homily 8, lines 110–20).

Evoking both worldly abundance and Christ's sacrifice for mankind ensures that the audience of this homily is suitably grateful, and that they will approach Rogationtide with the mixture of fear and reverence that it demands.

This world and the next are blurred at Rogationtide, with the hope that like the righteous during the Harrowing, the pious will be led in procession away from Hell. These processions must have been spectacular, but, because they could so easily become frivolous, the laity must be urged, in the strongest possible terms, to treat Rogation with awe. Preachers use vivid images of Judgement, Heaven, and Hell and render these even more intense for their audience through the introduction of familiar figures. The drunkards, liars, and little birds are reference points around which the otherworld can be imagined by a general populace. The audience comes to know how behaviour in this world, in these processions, will dictate the place they occupy in the next. References to agricultural prosperity present more immediate and concrete rewards for good behaviour. This incentivises the people to obey. Through stern admonitions and clear guidance, the large, and largely unlearned, audience of these texts is encouraged to recognise Rogationtide as an echo of the Last Judgement. They have been led out and assembled before God, and if they care for the state of their residence, in this world and the next, they must look to the state of their souls. Will Rogation work? Will the crops be plentiful and Adam's curse mitigated? Or will it be a bad year because the population is sinful? Will God's just anger destroy their crops? They cannot know, any more than they can know where their souls are going – there is only faith and good works. The audience of these Rogationtide homilies has to remain, poised somewhere between Hell and Heaven 'cum timore et tremore', just as the 747 Council of Clofesho demanded that they be.

Works Cited

Ælfric of Eynsham, *Ælfric's Catholic Homilies: The Second Series*, ed. M. R. Godden, Early English Text Society ss. 5 (Oxford, 1979)

Alcuin, *The Bishops, Kings, and Saints of York*, ed. and trans. Peter Godman (Oxford, 1982)

Bassi, Roberta, 'The accounts of Fursey and Dryhthelm in Bede's *Historia Ecclesiastica* and the Homilies of Ælfric', in *Art and Mysticism: Interfaces in the Medieval and Modern Periods*, eds Helen Appleton and Louise Nelstrop (Abingdon, 2018), 221–45

Bazire, Joyce, and James E. Cross, eds, *Eleven Old English Rogationtide Homilies* (London, 1989)

Bede, *Bede's Ecclesiastical History of the English People*, ed. and trans. Bertram Colgrave and R. A. B. Mynors (Oxford, 1969)

Bedingfield, M. Bradford, *The Dramatic Liturgy of Anglo-Saxon England* (Woodbridge, 2002)

Biblia Sacra Iuxta Vulgatam Versionem, 4th edn (Stuttgart, 1994)

Blair, John, *The Church in Anglo-Saxon Society* (Oxford, 2005)

Bosworth, J., and T. Northcote Toller, *An Anglo-Saxon Dictionary* (Oxford, 1898)

Cross, J. E., 'English Vernacular Saints' Lives before 1000 A.D.', in *Hagiographies: International History of the Latin and Vernacular Literature in the West from Its Origins to 1550*, ed. Guy Philippart (Turnhout, 1996), 413–27

Cross, J. E., and Thomas D. Hill, eds, *The Prose Solomon and Saturn and Adrian and Ritheus* (Toronto, 1982)

Cubitt, Catherine, *Anglo-Saxon Church Councils c.650–c.850* (London, 1995)

de Bruyne, D., 'L'origine des processions de la Chandeleur et des Rogations à propos d'un sermon inédit', *Revue bénédictine* 34 (1922), 14–26

Dictionary of Old English Web Corpus, compiled by Antonette diPaolo Healey with John Price Wilkin and Xin Xiang (Toronto, 2009). https://tapor. library.utoronto.ca/doecorpus/index.html [accessed 20 August 2020]

Doane, A. N., ed., *Genesis A: A New Edition* (Madison, 1978)

Fitzgerald, Jill M., 'Measuring Hell by Hand: Rogation Rituals in Christ and Satan', *The Review of English Studies* 68 (2017), 1–22

Förster, Max, *Zur Geschichte des Reliquienkultus in Altengland* (Munich, 1943)

Fowler, Roger, ed., *Wulfstan's Canons of Edgar* (London, 1972)

Gatch, Milton McC., 'Eschatology in the Anonymous Old English Homilies', *Traditio* 21 (1965), 117–65

Gittos, Helen, *Liturgy, Architecture, and Sacred Places in Anglo-Saxon England* (Oxford, 2013)

Godden, M. R., 'Old English Composite Homilies from Winchester', *Anglo-Saxon England* 4 (1975), 57–65

Haddan, A. W., and W. Stubbs, eds, *Councils and Ecclesiastical Documents Relating to Great Britain and Ireland*, 3 vols (Oxford, 1869)

Hall, Thomas N., 'Old English Religious Prose: Rhetorics of Salvation and Damnation', in *Readings in Medieval Texts: Interpreting Old and Middle English Literature*, eds Elaine M. Treharne and David F. Johnson (Oxford, 2005), 136–48

Hamilton, Sarah, *Church and People in the Medieval West, 900–1200* (London, 2013)

Hawk, Brandon W., *Preaching Apocrypha in Anglo-Saxon England* (Toronto,

2018)

Hill, Joyce, 'The *Litaniae maiores* and *minores* in Rome, Francia and Anglo-Saxon England: Terminology, Texts and Traditions', *Early Medieval Europe* 9 (2000), 211–46

Hughes, Anselm, ed., *The Portiforium of Saint Wulstan (Corpus Christi College, Cambridge Ms. 391)*, 2 vols (London, 1958–60)

Ker, N. R., *Catalogue of Manuscripts Containing Anglo-Saxon* (Oxford, 1957)

Kotzor, Günter, 'The Latin Tradition of Martyrologies and the Old English Martyrology', in *Studies in Earlier Old English Prose*, ed. Paul E. Szarmach (Albany, 1986), 301–34

Kramer, Johanna, *Between Earth and Heaven: Liminality and the Ascension of Christ in Anglo-Saxon Literature* (Manchester, 2014)

Napier, A. S., 'An Old English Vision of Leofric, Earl of Mercia', *Transactions of the Philological Society* 26 (1907–10), 180–8

Orchard, Nicholas, ed., *The Leofric Missal*, 2 vols (London, 2002)

Powell, Hilary, 'Following in the Footsteps of Christ: Text and Context in the Vita Mildrethae', *Medium Aevum* 82 (2013), 23–43

Rauer, Christine, ed. and trans., *The Old English Martyrology* (Cambridge, 2013)

Rollason, D. W., ed., *The Mildrith Legend: A Study in Early Medieval Hagiography in England* (Leicester, 1892)

Sawyer, P. H., *From Roman Britain to Norman England* (London, 1978)

Scragg, Donald, ed., *The Vercelli Homilies*, Early English Text Society o.s. 300 (Oxford, 1992)

Skeat, Walter W., ed., *Ælfric's Lives of the Saints*, Early English Text Society o.s. 76, 82, 2 vols (Oxford, 1881–85)

Tamburr, Karl, *The Harrowing of Hell in Medieval England* (Cambridge, 2007)

Tristram, Hildegard L. C., 'Die "Leohtfæt"-Metapher in Den Altenglischen Anonymen Bittagspredigten', *Neuphilologische Mitteilungen* 75 (1974), 229–49

––––, 'Stock Descriptions of Heaven and Hell in Old English Prose and Poetry', *Neuphilologische Mitteilungen* 79 (1978), 102–13

Wood, Ian, 'The Mission of Augustine of Canterbury to the English', *Speculum* 69 (1994), 1–17

Wright, Charles D., 'Old English Homilies and Latin Sources', in *The Old English Homily: Precedent, Practice, and Appropriation*, ed. Aaron J. Kleist (Turnhout, 2007), 15–66

––––, *The Irish Tradition in Old English Literature* (Cambridge, 1993)

Pandæmonium as Parallax: Metropolitan Underworlds and Anarchist Clubs in Nineteenth-Century London and its Literature[1]

CHARLOTTE JONES

Late nineteenth-century London's East End is notorious as a hellhole: an area of industrial furnaces, fumes, abject poverty, and moral degradation. The appalling conditions, and the work of the social reformers, writers, and journalists who sought to uncover the social injustices that caused such squalor, are now so well-known as to have become something of a commonplace in discussions of hell. The Victorian cityscape will however still have more to share with us about the application of infernal metaphors and rhetoric in the late-nineteenth century if we allow that our existing methodologies of literary and cultural recovery themselves require reassessment. Historical change becomes most visible when pre-existing generic structures are critiqued from alternative perspectives, but we tend to keep our inherited property, its sites and motifs, even as we invert its iconography. This essay will trace the rise of self-consciously subterranean political organisations within late-Victorian society and, in so doing, look again at how that society defined itself and how it made political meaning out of hell.

What is an 'underground', and how do you build one? It demands the construction of something more than a venue; it necessitates a whole new conceptual infrastructure. Underground cultural movements arise within particular urban contexts and those contexts also shape them. Critical work in urban studies and geography has demonstrated the importance of understanding cities not as bounded locations but in terms of their interrelations with other places and peoples, as nodes and meeting places within flows and networks.[2] What comes through most strongly in such an analysis is the significance of material urban spaces for these exchanges and

[1]   I would like to thank Scott McCracken for commenting on an early version of this essay, and the Paul Mellon Centre for Studies in British Art for a Research Continuity Fellowship which enabled the completion of this work at a particularly challenging time.
[2]   See, for example, Doreen Massey, *World City* (Cambridge, 2007).

circulations. These were exchanges that quite literally *took place*. Anarchism proposes a different way of inhabiting the world around us. The way anarchists actually lived in nineteenth-century London provides a vital counterpoint to their depiction in fiction of the time, and giving due attention to this representational gap will provide literary criticism with a set of tools to question conventional applications of the rhetoric of damnation. In order to meet the challenge, this essay recovers material contexts of cultural history and uses this approach to inform its analysis of infernal metaphors and rhetoric in late-nineteenth-century popular fiction. The essay tracks the logics that ground hell's operation as a set of literary metaphors for anarchist activities and organisation in the late nineteenth century. It shows how knowledge of the material spaces of anarchist clubs illuminates the struggle to represent a spatial aesthetics of revolution, as well as casting light on the varied subterranean relationships, circulations, and forces that are at work in constituting these urban spaces. It then concludes with some preliminary speculations about the significance of these urban forms and the social-spatial relations that emerge from them.

A 'vigorous search of person and premises'

In the early hours of Sunday, 30 September 1888, the body of Elizabeth ('Long Liz') Stride was discovered by the gates of Dutfield's Yard in Berner Street, Whitechapel. This was the infamous 'double event' when the killer known only as 'Jack the Ripper' struck twice within a matter of hours, first at Berner Street and then, even more brutally, at Mitre Square in the heart of the City of London. Reeling from the ferocity of these attacks, the *Evening Standard* newspaper described the killer as 'a human fiend' with an 'absolutely demonical thirst for blood'.[3] Two weeks later, as though to confirm the hysteria, the chairman of the Whitechapel Vigilance Committee was sent half a preserved human kidney alongside a letter addressed 'From hell'.

If the furnaces, smoke, and dust of industrialisation gave modern life the look of hell, the Whitechapel murders reinforced a public discourse that linked the slums of London to a criminal underworld of poverty, depravity, and the demonic. Hell is a recurrent metaphor in George Gissing's evocations of appalling urban squalor. In the opening paragraph of his first novel *Workers in the Dawn* (1880), the author-narrator bids us, in the guise of Virgil from Dante's *Inferno*: '[w]alk with me, reader, into Whitecross Street',

---

[3]   'Two More Murders in East London', *Evening Standard* (1 October 1888).

through the 'hubbub' and 'reddish light' under a 'yawning archway' towards 'unspeakable abominations'.[4] There is no question of discovering some kind of providential scheme for the masses of urban poor in Gissing's 'city of the damned'.[5] Only a madman could experience an angel visitation here. 'The life you are now leading', the angel announces to Mad Jack in *The Nether World* (1889), 'is that of the damned; this place to which you are confined is Hell! There is no escape for you'.[6] In the naturalist hellscape of Gissing's nether world, Arthur Morrison's Jago, or Jack London's abyss, there is only the atavistic life force of the troglodyte.

This topographical representation of overground space as if it were subterranean was reinforced by a common set of visual co-ordinates in the nineteenth century. In Gustave Doré's illustrations for Blanchard Jerrold's investigative survey *London: A Pilgrimage* (1872), published six years after his *Paradise Lost* and *The Vision of Hell*, the huddled figures in plates depicting the docks and the surrounding brothels, pubs, and opium dens adopt the postures of the damned.[7] William Booth's *In Darkest England and the Way Out* (1890) is typical of sociological accounts in this period, where to venture deeper into the urban environment was to undertake a kind of *katabasis*:

> [t]alk about Dante's Hell, and all the horrors and cruelties of the torture-chamber of the lost! The man who walks with open eyes and with bleeding heart through the shambles of our civilisation needs no such fantastic images of the poet to teach him horror.[8]

Booth ironically reworks the trope of 'Darkest Africa' promulgated by H. M. Stanley's accounts of his African journeys. In the first part, Booth describes the 'submerged tenth' of Darkest England – destitute, and possibly criminal – and then goes on to suggest the way to '[d]eliverance', which includes better housing, education, and training for work, as well as redistributing the urban poor to 'colonies', both overseas and in the British countryside. There is, therefore, a way out of this modern hell for Booth, a pathway anchored in sober social principles derived from Methodist faith.

---

[4]   George Gissing, *Workers in the Dawn* (London, 1976), pp. 1–2.
[5]   Gissing, *The Nether World* (Oxford, 2008), p. 164.
[6]   Gissing, *The Nether World*, p. 345.
[7]   Blanchard Jerrold, illus. Gustave Doré, *London: A Pilgrimage* (London, 1872).
[8]   William Booth, *In Darkest England and the Way Out* (London, 1890), p. 13. For more examples, see Peter Keating, ed., *Into Unknown England, 1866–1913: Selections from the Social Explorers* (Glasgow, 1976).

'Work for all' provides the keystone within the allegorical map accompanying Booth's book, which was 'intended to give a birdseye-view' of the Salvation Army's reform program (Illus. 1). The map's schema provides a structural frame for understanding the shape of liberal social reform in the nineteenth century, using the vertical topography to provide a clear model for social improvement which, in its conceptual structure, depends on longstanding religious tropes of transcendence. William Booth was unrelated to his contemporary Charles Booth, who around the same time produced a series of 'Maps Descriptive of London Poverty', but the graphic distribution of colour in those charts offers a similar socio-political cartography, as a black stain yawns like a void across the eastern sector of the city.

There is a complex intersection of physical, metaphysical, and metaphorical appropriations of hell in the world-space of industrial capitalism, as actual subterranean networks – sewers, tunnels, mines, railways, storage vaults, covered passages, cemeteries – began to proliferate in cities such as London and Paris.[9] The ever more varied underground infrastructure associated with the second industrial revolution complicated contemporary understandings of mythic or metaphorical underground spaces of poverty and crime.[10] In the new genre of the 'scientific romance', the idea of life underneath the Earth's surface cast the class structures that stratified the world above into vivid imaginative relief, as when urban workers evolve to dwell underground alongside the machinery they tend in H. G. Wells's *The Time Machine* (1895). On the one hand, broaching new telluric frontiers gave concrete form to the abstract divisions of the city between rich and poor, virtue and crime. On the other hand, the increasing presence of physical thresholds between the underground and the world above provided evidence of the instability of these conceptual divisions. As David

---

[9]   David L. Pike, *Subterranean Cities: The World beneath Paris and London, 1800–1945* (Ithaca, 2005).
[10]   Most scholarly work on underground space in London focuses on its material development and impact – for instance, Richard Trench and Ellis Hillman, *London Under London* (London, 1984); Peter Ackroyd, *London Under: The Secret History Beneath the Streets* (London, 2011). Studies that address both the material and metaphorical underground, such as Rosalind Williams, *Notes on the Underground* (Cambridge, MA, 1990) and Wendy Lesser, *Life Below the Ground* (London, 1987), take note of the sea change brought about by the Industrial Revolution but do little to further historicise the imagery related to those spaces. David L. Pike, *Passage Through Hell: Modernist Descents, Medieval Underworlds* (Ithaca, 1997) and Rachel Falconer, *Hell in Contemporary Literature: Western Descent Narratives since 1945* (Edinburgh, 2005) have done much to explore the cultural and imaginary engagement with some of these underground spaces.

Illus. 1. William Booth, *In Darkest England and the Way Out*, Salvation Army Social Campaign (1890) © The Salvation Army International Heritage Centre, London.

Pike observes, 'the language with which the underground is represented in discourse was influenced by and helped to produce the confusion between the moral and the physical, the imaginary and the material'.[11]

But if recent scholarly work has sharpened our sense of the complex uses to which industrial modernity has put the vast armature of underworld topoi, either as material or archetypal space, we still need to attend to the role of lived landscape in this process of making meaning out of hell. To return to the night of 30 September 1888: Berner Street has always held the most historical interest of all Jack the Ripper murder sites. Dutfield's Yard was a narrow passageway wedged between No. 42 and No. 40, the premises of the International Working Men's Educational Club. The club was founded in 1884 by the Society of Jewish Socialists as a popular assembly place for social democrats, anarchists, and other déraciné radicals, especially newly arrived immigrants. The club hosted lectures, language classes, and social evenings for its eighty or so members, and at its rear were the printing and editorial offices of the weekly Yiddish newspaper *Arbeter Fraint* ('Worker's Friend'). Berner Street 'is a very notorious part of Whitechapel', observed the *Evening Standard*, noting the scene's proximity to the home of murderer Israel Lipski and reminding readers, with an anti-Semitic whisper, 'the bulk of the residents are Jews'.[12] The area was described invariably as 'a neighbourhood of evil repute', while the club itself was 'a regular hell' according to the census.[13]

It was the club's steward, Louis Diemschutz, who drove his barrow into the yard within minutes of the time Stride must have been killed and so discovered her body. Almost immediately, conspiracies linking Jewish anarchists to the murder began to emerge. A 'vigorous search of person and premises was instituted', reported the *Daily News*, 'much to the annoyance of members', but the police found nothing suspicious.[14] Despite interviewing neighbours, the press conceded that 'there is not the slightest tittle of evidence to show that the yard in question has been habitually used for immoral purposes'.[15] In the weeks after the murder, however, a series of stories circulated about the guilt of one Nikolai Vasiliev, a 'fanatical

[11]   David L. Pike, *Metropolis on the Styx: The Underworlds of Modern Urban Culture, 1800–2001* (Ithaca, 2007), p. 6. For a full account of the major doctrinal battles over hell and eternal punishment in the nineteenth century, see Michael Wheeler, *Heaven, Hell, and the Victorians* (Cambridge, 1994), pp. 175–218.
[12]   'Two More Murders in East London', *Evening Standard* (1 October 1888).
[13]   *Sheffield Daily Telegraph* (1 October 1888).
[14]   'Another Account', *Daily News* (1 October 1888), 6.
[15]   'The Whitechapel Horrors', *Evening News*, 5th edition (1 October 1888).

anarchist'. It seems unlikely that Vasiliev ever existed; the involvement of Olga Novikova (the notorious Russian 'M.P. for London' who established a salon at Claridge's Hotel) in disseminating the rumours suggests that the story was an attempt by the Tsarist secret police to discredit the revolutionary movement in London and collect information about Russian exiles.[16] Yet however far-fetched these theories were, the Berner Street club became the subject of intrigue for a popular press clamouring to connect lurid violence on the continent with the more mundane realities of Britain's domestic life. Radical social clubs, though not illegal or even particularly clandestine, were accustomed to operating below the threshold of visibility. With first the Berner Street murder, then the 1894 Greenwich Bomb Outrage by a card-carrying member of the Autonomie Club, then the 'Houndsditch murders' of three police officers in 1910 by alleged frequenters of the Jubilee Street Club, clubs across London were thrust into the glare of media attention. The explosion in domestic violence stoked fears that immigrants were exporting conspiratorial tactics, and that clubs were sheltering terrorist cells who would incubate insurrectionary ideas and habits until the conditions for revolution were ripe.

Yet, if the occupation of an urban underworld was a charge laid at political subversives, it also provided a way for insurgents to conceptualise their own place in the metropolis, and to challenge existing cartographic systems of classification and control. It was both a threatening zone from which carnage might erupt, and a liberating space of political resistance during a period when radicals in Russia and Europe were forced into hiding and exile by repressive regimes. The *Oxford English Dictionary* maps the word's transformation from 'region below the earth' to a symbolic reference to what is 'hidden, concealed, secret', tracing its political usage in the nineteenth century through Sergei Kravchinsky's nihilist tract *Underground Russia* (1883).[17] Mikhail Bakunin, the Russian revolutionary and founder of collectivist anarchism, used the figure of the tunnel to evoke the manner in which radical spirit survives under such conditions: 'the spirit of revolution is not subdued, it has only sunk into itself in order soon to reveal itself again as an affirmative, creative principle, and right now it is burrowing [...] like a mole under the earth'.[18] Socialists, anarchists, nihilists, and

16   W. T. Stead, *The M. P. for Russia*, 2 vols (London, 1909), vol. 1, p. v.

17   'Underground, adj. and n.' OED Online. December 2020. Oxford University Press.   https://ezproxy-prd.bodleian.ox.ac.uk:2446/view/Entry/211700? rskey=1bcQy3&result=2&isAdvanced=false (accessed December 06, 2020).

18   Mikhail Bakunin, 'The Reaction in Germany [1842]', in *Bakunin on Anarchy*, trans. and ed. Sam Dolgoff (New York, 1972), pp. 55–7 (p. 56).

others all found revolutionary appeal in the subterranean metaphor. Being underground meant an ethos of subversion and subterfuge; of dissimulation and double-crossing. Their vocabulary combined physical areas under the earth – basements and bunkers and bolt-holes – with secret social spaces and organising centres above ground.

The organisation and operation of anarchist social clubs in late-nineteenth-century London offers a metaphorics of 'underground' that cannot be accommodated to a vertical schema of surface and depth, visibility and invisibility, or a corresponding moral or religious topography. These clubs were all appropriated buildings subsequently restructured for new use and, subject to incessant police raids and chronic poverty, they rarely lasted more than a few years at a time. Their radical potential is not submerged but superimposed upon the surface of the urban fabric. It hides in plain sight. As such, clubs provide a useful case study for thinking about why hell has proven such a tempting yet imperfect metaphor, to those looking back at the period as well as those who lived in it, and for exploring its imbrication with hegemonic modes of social thinking. In many ways, the most positive metaphor of hell the nineteenth century can offer is an inheritance of the Romantic interpretation of John Milton's Satan in *Paradise Lost* (1667) as the charismatic rebel, for whom revolution is glorious in its inevitable failure. Hell is thus curated as both a religious and secular metaphor in order to map and control space, and to police the borders of what is deemed politically, morally, and conceptually possible. Anarchist presence, both real and imagined, provokes a crisis of this representational framework.

To recover the architectural principles of these clubs, and examine their wider cultural representations, will reveal the extraordinarily generative power of a crisis where multiple discourses – public, private, political, literary, architectural, urban – are entangled. This plurality is a facet of anarchism's commitment to praxis. Anarchism is a protean idea derived broadly from the ancient Greek ἀναρχία (anarkhía, 'without command structure'), but the political philosophy received sharper contours when adopted by Pierre-Joseph Proudhon in his 1840 treatise, *What is Property?*, to advocate self-governed societies based on free and voluntary associations.[19] Anarchism of the late nineteenth century is distinguished from its parallels in utopian socialist and communist movements by its belief in the emancipatory power of authentic social relations, that the future world ought to be lived in the present. As the German anarchist Rudolf Rocker recalled, anarchist principles are 'not something only to dream about [...]

[19]   Peter Marshall, *Demanding the Impossible: A History of Anarchism* (London, 2008), pp. 3–50.

they must be translated into our daily life, here and now; they must shape our relations with our fellow-man'.[20] London's anarchist clubs connect political ideology to practical organisation, eschewing forms of private property necessarily backed by and interlinked with state power. The clubs take the habitation of the underground – as a space of enclosure, exclusivity, and capitalist extraction – and redefine it as one of radical inclusivity and collectivity. To focus on the underground in this way as both a material and metaphorical space of movement, diversity, encounter, refuge, and political action, is to attend also to the aesthetic, performative, and sociophilosophic strategies used by underground groups, thinkers, and activists to re-imagine established images of London.

'Fiends of Destruction': Mapping Hellscapes

Fenians were the first revolutionaries to attack underground space in London. The bombs, beginning with two explosions on Praed St, between Charing Cross and Westminster, on 30 October 1883, marked the start of a new form of subterranean terror. A large explosion at Victoria Station followed one year later, while bombs primed to detonate simultaneously were also found at Charing Cross, Paddington, and Ludgate Hill. In press coverage of the explosions, underground railways became a locus of fear:

> [a]s reported yesterday, infernal machines were discovered at Charing-cross and Paddington Stations under circumstances which clearly prove that the explosion at Victoria Station was only part of a diabolical plan to destroy property and probably life.[21]

Bombs are constantly referred to in journalism and fiction of this period as 'infernal machines', planted by 'dynamite fiends' (Illus. 2). In 1894, *Strand Magazine* sent a correspondent into the Crime Museum of New Scotland Yard to report on a new exhibit of 'dynamite relics', used to educate officers about the 'infernal machine', or improvised bomb.[22] John Coulson Kernahan's 1906 novel *The Dumpling* opens with a terrorist planting an elaborately symbolic device on an underground train: 'what appeared to be a parcel of volumes from a circulating library was in reality a case, cunningly covered with the backs, bindings, and edges of books, and [...] this

---

20   Rudolf Rocker, *The London Years* (Nottingham, 2004), p. 8.

21   'The Discovery of Infernal Machines', *Pall Mall Gazette* (29 February 1884), 7.

22   'Crimes and Criminals. No. 1 – Dynamite and Dynamiters', *Strand Magazine* 7 (1894), 119–32, p. 119.

Illus. 2. 'The Dynamite Fiend', *Illustrated Police News* (15 March 1884).
Newspaper image © The British Library Board. All rights reserved. With
thanks to The British Newspaper Archive.

case contained an infernal machine of the most deadly description'.[23] It was a lexis reproduced, at times, by anarchists themselves. Auguste Coulon, a French anarchist close to Louise Michel who was later revealed to be a police agent, wrote enthusiastically in the *Commonweal* in 1891, '[o]nly last week, I mentioned two bomb explosions in Ruchenberg, and here again, we record another infernal and diabolical Machine that has thrown terror and dismay into the mind of the capitalist class'.[24] In their fictionalised memoir *A Girl Among the Anarchists* (1903), Helen and Olivia Rossetti – writing under the *nom de plume* Isabel Meredith – consider the possible intentions of the Greenwich Park bomber, 'having manufactured his infernal machine for some nefarious purpose'.[25]

Several layers of obfuscation take place in these accounts. While there were notorious anarchist bombing campaigns on the continent, most attacks on British soil were perpetrated by Irish nationalists. In fiction and the popular press, however, dynamite is predominantly associated with anarchism, and anarchism with 'infernal' intent. As *The Times* noted, '[e]very month brought its quota of horrors and made the name of Anarchist a by-word'.[26] Anarchism provided a rhetorical frame that gave the bombing campaigns minimal intelligibility. Certain figurative tropes of the fictional terrorist mobilise diabolism as a moral referent, stripped of any theological content, so that political action is routinely translated into a metaphysical register. Indeed, contrary to what one might expect, the typical and most dangerous anarchist in literature is not the activist in working men's clubs nor the orator on street corners.[27] Such social geography features at length only in H. Barton's *Robert Miner: Anarchist* (1902). Anarchists are most often deviant upper-class caricatures, as in Richard Henry Savage's *The Anarchist* (1894), where plotters seek to infiltrate a society family and claim the fortune of an heiress. Davidoff, the chairman of the anarchist conspiracy, is '[h]ell's high priest', while Carl Stein, the central anarchist, is described as 'the apostle of destruction'.[28] These cosmopolitan villains become empty ciphers for the playing out of a manichean struggle between good and evil. The hero of *An Apostle of Freedom* (1895)

23   John Coulson Kernahan, *The Dumpling* (London, 1906), pp. 4–5.
24   Auguste Coulon, 'International Notes', *Commonweal* (24 October 1891), 136.
25   Isabel Meredith, *A Girl Among the Anarchists* (London, 1903), p. 40.
26   'Latest Intelligence', *The Times* (1 January 1895), 3.
27   Haia Shpayer-Makov, 'A Traitor to His Class: The Anarchist in British Fiction', *Journal of European Studies* 26 (1996), 299–395.
28   Richard Henry Savage, *The Anarchist: A Story of To-Day*, 2 vols (London, 1894), vol. 1, pp. 81, 397.

names the anarchists interchangeably 'Satans', 'devils', and 'armoury of Satan'.[29] Sir Robert le Camps evokes the same association in *Desrues the Anarchist, or The Devil's Son* (1894).[30]

Dynamite fiction, as such novels were collectively known, was a conservative genre, predominantly invested in the idea of containment: preventing explosions, neutralising dissent, regulating middle-class anxiety. Consumption of these shocks by way of forms such as dystopian and science fiction helped to desensitise and mystify the public about the political motivations that inspired terrorism, and it distanced the sphere of action from everyday reality. By emphasising the shadowy presence of an aberrant upper class (usually foreign) conspirator, these narratives portray revolutionary violence as a result of the psychological tics of maniacs, not evidence of political or cultural crises at the heart of British empire.[31] Revolution is figured as eschatology in Edward Douglas Fawcett's science fiction novel *Hartmann the Anarchist, or, The Doom of the Great City* (1893), where the unleashing of 'pandemonium on earth' is preceded by a renewal of anarchist outrages. The plot centres around Mr Stanley, a young gentleman who aims to stand for election as a Labour party candidate. Through his associations with many of London's most prominent socialists and anarchists, he encounters and befriends Rudolph Hartmann and 'goes along' with Hartmann's plan to attack London using his airship *The Attila*. During the final 'tempest of dynamite', Hartmann's machine unleashes liquid petroleum on London, in an echo of the *petroleuses* prepared to ignite Paris in the final days of the Commune.[32] Fawcett's treatment of these 'fiends of destruction' demonstrates how the challenge set by anarchists needed to be re-enfolded into a structure that manages their dissent.

In another example, Gustave Linbach creates an immediate connection between anarchism and Satan by entitling his novel *The Azrael of Anarchy* (1894).[33] The titular Azrael – Angel of Death in some Jewish and Islamic traditions – is Sir Dunstan Gryme, the son of an English army surgeon and

---

[29]   Edwin Hughes, *An Apostle of Freedom* (Bristol, 1895), p. 124.

[30]   Robert le Camps, 'Desrues the Anarchist, or, The Devil's Son', *The Halfpenny Monarch* 21 (31 July 1894).

[31]   For variations on this argument, see Deaglán Ó Donghaile, *Blasted Literature: Victorian Political Fiction and the Shock of Modernism* (Edinburgh, 2011) and Barbara Melchiori, *Terrorism in the Late Victorian Novel* (London, 1985).

[32]   Edward Douglas Fawcett, *Hartmann the Anarchist, or, The Doom of the Great City* (London, 1893), p. 169.

[33]   'Gustave Linbach' is a pseudonym for Charles Carlson, editor of theatrical periodical *The Stage*, and Henry Edlin, a librettist. See 'The Authorship of "The Azrael of Anarchy"', *The Westminster Budget* (22 February 1895), 29.

Indian princess, who was raised by his mother to hate England.[34] Sir Dunstan trains as both a physician and an occultist, and he devises an array of deadly poisons. He joins a group of anarchists, but only because he sees an opportunity when they topple the government to become Dictator of Empire. When a cholera epidemic hits England, Sir Dunstan is appointed Special Royal Commissioner for fighting the disease but spreads it instead. Linbach reiterates this motif throughout the book, calling his antagonist an 'archfiend in human form' and his deed a 'mephistophelian crime'; even Gryme's name puns on the Miltonic construction of Satan as an infernal industrialist, building hell with his 'industrious crew' of miners.[35]

One of the main things to be learned is the unreflective repetition evident in the majority of these examples. Deploying this set of archetypal referents sought to evacuate terrorist activities, and the ideology that underpins them, of historical particularity or political traction. Satan's syncretic quality allowed this figure to function as 'the locus within capitalist space where belief systems and modes of representation alien or marginal to that space came to be appropriated by it', in David Pike's words, 'and through whom the difficult negotiations of that process of appropriation can be seen to be expressed'.[36] The visual rhetoric of a cartoon in the satirical magazine *Punch* is particularly fascinating on this note, depicting Liberty, the figure of old Republican revolutionary zeal, in her iconic pose, one arm raised defiantly, crushing the serpent of anarchy beneath her 'unfaltering' feet.[37] Hell imagery becomes a kind of control mechanism that pre-emptively condemns alterity along hegemonic state–Christian binaries, in ways that deliberately exploit some of the contradictions in Milton's depiction of Satan, such as his allegory of a revolutionary who rules Chaos amid '[e]ternal anarchy'.[38] And yet the Greenwich Park bomber, Martial Bourdin, carried in his pocket a copy of a sensational article from a few days earlier by the *Pall Mall Gazette*, warning that England was 'warming a snake in our bosom in harbouring in this country the anarchical refuse of the world'.[39]

---

[34]   '"Azrael" [...] is the name of the Angel of Death' remarks one character prophetically of a former Communard with this name in Richard Whiteing's *No. 5 John Street* (London, 1902), p. 66.

[35]   Gustave Linbach, *The Azrael of Anarchy* (London, 1894), p. 134. John Milton, *Paradise Lost*, ed. Alastair Fowler, 2nd edn (Harlow, 1998), I.751.

[36]   Pike, *Metropolis on the Styx*, p. 68.

[37]   'Vive La République', *Punch* 107 (7 July 1894), 7.

[38]   John Milton, *Paradise Lost*, ed. Alastair Fowler, 2nd edn (Harlow, 1998), II.896.

[39]   'The Anarchists in London: By One Who Studies Them', *Pall Mall Gazette* (13 February 1894), 1.

'Sudden Holes in Space and Time': Building Hell

After the explosion in Greenwich Park, several debates in the House of Commons over the anarchists' right to hold demonstrations eventually agreed to censor their public presence.[40] The streets of London became disputed territory: the French anarchist Charles Malato noted that in Britain political life was 'all interior [...] the cold street without benches is a place which you only go through, and do not step in'.[41] Instead, anarchism found momentum during and as a result of the golden age of '[m]etropolitan clubland'.[42] Here, complex and shifting relations between buildings and bodies, structures and sites, characterise not just the particular form of this organising metaphor – underground as hell – but also its attendant structuralisation in the actual spaces where anarchists gathered. The underground becomes particularised, embodied in architectural forms that express the precarious relationship between legitimacy and subterfuge.

The particular threat of the anarchist was underlined by their imperceptibility among the thronged crowds of the metropolis, their subversion of the modern state along with the power of its policing and surveillance systems. As Inspector Heat laments in Joseph Conrad's *The Secret Agent* (1907):

> [i]n the close-woven stuff of relations between the conspirator and police there occur unexpected solutions of continuity, sudden holes in space and time. A given anarchist may be watched inch by inch and minute by minute, but a moment always comes when somehow all sight and touch of him are lost for a few hours, during which something (generally an explosion) more or less deplorable does happen.[43]

The possibility of an episode unconnected to a general scheme is precisely what threatens the efficiency of surveillance, as if anarchists occupy unseen interstices in the urban fabric and thereby insert cavities into the chain of cause and effect. As Havelock Ellis warned in 1890, the 'political criminal [...] does not easily admit of scientific discussion'.[44]

---

[40]   *Hansard*, 4, xviii (14 November 1893), col. 875, and *Hansard*, 4, xviii (28 November 1893), col. 1910.

[41]   Charles Malato, *Les Joyeusetés de l'exil* (Paris, 1985), p. 15.

[42]   Stan Shipley, *Club Life and Socialism in Mid-Victorian London* (London, 1971), p. 21.

[43]   Joseph Conrad, *The Secret Agent* (Oxford, 2008), p. 63.

[44]   Havelock Ellis, *The Criminal* (London, 1890), p. 2.

Conrad is unusual in staging his anarchist tale in a domestic space, rather than a continental café or filthy public house, such as the little tavern called the 'Sun and Moon' in Henry James's *The Princess Casamassima* (1886) 'which presented so common and casual a face to the world and yet, in its unsuspecting rear, offered a security as yet unimpugned to the machinations going down to the very bottom of things'.[45] *The Princess Casamassima* is a novel less about anarchism than it is about the language which frames anarchist operations, most of which James borrowed from the press. The sensationalist language of journalists was particularly potent because this was the medium through which the findings of police investigators were filtered through to novelists. Young bookbinder Hyacinth Robinson remarks turbidly to the Princess of the anarchist movement with which he has become briefly involved:

> [i]t is more strange than I can say. Nothing of it appears above the surface; but there is an immense underworld, peopled with a thousand forms of revolutionary passion and devotion. The manner in which it is organised is what astonished me; I knew that, or thought I knew it, in a general way, but the reality was a revelation. And on top of it all, society lives! People go and come, and buy and sell, and drink and dance, and make money and make love, and seem to know nothing and suspect nothing and think of nothing. [...] In silence, in darkness, but under the feet of each of us, the revolution lives and works. [...] The invisible, impalpable wires are everywhere, passing through everything, attaching themselves to objects in which one would never think of looking for them.[46]

Even discounting the fact that Hyacinth's speech is designed to keep the Princess's attention firmly focused on the plotters, and upon himself in particular, it is one of the best descriptions to be found of the sense of foreboding and threat which pervaded the dynamite years.

Anarchist clubs were pictured in the press as fearsome places, reminiscent of the infernal council in Milton's Pandæmonium. 'The remarkable outburst of Anarchist crime', reported the *Spectator* in 1893, 'has naturally increased the presumption that such crimes are the work of a Secret Society which has declared war on the human race'.[47] One year later, the *Evening News* ran a series of investigative reports, fanning readers' fears about '8,000 anarchists in London' and 'where these enemies of society live in the great metropolis'.[48]

45   Henry James, *The Princess Casamassima* (London, 1987), p. 270.
46   James, *The Princess Casamassima*, p. 330.
47   'The Anarchist Wave', *Spectator* (30 September 1893), 424.
48   *Evening News* (17 December 1894), p. 2.

One visit to 'a London club' takes on an almost nightmarish quality, and compares the reporter 'Zitrik' to Dante. The voices of the anarchist crowd as they debate the notorious murderer Ravachol sound like 'strange wild beasts' calling for bloodshed and massacre.[49] These clubs – simultaneously esoteric enclaves and destinations for press tours – helped to construct a sphere of relations sufficiently opaque to larger publics and at the same time translucent. This sphere could be characterised as 'indefinite' in its extent, 'mediated by print, theatre, diffuse networks of talk', to borrow the language of Michael Warner's *Publics and Counterpublics*.[50] We might conclude that anarchist clubs are vital architects of an emergent anarchist counterpublic. This is a social world defined by its 'tension with a larger public', its constituency 'marked off from persons or citizens in general'.[51] Such a counterpublic was visible, but maintained a vigilant, and at times painful, consciousness of its subordinate or subaltern relationship to the larger (and hostile) public within which it is embedded.

The apparent mysteriousness of anarchist counterpublic discourse is accentuated when it unfolds as part of a global diaspora. The originating function of these clubs was refuge, as emigrants from Europe and Russia sought shelter under Britain's comparatively liberal asylum policies. It was to 'a little Club instituted by their compatriots in Francis-street, Tottenham-court-road' that twelve beleaguered Communards first went for assistance in 1872, having hiked from Dover to London, 'penniless' with 'swollen limbs' and 'blistered, if not lacerated, feet'.[52] The Social Democratic Club met in pubs around Soho from its foundation in August 1877 until it established premises in Rose Street in 1878, and this then formed the model, along with the Eclectic Hall in Denmark Street, for a plethora of radical clubs from the 1880s onwards.[53] The move to a fixed location was important, according to Frank Kitz, because discussion and organisation could proceed without the interference of landlords or the expense of hired rooms, and so 'we were enabled to hold public meetings with greater frequency'.[54] When another wave of refugees arrived

[49]   *Evening News* (18 December 1894), p. 2.
[50]   Quoted in Kathy E. Ferguson, 'Anarchist Counterpublics', *New Political Science* 32.2 (2010), 193–214, p. 195.
[51]   Michael Warner, *Publics and Counterpublics* (New York, 2002), p. 56.
[52]   'The Banished Communists', *Daily News* (18 May 1872), p. 5.
[53]   See John Quail, *The Slow Burning Fuse* (London, 1978) and Hermia Oliver, *The International Anarchist Movement in Late Victorian London* (London, 2015 [1983]), p. 5.
[54]   Frank Kitz, 'Recollections and Reflections', *Freedom* (February 1912), 10.

from Germany after the passage of the 1878 Anti-Socialist Laws, the Rose Street club became a central point for aid, hospitality, shelter, and advice.[55] Something of this heterogeneity is alluded to in the office of the fictional 'Tocsin' paper in *A Girl Among the Anarchists*, which Meredith remembers 'besides being a printing and publishing office, rapidly became a factory, a debating club, a school, a hospital, a mad-house, a soup-kitchen, and a sort of Rowton House, all in one'.[56]

As the political context changed, however, this benign feature of club life would find increasingly little purchase in how the clubs came to be represented. Once again, this feature finds its touchstone in a Satanic parallel. A primary element of the devil's mythic identity is his character as a nomadic wanderer. While the Dantean hell fixed Satan at the bottom of his own infernal city and condemned the souls around him to an endless repetition of identical punishment, Milton's Satan had looser bonds. Daniel Defoe took this nomadism a step further, arguing at length against Milton that the devil was not consigned to hell but was 'more of a vagrant than a prisoner', condemned to 'wander' the earth.[57] The wider cultural anxiety attendant upon these clubs was less Zitrik's sense of venturing into a fixed and bounded inferno, and more its itinerant inhabitants' dispersal throughout the capital. The cosmopolitan anarchist community of refugees in London gave some indication of international cooperation which, with a little imagination, could be elaborated into a grand conspiracy. The greatest fear expressed was that anarchist networks operating for the diffusion of propagandist material – both Berner Street and Rose Street sponsored papers – also sustained terrorist activities.[58]

The reality was much messier, more chaotic, and more provisional. Insofar as there had been any anarchist organisation at all it had been gathered under the London Socialist League. It was not until mid-1892 that a federation of anarchist groups was formed in London, and even then

By contrast, the Homerton Social Democratic Club (1881–2), which held open meetings on Sunday evenings at the Lamb and Flag public house in Homerton High Street, was suppressed by police pressure on the landlord. Nicolas Walter, 'Homerton Club', *History Workshop Journal* 7.1 (1979), 211–13.

[55]   Adolphe Smith, 'Political Refugees', in *London in the Nineteenth Century*, ed. Walter Besant (London, 1909), pp. 404–45 (p. 404).

[56]   Meredith, *A Girl Among the Anarchists*, p. 133.

[57]   Daniel Defoe, *The Political History of the Devil* (London, 1726), p. 63.

[58]   Daniel Laqua, 'Political Contestation and Internal Strife: Socialist and Anarchist German Newspapers in London, 1878–1910', in *The Foreign Political Press in Nineteenth-Century London*, ed. Constance Bantman and Ana Cláudia Suriani da Silva (London, 2018), pp. 135–54.

the assemblages remained volatile. The Autonomie Club, where Martial Bourdin was a member, was designated the 'centre of the whole Anarchist organisation in the Metropolis' in the press.[59] In reality, it lasted barely eight years. Here is German anarchist John Henry Mackay's version of the same period:

> in none is their swarm so mixed as in London. Nowhere does it draw so closely together; nowhere does it go so far apart. [...] Nowhere does it speak in so many languages, and nowhere does it give expression to a greater variety of opinions in a greater variety of accents.

> [...] It seems at times as if the refugees had forgotten their distinct enemy, so bitterly they fight among themselves. Individual groups secede from the sections of the parent society, and refuse to retain even the old name. A few individuals, filled with restlessness and ambition, try to avail themselves of the dissension for the purpose of gathering up the severed threads and keeping them – in their own hands. The controversies for and against them are carried on for weeks and for months to the degree of exhaustion, when they cease and leave no other traces than estrangement, a pile of papers full of insinuations and suspicions, and a useless pamphlet.[60]

Without the press attention that terrorist attacks generated, historians would struggle to say much of consequence about the clubs, whose existence is otherwise only alluded to in scattered diary references, letters, and occasional accounts in the anarchist press itself. As Antonio Gramsci maintains in his study of social structures that lie beyond hegemonic institutions, 'the history of subaltern social groups is necessarily fragmented and episodic'.[61] The underground, as a space of alterity, could not be articulated as a coherent structure. The newly formed Special Branch targeted the clubs relentlessly, but little is now extant from what were extensive reports.[62] Anarchism in English writing accordingly inhabits, in the words of Valentine Cunningham, the 'condition of a real-presence which is also

[59] 'Anarchism in London', *Graphic* (24 February 1894), 207–8, p. 207.
[60] John Henry Mackay, *The Anarchists*, trans. George Schumm (Boston, 1891), pp. 231–3.
[61] Antonio Gramsci, *Selections from the Prison Notebooks*, trans. Geoffrey Smith and Quintin Hoare (New York, 1971), p. 55.
[62] The reports of foreign police services, tailing their citizens in exile, seem more extensive. See Constance Bantman, *The French Anarchists in London, 1880–1914* (Liverpool, 2013).

clamantly an absence'.[63] How then to eschew the hellscapes imposed upon anarchist culture by the press and fiction at this time, in order to grasp this shiftingness on its own terms? Is it possible to plot a new set of co-ordinates to survey these loose political groupings and regroupings?

'Beer and Billiards': Beyond Hell

The actual architecture of these clubs created a dilemma for sensation-seeking journalists. The Autonomie Club, initially set up at 32 Charlotte Street in Fitzrovia in 1886 before relocating to 6 Windmill Street, offers a particularly infamous example. The explosion in Greenwich occurred three days after Émile Henry bombed the Café Terminus in Paris, killing one and injuring twenty. Lord Salisbury drew on fears of a transnational anarchist conspiracy in his speech to the House of Lords to claim (falsely) that it was 'now known' that the Autonomie had housed the ingredients for Henry's bomb. In response, Lord Halsbury announced that, though he had 'no information as to the offence which these people were supposed to have committed; nor do I know upon what authority the raid of the police was made', he did not believe 'any human being [can] doubt that the Autonomie Club was a club of foreign conspirators with aims that are inhuman, for anarchists are *hostes humani generis*'.[64] Such rhetoric built a formidable image of the Autonomie Club: *The Times* described it as 'the headquarters' of London's 'dovecote of anarchists'.[65]

By the time the club was raided, its inflated public image was being noted (ironically):

[i]t was there, claimed reporters lacking inspiration and happy to speculate on bourgeois terrors for three pennies a line, that all the conspiracies meant to explode on the continent were plotted, that all the tragic resolutions were made, that dynamite, potassium chlorate, nitrobenzene, rack-a-rock and green powder were fabricated.[66]

---

[63]   Valentine Cunningham, 'Litvinoff's Room: East End Anarchism', in *'To Hell with Culture': Anarchism and Twentieth-Century British Literature*, ed. H. Gustav Klaus and Stephen Knight (Cardiff, 2005), pp. 126–40 (p. 145).

[64]   *Hansard*: HL Deb 17 July 1894, vol. 27, cols 117–56. 'Hostis humani generis' is Latin for enemy of mankind, and originates in laws against pirates and slavers, determining them to be beyond the protection of any nation's law.

[65]   'The Explosion in Greenwich Park', *The Times* (17 February 1894).

[66]   'Là [...] se tramaient tous les complots destines à exploser sur le continent, se prenaient toutes les resolutions tragiques, se fabriquaient la dynamite, le chlorate de potasse, la nitrobenzene, le rack-a-rock et la poudre verte'. Malato, *Joyeusetés de l'exil*, p. 57.

Even the most prolific and sensationalist writers acknowledged that it was 'doubtful whether these clubs were ever the hotbeds of conspiracy that has sometimes been represented'.[67] Longstanding members briefed the Press Association that the Autonomie had actually become 'infested with the police spies of various governments'; Inspector Melville gained admission for his raid through knowing the 'peculiar' knock – or so the papers alleged.[68] Indeed, as a generic Fitzrovia townhouse in a terraced backstreet, the Autonomie projected an image more of unobtrusive domesticity than insurrectionary laboratory. Nothing of its exterior revealed the code to the presence or absence of subjects that would give the form meaning. Its political function was entirely subsumed into a continuous surface inside which habitation cannot be predicted. If the anarchists really were '*hostes humani generis*', their choice of location placed them, geographically and iconographically, at the heart of the metropolis. 'The Club', noted the *Graphic*, with perhaps the faintest hint of bathos, 'is an ordinary house'.[69]

The club's portrait accompanying the *Illustrated London News* report (Illus. 3) seems an attempt to reconcile the problem presented by the building's formal gestures of apparent normality. The field of view is restricted by a circular frame with a dark surround, as though the observer is peering through a spyglass – an estranging gesture which takes the gaze of the imperial explorer and turns it inward. Subtle contrast is drawn with the dwellings that flank the building to either side. The club's façade is sketched slightly darker and the blinds are mostly down, as though to signal that this is but an eldritch imitation of a generic urban terrace. The layout of the spread as a whole encourages the conclusion that the club was responsible for the events at Greenwich Park: the borders of the image depicting the Autonomie are permeable, intersecting with others of Bourdin's house and workroom. Its juxtaposition to the site of the explosion completes a chain of causation ordered by the sequential structuring of the images: what begins in the club ends at the bombsite.

In such popular culture representations, the theme of hell serves to join architectural speculation on political underworlds to more general reflection on questions of social and individual estrangement, alienation, and terror. But beyond this largely theatrical role, the architecture of these clubs reveals forms of the underground in a more analogical way, demonstrating a disquieting slippage between what seems visible and what is

---

[67] Félix Dubois, *The Anarchist Peril*, trans. Ralph Derechef (London, 1894), pp. 270–1.
[68] 'Anarchist Conspiracies', *Western Mail* (17 February 1894), p. 5.
[69] 'Anarchism in London', p. 208.

Illus. 3. 'The Anarchist Conspirators in London' *Illustrated London News* (24 February 1894), 288. © Illustrated London News Ltd: Mary Evans Picture Library.

definitely hidden. Structural adjustments had been made at the Autonomie to the reappropriated residential space, which was 'slightly modified by the creation of an underground hall for its special purpose'.[70] In 1908 Peter Latouche described the interior as a 'very dingy, badly furnished, ramshackle' place. Beside bare floorboards and wooden panelling, a 'few rough benches, chairs, and tables was the only accommodation afforded to the regular frequenters or the casual visitor'.[71]

Austerity was an unavoidable reality for these clubs. The building on Rose Street was almost derelict.[72] 'A more unlovely place than this club could scarcely be conceived', reported one visiting journalist to Berner Street, adding that it 'wears a most poverty-stricken aspect'. 'It is such institutions as these', the reporter warned, 'wherein is sown the seed of violent methods which threaten the lives and property of the community'.[73] Portraits hung on the walls of Berner Street depicting radical icons such as Marx, Proudhon, Lasalle, and Michel, but neither visitors nor members had much to say about the building itself, a rickety three-storey construction that seemed to belie its supposed political purpose (Illus. 4).

If the Rose, Autonomie, and Berner Street clubs' aesthetic was partly a result of material circumstances, it seems also to be one of calculated disequilibrium. In an image of the Autonomie club bar, an attendant can be seen dressed in formal attire: peaked cap, white shirt, tie, and vest. At Berner Street, the first floor offered an entertainment room which was adapted to provide capacity for around 200 people, with benches and a small stage at the front. One member recalled:

[h]ere were performed by amateurs mostly in Russian language plays by well known Russian revolutionists – Tchaikovsky (not the famous composer), Volchovksy, Stepniak, Winchevsky, Gallop [...]. Quite often the renowned radical poet, William Morris was seen there reading his splendid verses. It may be said that there, in Berner Street, was laid the foundation for the true International Brotherhood of Mankind.[74]

[70] 'Anarchism in London', p. 208.
[71] Peter Latouche, *Anarchy! An Authentic Exposition of the Methods of Anarchists and the Aims of Anarchism* (London, 1908), p. 63.
[72] Henry Solly, *'These Eighty Years': Or, The Story of an Unfinished Life* (Cambridge, 2011), p. 236.
[73] *Evening News* (25 April 1892), 3.
[74] Thomas B. Eyges, *Beyond the Horizon: The Story of a Radical Emigrant* (Boston, MA, 1944), p. 79.

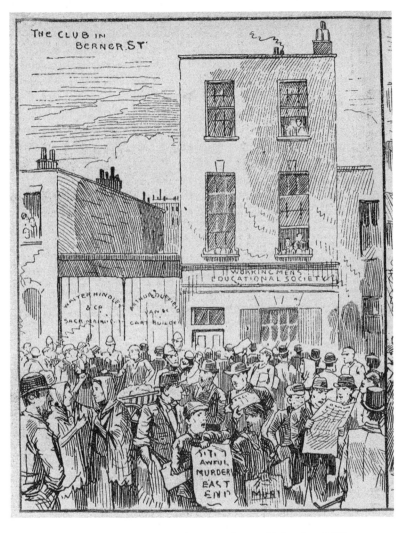

Illus. 4. 'The Club in Berner Street', *Pictorial News* (6 October 1888).
© British Library Board, MFM.M39880 [1888].

The combination of lectures and entertainment on offer at these clubs, where music, dances, and theatrical performances were all common, is in line with Frank Kitz's lament that the character of working-men's and radical clubs changed in the late 1870s, with 'beer and billiards' increasingly prevalent and 'the amateur [...] minstrel standing where the lecturer should be'.[75] These practical gestures meant that in the same space as the *Evening News* found a version of hell, the *Graphic* in 1892 spoke of '[e]verything [...] attuned to gaiety', the roof-beams 'hung with Chinese lanterns, and [...] gas-brackets [...] pink with twisted paper'. Instead of the imposing 'chairman's seat' found at the Communist Club, Berner Street had a small wooden platform, allowing for speeches without necessitating or institutionalising hierarchy – and on this occasion providing a stage 'set in a cheerful representation of a dungeon'.[76]

Irony is the figurative mode of these clubs, an irony embodied in the formal structure of the buildings themselves. An element of propriety seems inherent to the self-image of these clubs, a fact that in itself infuriated hostile commentators like W. C. Hart, who fumed that 'some of the groups, for obvious reasons, adopt a disguise of respectability!'[77] Anarchists may well have taken an element of satirical enjoyment in adopting the affectations of grandiloquent West End clubland. In some images, the words 'Club Autonomie' can be seen etched onto the fanlight above its doorway, asserting both public legitimacy and the hint of parody.

'A Virtual Space of New Possibilities'

Slavoj Zizek's notion of the architectural parallax might provide us with a means of grappling with the necessary recalcitrance of extant structures for sheltering underground or anarchist existence. The chapter on architecture in Zizek's *Living in the End Times* (2011) consists of a fascinating 'interlude', as he calls it, in which he develops the concept of the 'architectural parallax'.[78] The word 'parallax' derives from *parallassein* ('to alternate'). It is in its ordinary sense the apparent difference in an object, or the position of an object, when it is viewed from different perspectives. Cubist painting, to develop an example at which Zizek hints, could be productively characterised as a sustained and elaborate attempt to capture a parallax view

75   Kitz, 'Recollections and Reflections', p. 10.
76   'The Anarchist at Play', *Graphic* (30 July 1892), 132.
77   W. C. Hart, *Confessions of an Anarchist* (London, 1906), p. 37.
78   Slavoj Zizek, *Living in the End Times* (London, 2011), p. 244.

of the object; the painter reconstitutes the image of the object itself, and its relation to its surrounding environment, as if the painter is repeatedly shifting his perspective. This apprehends the object not simply as a three-dimensional entity but as a four-dimensional one; that is, an object situated in time as well as space. The painter's dynamic, unstable point of observation compels the shapes, planes, and angles of the composition to intersect with one another as if they are moving in time. In addition, the 'parallax' form of the cubist aesthetic folds the viewer herself into the dynamics of the picture, collapsing subject into object.

Zizek emphasises that, philosophically speaking, this apparent difference in an object when it is viewed from alternative perspectives is more than simply subjectivism. 'An "epistemological" shift in the subject's point of view', he writes, 'always reflects an "ontological" shift in the object itself.'[79] The Cubist object, to return to that example, is constitutively transformed by the dynamic decomposition that is the result of the painter's shifting perspectives. The object, in the shifting perspective of the parallax, is both itself and not itself. The parallax view renders it non-identical with itself. Think of a photograph in which, because the camera has been accidentally moved during the exposure, the object or person captured is not only blurred but visible from two slightly distinct angles. This effect registers the inscription of what Zizek calls the 'parallax gap', the interval or passage between changing, competing perspectives.

How does this relate to architecture? Zizek underlines his point that the parallax gap is 'not just a matter of shifting perspective (from one standpoint, a building looks a certain way – if I move a bit, it looks different)'.[80] It also marks a radically destabilising shift in the building's very identity, its individuality, and indivisibility. 'Things get interesting', he suggests, 'when we notice that the gap is inscribed into the "real" building itself – as if the building, in its very material existence, bears the imprint of different and mutually exclusive perspectives'. He continues:

[w]hen we succeed in identifying a parallax gap in a building, the gap between the two perspectives thus opens up a place for a third, virtual building. In this way, we can also define the creative moment of architecture: it concerns not merely or primarily the actual building, but the virtual space of new possibilities opened up by the actual building. Furthermore, the parallax gap in architecture means that the spatial disposition of a building cannot be understood without reference to the temporal dimension: the

79 Zizek, *Living in the End Times*, p. 244.
80 Zizek, *Living in the End Times*, p. 244.

parallax gap *is* the inscription of our changing temporal experience when we approach and enter a building.[81]

If the urban fabric is grasped in these ontological terms, then a 'virtual building' is necessarily precipitated by the interaction between the building's architectural form and the individual subject, moving through space and time in the context of everyday life. I propose to refine Zizek's concept a little here, or to displace it slightly, by situating it more explicitly in relationship to the ideological operations of buildings as we move about in their spatio-temporal orbit. The dynamics of this force field, which is necessarily constituted and reconstituted not in the abstract but in the historical conditions of time and space, are of course extremely complicated.[82] But my specific claim, in spite of the risk of simplification, is that the parallax gap that opens up between two or more competing, interpenetrating perspectives on a particular building is, precisely, the spectral architectural point from which the underground becomes apparent. It is the aperture at which underground as a condition of occupying space – a 'virtual space of new possibilities' – materialises or momentarily becomes visible. In these clubs, the underground is not a property of space itself nor can it be provoked by any particular spatial configuration; it is, in its aesthetic dimension, a play of forms that precisely eludes the boundaries of real and unreal in order to provoke a disturbing ambiguity. In this way, anarchist occupation of underground space would seem to be precisely that which eludes the far-reaching urban mapping projects evinced by Charles Booth and William Booth. A system of form seems to be at work in these clubs that does not rely on immediate referents for its existence, and, indeed, does not refer to them at all. The clubs exist as sites not so much to define the events that take place around them but to suppress the signifying elements of architecture, to identify and situate actions that are not necessarily events. One fundamental aim of the anarchist underground was to disrupt all previous natures and to dislocate private property.[83] This is architecture dissociated from cultural obligations of signification – as both representation and instrument for the display of history – and from its contexts, real and ideological.

[81] Zizek, *Living in the End Times*, pp. 244–5.

[82] See David Harvey, *Social Justice and the City* (Athens, 2009).

[83] Jonathan Moses attributes the sparse aesthetic politics of Berner Street to the influence of Russian nihilism on the anarchist movement in Britain. 'The Texture of Politics: London's Anarchist Clubs, 1884–1914', *Royal Institute of British Architects* (2016).

'That Strange Fermenting Underworld'

A buried world, hidden from the state, creates forms of solidarity and self-understanding that shape what is politically possible. For James, the organisation of 'that strange fermenting underworld' is vital to its revolutionary potential.[84] 'Are we on the eve of great changes, or are we not?' asks Madame Grandoni:

> [i]s everything that is gathering force, underground, in the dark, in the night, in the little hidden rooms, out of sight of governments and policemen and idiotic 'statesmen' – heaven save them! – is all this going to burst forth some fine morning and set the world on fire? Or is it to splutter out and spend itself in vain conspiracies, be dissipated in sterile heroisms and abortive isolated movements?[85]

Hyacinth, drawing on direct contact with these groups, fears:

> that the forces secretly arrayed against the present social order were pervasive and universal, in the air one breathed, in the ground one trod, in the hand of an acquaintance that one might touch, or in the eye of a stranger that might rest a moment on one's own. They were above, below, within, without, in every contact and combination of life; and it was no disproof of them to say it was too odd that they should lurk in a particular improbable form. To lurk in improbable forms was precisely their strength [...].[86]

The revolutionary forces' strength lies in their 'improbable forms', in their protean amorphousness that pervades the city like an intangible contagion. The shapelessness of the revolution, however, is also its weakness here, as action becomes further attenuated in the surfeit of discourses surrounding the movement.

How do such groupings occupy space in the social world of an emergent global capitalist modernity? Theodor Adorno, in his one essay devoted to architecture, argues that:

> [architectural work] is conditioned by a social antagonism over which the greatest architecture has no power: the same society which developed human productive energies to unimaginable proportions has chained them

---

84   James, *The Princess Casamassima*, p. 332.
85   James, *The Princess Casamassima*, p. 200.
86   James, *The Princess Casamassima*, p. 486.

to conditions of production imposed upon them. [...] This fundamental contradiction is most clearly visible in architecture.[87]

It is this visibility – its formal and phenomenological registering of the disjunction between the (technological and social) possibilities and actuality of industrial modernity – that gives architecture something of what Jameson calls its 'emblematic significance' or 'its immediacy to the social'.[88] Anarchist clubs occupy architectural forms differently. So what does the discursive maintenance of two interlinked imaginaries – the underground and the urban – reveal about the relationship between abstract conceptualisation and the imaginaries that ground and determine social life? To think about anarchist clubs and their complex relationship to a sociological discourse of hell is to discover a more ideologically provocative set of architectural aesthetics and functions. It allows us to see how structure relates to physical environment, and how this relationship represents and influences one's actions in the world.

In popular culture representations, anarchists are never conceived in isolation. In such plots, a secret organisation oversees all, and contrary to anarchist principles, this organisation is usually rigidly hierarchical, highly centralised, and conspicuously undemocratic. In reality, anarchist organising in nineteenth-century clubs is marked by the effort to articulate emergent forms of collectivity. What looks like disunity, chaos, or formlessness often stems from creative efforts to experiment with alternative modes of organisation: cells, councils, committees, constellations, militias, citizens' assemblies. Benedict Anderson has characterised such assemblages as a 'vast rhizomal network'.[89] This becomes apparent if one follows Caroline Levine in understanding modern politics as a set of formal protocols for 'enforcing restrictive containers and boundaries – such as nation-states, bounded subjects, and domestic walls', while also wondering what happens to bodies, groups, objects, or other phenomena that do not correspond to the properties or affordances of prescribed 'shapes and arrangements'.[90] We might imagine the parallax sites of anarchist clubs as the basis of some

---

[87]   Theodor Adorno, 'Functionalism Today', in *Rethinking Architecture: A Reader in Cultural Theory*, ed. Neil Leach (London, 1997), pp. 5–20 (p. 16).

[88]   Fredric Jameson, *The Cultural Turn: Selected Writings on the Postmodern, 1983–1998* (London, 1998), p. 163.

[89]   Benedict Anderson, *Under Three Flags: Anarchism and the Anti-Colonial Imagination* (London, 2005), pp. 3–4.

[90]   Caroline Levine, *Forms: Whole, Rhythm, Hierarchy, Network* (Princeton, 2015), p. 3.

transnational social interconnectedness or form of collectivity conceived in non-economic and non-hierarchical terms.

David Cunningham suggests that the forms of spatial relationality characteristic of urban 'exchangeability' mean that units of form are always subject (in however minor a way) to a kind of potential *détournement*: '[a] church can, in the formal structure of universal equivalence, become a café, an art gallery, a recording studio, a set of apartments, a recording studio, or whatever'.[91] Radical clubs, as reappropriated spaces, inscribe a similarly mutable experience, in that they partake nothing of the intrinsic qualities of certain sites. Instead they empty these sites of specific content, including specific political and cultural content, and are thus not determined in advance by the abstract structuring of the conditions of capital accumulation. If there is no metropolis without the hegemony of capital, the parallax gap produced by the conditions of use of these clubs asks that we equally recognise that such hegemony is never, in itself, total or complete. It is here that the idea of an urban underground reveals both its possibilities and its immense difficulties.

Works Cited

Ackroyd, Peter, *London Under: The Secret History Beneath the Streets* (London, 2011)

Adorno, Theodor, 'Functionalism Today', in *Rethinking Architecture: A Reader in Cultural Theory*, ed. Neil Leach (London, 1997), 5–20

'Anarchism in London', *Graphic* (24 February 1894), 207–8

'The Anarchist at Play', *Graphic* (30 July 1892), 132

'Anarchist Conspiracies', *Western Mail* (17 February 1894), 5

'The Anarchist Wave', *Spectator* (30 September 1893), 424

'The Anarchists in London: By One Who Studies Them', *Pall Mall Gazette* (13 February 1894), 1

Anderson, Benedict, *Under Three Flags: Anarchism and the Anti-Colonial Imagination* (London, 2005)

'Another Account', *Daily News* (1 October 1888), 6

'The Authorship of "The Azrael of Anarchy"', *Westminster Budget* (22 February 1895), 29

Baker, H. Barton, *Robert Miner: Anarchist* (London, 1902)

Bakunin, Mikhail, 'The Reaction in Germany [1842]', in *Bakunin on Anarchy*, trans. and ed. Sam Dolgoff (New York, 1972), 55–7

---

[91]   David Cunningham, 'The Concept of Metropolis: Philosophy and Urban Form', *Radical Philosophy* 133 (2005), 13–25, pp. 21–2.

'The Banished Communists', *Daily News* (18 May 1872), 5

Bantman, Constance, *The French Anarchists in London, 1880–1914* (Liverpool, 2013)

Bloch, Ernst, *The Principle of Hope*, trans. Neville Plaice, Stephen Plaice, and Paul Knight (Oxford, 1986)

Booth, William, *In Darkest England and the Way Out* (London, 1890)

le Camps, Robert, 'Desrues the Anarchist, or, The Devil's Son', *The Halfpenny Monarch* 21 (31 July 1894)

Conrad, Joseph, *The Secret Agent* (Oxford, 2008)

Coulon, Auguste, 'International Notes', *Commonweal* (24 October 1891), 136

'Crimes and Criminals. No. 1 – Dynamite and Dynamiters', *Strand Magazine* 7 (1894), 119–32

Cunningham, David, 'The Concept of Metropolis: Philosophy and Urban Form', *Radical Philosophy* 133 (2005), 13–25

Cunningham, Valentine, 'Litvinoff's Room: East End Anarchism', in *'To Hell with Culture': Anarchism and Twentieth-Century British Literature*, ed. H. Gustav Klaus and Stephen Knight (Cardiff, 2005), 126–40

Defoe, Daniel, *The Political History of the Devil* (London, 1726)

Dick, Nellie, interview with Andrew Whitehead, 5 November 1985, Sound Recording, 'Andrew Whitehead Oral History Interviews with Political Radicals', CD 26, British Library Sound Archive C1377

'The Discovery of Infernal Machines', *Pall Mall Gazette* (29 February 1884), 7

Dubois, Félix, *The Anarchist Peril*, trans. Ralph Derechef (London, 1894)

Ellis, Havelock, *The Criminal* (London, 1890)

Evening News (25 April 1892)

Evening News (2 October 1894)

Evening News (17 December 1894)

Evening News (18 December 1894)

'The Explosion in Greenwich Park', *The Times* (17 February 1894)

Eyges, Thomas B., *Beyond the Horizon: The Story of a Radical Emigrant* (Boston, MA, 1944)

Falconer, Rachel, *Hell in Contemporary Literature: Western Descent Narratives since 1945* (Edinburgh, 2005)

Fawcett, Edward Douglas, *Hartmann the Anarchist, or, The Doom of the Great City* (London, 1893)

Ferguson, Kathy E., 'Anarchist Counterpublics', *New Political Science* 32.2 (2010), 193–214

Gissing, George, *The Nether World* (Oxford, 2008)

––––––, *Workers in the Dawn* (London, 1976)

Gramsci, Antonio, *Selections from the Prison Notebooks*, trans. Geoffrey

Smith and Quintin Hoare (New York, 1971)

Hansard: HL Deb 17 July 1894, vol. 27, cols 117–56. https://api.parliament. uk/historic-hansard/lords/1894/jul/17/second-reading

Hansard, 4, xviii (14 November 1893), col. 875. https://api.parliament.uk/ historic-hansard/commons/1893/nov/14/ anarchist-meeting-in-trafalgar-square#column_875

Hansard, 4, xviii (28 November 1893), col. 1910. https://api.parliament.uk /historic-hansard/commons/1893/nov/28/ anarchist-meetings-in-trafalgar-square#column_1910

Hart, W. C., *Confessions of an Anarchist* (London, 1906)

Harvey, David, *Social Justice and the City* (Athens, 2009)

Hughes, Edwin, *An Apostle of Freedom* (Bristol, 1895)

James, Henry, *The Princess Casamassima* (London, 1987)

Jameson, Fredric, *The Cultural Turn: Selected Writings on the Postmodern, 1983–1998* (London, 1998)

Jerrold, Blanchard, illus. Gustave Doré, *London: A Pilgrimage* (London, 1872)

Keating, Peter, ed., *Into Unknown England, 1866–1913: Selections from the Social Explorers* (Glasgow, 1976)

Kernahan, John Coulson, *The Dumpling* (London, 1906)

Kitz, Frank, 'Recollections and Reflections', *Freedom* (February 1912), 10

Kravchinsky, Sergei, *Underground Russia* (London, 1883)

Laqua, Daniel, 'Political Contestation and Internal Strife: Socialist and Anarchist German Newspapers in London, 1878–1910', in *The Foreign Political Press in Nineteenth-Century London*, ed. Constance Bantman and Ana Cláudia Suriani da Silva (London, 2018), 135–54

'Latest Intelligence', *The Times* (1 January 1895), 3

Latouche, Peter, *Anarchy! An Authentic Exposition of the Methods of Anarchists and the Aims of Anarchism* (London, 1908)

LCC Building Act Case File 1361:GLC/AR/BR/07/1361 (LMA)

Lesser, Wendy, *Life Below the Ground* (London, 1987)

Levine, Caroline, *Forms: Whole, Rhythm, Hierarchy, Network* (Princeton, 2015)

Linbach, Gustave, *The Azrael of Anarchy* (London, 1894)

Mackay, John Henry, *The Anarchists*, trans. George Schumm (Boston, 1891)

Malato, Charles, *Les Joyeusetés de l'exil* (Paris, 1985)

Marshall, Peter, *Demanding the Impossible: A History of Anarchism* (London, 2008)

Massey, Doreen, *World City* (Cambridge, 2007)

Melchiori, Barbara, *Terrorism in the Late Victorian Novel* (London, 1985)

Meredith, Isabel, *A Girl Among the Anarchists* (London, 1903)

Milton, John, *Paradise Lost*, ed. Alastair Fowler, 2nd edn (Harlow, 1998)

Moses, Jonathan, 'The Texture of Politics: London's Anarchist Clubs, 1884–1914', Royal Institute of British Architects (2016). https://www.architecture.com/-/media/GatherContent/RIBA-Presidents-Awards-for-Research/Additional-Documents/106897TextureofPoliticsDDpdf.pdf

Ó Donghaile, Deaglán, *Blasted Literature: Victorian Political Fiction and the Shock of Modernism* (Edinburgh, 2011)

Oliver, Hermia, *The International Anarchist Movement in Late Victorian London* (London, 2015 [1983])

Pike, David L., *Metropolis on the Styx: The Underworlds of Modern Urban Culture, 1800–2001* (Ithaca, 2007)

––––––, *Passage Through Hell: Modernist Descents, Medieval Underworlds* (Ithaca, 1997)

––––––, *Subterranean Cities: The World Beneath Paris and London, 1800–1945* (Ithaca, 2005)

Quail, John, *The Slow Burning Fuse* (London, 1978)

Rocker, Rudolf, *The London Years* (Nottingham, 2004)

Savage, Richard Henry, *The Anarchist: A Story of To-Day*, 2 vols (London, 1894)

Sheffield Daily Telegraph (1 October 1888)

Shipley, Stan, *Club Life and Socialism in Mid-Victorian London* (London, 1971)

Shpayer-Makov, Haia, 'A Traitor to His Class: The Anarchist in British Fiction', *Journal of European Studies* 26 (1996), 299–395

Smith, Adolphe, 'Political Refugees', in *London in the Nineteenth Century*, ed. Walter Besant (London, 1909), 404–45

Solly, Henry, *'These Eighty Years': Or, The Story of an Unfinished Life* (Cambridge, 2011)

Stead, W. T., *The M. P. for Russia*, 2 vols (London, 1909)

Trench, Richard, and Ellis Hillman, *London Under London* (London, 1984)

'Two More Murders in East London', *Evening Standard* (1 October 1888)

'Vive La République', *Punch* 107 (7 July 1894), 7

Walter, Nicolas, 'Homerton Club', *History Workshop Journal* 7.1 (1979), 211–13

Warner, Michael, *Publics and Counterpublics* (New York, 2002)

Wheeler, Michael, *Heaven, Hell, and the Victorians* (Cambridge, 1994)

'The Whitechapel Horrors', *Evening News*, (1 October 1888)

Whiteing, Richard, *No. 5 John Street* (London, 1902)

Williams, Rosalind, *Notes on the Underground* (Cambridge, M. A., 1990)

Zizek, Slavoj, *Living in the End Times* (London, 2011)

Hell's Museum, Singapore

MARGARET KEAN INTERVIEWS JEYA AYADURAI

At Haw Par Villa in Singapore, Hell's Museum confronts visitors with the realities of death, and provides comparative information on Asia's death rituals, funerary practices, and various religious beliefs on the afterlife. The new museum area is the first step on a journey to hell which will take the visitor, by way of dioramas that depict the Buddhist and Daoist concepts of the afterlife, through the Ten Courts of Hell. In the First Court, the virtuous will be led over the 'Golden Bridge' to paradise but most souls must submit to hell's penal system. The walk-through exhibit depicts, in agonising detail, the just punishments levied for different types of wrong-doing: robbery and murder result in dismemberment, those who evaded their taxes are pounded by a stone mallet, those who neglected the elderly are crushed under boulders, and, should you misuse books, expect to have your body sawn in two. At last, in the Tenth Court, comes a depiction of the now-purged sinner being offered the 'Cup of Forgetfulness', and rebirth on the Wheel of Reincarnation.

MK You are the Director of *Journeys Pte*, and the driving force behind the construction of the world's first museum of hell. This project has been an integral part of the revitalisation of Haw Par Villa as a twenty-first-century leisure venue. Haw Par Villa holds iconic status within Singapore, but, for those less familiar with the site, please take us on a brief tour.

JA Today, this heritage site is essentially the largest outdoor art gallery in Singapore. Locals and guests come here to relax a little, and to escape from the hectic pace of life in the metropolis. They can visit the themed museums, join one of our guided tours, or just meander through the park to view the sculptures and dioramas. The sculpture collection is at first glance eclectic, but mostly relates to Chinese classical literature, history, and Buddhist, Daoist, and Confucian philosophy. By far the best-known and best-loved of the installations is the underworld display of the Buddhist Ten Courts of Hell. This series of dioramas graphically itemises the separate punishments meted out to sinners for specific crimes. The visitor enters the installation through a dark cave-like mouth, guarded by two huge monstrous figures: Ox-Head and Horse-Face. These terrifying entities are, according to Chinese mythology, the escorts for dead souls being brought to judgement in the courts below. Many Singaporeans have shared

Illus. 1. The entrance to the Ten Courts of Hell at Haw Par Villa, Singapore. Horse-Face and Ox-Head are featured at the entrance. Courtesy of Singapore History Consultants.

with us their memories of being brought here as children, and admonished by their parents to behave better ... or else!

MK What is the early history attached to this site?

JA The story of Haw Par Villa intersects with the history of Singapore across the twentieth century: its economic expansion, diverse cultural heritage, and multicultural present. In 1937 Aw Boon Haw built a handsome art-deco villa here, in the hope of persuading his brother and business partner, Aw Boon Par, to leave Burma and settle in Singapore. The brothers were co-owners of the famous Tiger Balm brand [a branded herbal pain-relief ointment], and among the richest families in South-East Asia. They were also great philanthropists. They allowed free access to the gardens of their villa, in part to promote their brand and in part to offset the paucity of recreational spaces available to Asians during the colonial period. From its inception, this was a place to refresh the spirit, with the sculptures functioning as memory triggers to recall mythological stories and prompt inspiration and moral guidance.

Unfortunately, the villa was damaged during the Japanese occupation of Singapore in the Second World War, and Boon Par died in 1944 in Burma.

His brother was grief-stricken. He channelled his creative energies into increasing the number of sculptures in the park. Around three-quarters of the stock we see today was created between 1946 and 1954 (when Boon Haw died).

The sculptures, such as the most prominent grouping, the 'Virtues and Vices', are informed by Chinese classical literature and the teachings that underpin it. In particular, they draw on the sixteenth-century Chinese novel *Journey to the West*. This recounts how the Monkey King assists the pilgrim monk Xuanzang on his perilous journey to collect the holy sutras [Buddhist scriptures] from India and bring them back to China. The Monkey King was one of the few who could, according to this story, overthrow hell's guardians, Ox-Head and Horse-Face, but this heroic feat of strength also indicated his arrogance and want of virtue. Thus, his adventures in hell stand as an early indicator of the need for enlightenment.

MK So Haw Par Villa uses its physical topography to educate and edify: a visitor to the gardens is to reflect upon virtuous acts, to walk away from vices, and is given a final warning on what will happen if they fail to heed this message, in the uncomfortably vivid Ten Courts of Hell?

AJ That would certainly have been how previous generations of Singaporeans, and the Chinese community in particular, would have interpreted the statuary. But today's visitors have become divorced from such interpretative frameworks, in part because such cultural knowledge is no longer deemed relevant in modern society. We want to offer information which can promote a deeper understanding of the Asian allegorical and cultural resonances behind the statuary, but also encourage a better comprehension of comparative religious thinking and literary cultures across the world.

MK So *Journeys Pte*'s contemporary curatorial practice has placed the visitor's encounter with the Buddhist Ten Courts of Hell in a new interpretative frame? Your focus is on Asia, and, in particular, local Singaporean Chinese culture, but you also explain the conceptual division between a teleological belief in a judgement day, found in the Christian and Islamic faiths, and the more cyclical understanding of Samsara [the cycle of death and rebirth] in Buddhist thought.

AJ Hell's Museum is not proselytising, nor is it exclusive in approach. Our intent is to embrace current multiculturalism and its needs. Death and the afterlife are, after all, themes of universal interest. This serious and respectful approach to a difficult but pressing subject meets, we are delighted to find, with the approval of our visitors. In the 1980s, a very different attempt to 'market' the location as a modern commercial leisure venue was made. The gardens were redesigned to become a theme park with rides (on the model of Disney Land), and renamed 'Haw Par Villa Dragon World'. The Ten Courts became a water ride, with entry by boat through the mouth of the dragon: a sixty-five metre concrete dragon was constructed specially for the new theme park launch! Though initially successful, the enterprise failed to sustain a sufficient customer base.

MK One eminent art historian, Robert Hughes, has traced the decline of the hellmouth in Western art to little more than a fairground attraction.

AJ Perhaps our experience at Haw Par Villa reflects something that is happening in many countries: a loss of interpretative memory. Yet we continue to enjoy familiar festivals and rituals, and to recognise the obvious features of key characters from old stories, even when we have become unfamiliar with the literary and philosophical thinking that once underpinned them. There is still a hunger to engage with ideas as well as to be entertained. After all, native Singaporeans complained that, at the 1980s water ride, the boats moved too quickly to allow visitors to appreciate the detail in the dioramas of the Ten Courts of Hell.

MK Concepts and tales about the afterlife are in effect encouraging us to consider how we should live today: today's tourists will not want to be preached to, but perhaps they are nonetheless seeking to be challenged by what they find on their travels.

AJ At Haw Par Villa, visitors go through the first building hosting new galleries of Hell's Museum, and then must pass the guarded cave mouth, in order to brave a fully immersive experience: the walk past the courts of hell and their gory exposition of the penalties imposed on sinners.

MK Visitors might be struck, in terms of their own morality, by the dioramas' representations of how a method of punishment fits a crime (what Dante calls the 'contrapasso'). There is a particular condemnation of those who lack respect or show no charity, such as failing to support the more vulnerable in society (like widows and orphans).

AJ Yes, and this perhaps encourages visitors to think about our own global society, and how best to improve our interaction with one another. After taking the slow path through the courts, they re-emerge into daylight and

Illus. 2. A depiction of the Sixth Court of Hell within the Ten Courts of Hell at Haw Par Villa, Singapore. The punishment for the misuse of books, possession of pornographic material, breaking written rules and regulations and wasting food is to have your body sawn into two. Courtesy of Singapore History Consultants.

conclude their journey at a reconstruction of a Daoist temple. This final location helps them see afresh how current religious practices function, and the ways in which ritual still helps us find ways to cope with our fears and endeavours. The new development at Haw Par Villa frames hell for the twenty-first century. It offers contextual information to guide the visitor, an immersive, entertaining, and slightly scary experience of the under-world, and a final challenge: to reassess the way we live today, our personal moral outlook, and our views on religious practice in the world around us.

MK One thing I learnt from the museum was the impact of Buddhism on Chinese thought, and the ways in which a concept of the afterlife, Samsara, has inflected Daoism. What would you see as specifically Chinese in the Aw Brothers' Courts of Hell installation?

AJ Daoist thinking would allow either ten or eighteen courts for hell. There is a dynamic in the atonement for sin, conceived of as a journey in space and time through the separate courts. The soul will eventually come to the point when re-entry onto the Wheel of Life is achievable. It drinks a Cup of Forgetfulness and can be reborn into a new existence: anything from a heavenly spirit to an animal or even a hungry ghost. The Chinese approach leans heavily on hell's legal team and civil servants: there is a strong focus on bureaucracy, with judges and magistrates named for each court, and a scribe assigned to record all the sins and punishments that are to be meted out. This is very clearly depicted at Haw Par Villa. What we are now adding to the framework (using the Daoist temple setting) is more local context for Singaporeans, such as explaining the context of the annual Hungry Ghost Festival [held on the fifteenth day of the seventh month to appease the anger of the ghosts that are let out of hell during this month of the lunar year]. There is a tendency to think that contemporary Chinese religion is just about superstition, but a journey to Hell's Museum will help you to respond more fully to the vibrancy of festival time in our city.

MK I retain a very strong memory of how it felt to exit the Ten Courts of Hell, to come back out from that under-space, where the lighting was low and the temperature cool, into the midday sun of the tropics. For me at the time it felt like a release. I was conscious of relishing the warmth and light of the natural world, after a sojourn in the dark.

Hell's Museum in the gardens of Haw Par Villa now relates hell to a twenty-first-century cityscape in ways that are innovative and positive. You are supporting local cultural history but also addressing the questions of why human beings across the globe have told (and continue to tell) stories of an afterlife, and what we now remember from the myths and foundation narratives with which we grew up. Singapore as a hub for world trade and travel, a multicultural nation defined by immigration and economic expansionism, seems the ideal place to take this endeavour forward. Thank you for sharing the story of Haw Par Villa and the reasoning behind the construction of Hell's Museum.

Works Cited

Hughes, Robert, *Heaven and Hell in Western Art* (London, 1968)

Part II

Out into this World:
Sensory Hells

The Taste of Food in Hell:
Cognition and the Buried Myth of Tantalus in Early Modern English Texts[1]

LAURA SEYMOUR

In Seneca's *Thyestes* (c. 62 CE), the Ghost of Tantalus poses a question:

> peius inuentum est siti
> arente in undis aliquid et peius fame
> hiante semper?

> (has something been devised that's worse than parching thirst amid the waves, and worse than gaping forever in hunger?)[2]

Tantalus is doomed to spend eternity starved and parched, grasping at elusive fruits and water. The Fury who has raised his ghost from the underworld promises (in anticipation of the play's conclusion, where Thyestes unwittingly eats his own children) events so terrible that they will ironically reverse Tantalus's stricken situation: 'I've planned a feast even you will flee from' ('inueni dapes/ quas ipse fugeres').[3] The play *Thyestes* not only poses but also answers Tantalus's question: a father cannibalising his own children is something worse than eternal hunger and thirst. Several early modern authors, however, were not satisfied with this. They took up Tantalus's question like a dare and competitively explored ever more terrible answers. The three texts I examine in this essay – Christopher Marlowe's *Tamburlaine the Great* (first performed 1587), Thomas Dekker's *If It Be Not Good, The Diuel Is In It* (first performed 1611), and John Milton's *Paradise Lost* ([1667], 1674) – rise to this challenge with explorations of multisensory triggers and ensouled punishments. Without explicit mention of Tantalus, all three authors choose to present versions of his punishment,

[1]   I am very grateful to Margaret Kean, Susan Wiseman, Stephen Clucas, and Faisal Alramah for their advice on this essay.
[2]   Seneca, *Thyestes*, ed. R. J. Tarrant (Oxford, 1985), lines 4–6. All English translations from Seneca are mine.
[3]   Seneca, *Thyestes*, lines 66–67. 'Aliquid' ('something') homophonically suggests to my ear the sought-after 'liquidus' ('liquid').

drawing not only on classical mythology but also ideas from Abrahamic religions. They employ a range of methods, including tableaux, dialogue, stagecraft, and amphibolous poetic descriptions, to present torments that involve but also exceed the pangs of eternal hunger and thirst.

Thomas Kyd's play *The Spanish Tragedy* (1587) was inspired by *Thyestes*, perhaps via Jasper Heywood's 1560 translation. Kyd mirrors the Senecan dialogue between Tantalus and the Fury when he has the Ghost of Andrea describe hell to Revenge, and Revenge promise lavishly bloody vengeance. Here, the Senecan augmentation of Tantalus's punishment has been submerged within a lengthy hypotyposis of a hell,

> Where Vsurers are choakt with melting golde,
> And wantons are imbraste with ougly snakes:
> And murderers grone with neuer killing wounds,
> And periurde wights scalded in boyling lead.[4]

The success of *The Spanish Tragedy* helped it become a touchstone, as later playwrights attempted to outdo Kyd, and each other. Playwrights working within the genre of revenge tragedy escalated Senecan conventions, multiplied ghosts, and devised ever-bloodier torments. Often, as in Cyril Tourneur's 1611 *The Atheist's Tragedy*, where an amateur bedsheet-based ghost disguise appears in the same play as a pious Ghost who advocates against revenge, ludicrous elements were incorporated.

In connecting *Thyestes* and *The Spanish Tragedy* I do not aim to intervene in debates about the extent of Seneca's influence on Kyd.[5] Rather, foregrounding the role of imagination and cognition, this essay unearths the ways in which the buried myth of Tantalus shapes Renaissance literary evocations of infernal eating. In *Tamburlaine the Great*, Marlowe's Orcanes describes his enemy eating unsatisfyingly bitter hellish fruit. Thereafter, Thomas Dekker stages what Kyd merely describes: the consumption of blood, molten gold, and snake venom. Dekker's murderers, usurers, and 'perjur'd wights' experience a feast from which they would flee, even as they simultaneously crave nourishing food. Milton's devils guzzle seemingly delicious fruit which tastes of ash. The hells constructed by Marlowe, Dekker, and Milton simultaneously repulse and entice their audiences, invoking a cognitively broad spectrum of embodied response, memory, and religious and moral judgements to afflict both body and soul.

---

[4]   Thomas Kyd, *The Spanish Tragedie* (London, 1592), A3r.
[5]   Eugene Hill, 'Senecan and Vergilian Perspectives in *The Spanish Tragedy*', *ELR* 15.2 (1985), 143–65.

Torments of taste may seem an overly niche topic. When it comes to eating in hell, the damned themselves are perhaps more commonly treated *as* food, to be consumed by demons or by hell itself.[6] However, a focus on what the damned can taste illuminates broader questions about personhood in the afterlife. Tantalus was tormented because, though dead, he still yearned to satisfy bodily desire and engage in nourishing acts of eating and drinking. If the damned are tortured through taste, they have (quasi-)sensory experiences. Discussing 'the quality of the soul after leaving the body, and the punishment inflicted on it by material fire', Thomas Aquinas (c. 1225–74) considers the idea, attributed to St Augustine, that 'man alone has a substantial soul, which lives though separated from the body, and clings keenly to its senses and wits'.[7] Aquinas grapples with, and rejects, the idea that the soul might retain its 'sensitive powers' and experience passions and sensations when separated from the body.[8] Nevertheless, sensory torments of disgusting or pain-inducing foods, and delicious tastes offered and denied, seem to be the worst that many Renaissance authors can imagine. Recent psychophysiological work on memory and imagination's roles in taste and olfaction suggests that images or descriptions of food alone can provoke in humans a strong physical anticipation of eating. The physically affecting power of performed and described images of eating is certainly one reason why these early modern authors foreground feasts in hell.

In *death* (2012), taste disrupts the atheist philosopher Shelly Kagan's attempt to reject the dualist argument that humans consist of both bodies and souls. He maintains that the emotional, qualitative experience of taste cannot be explained in purely physical, bodily terms. Thus, it seems, only ensouled beings, or at least beings that are more than bodies, can taste:

'What's it like to see red? What's it like to smell coffee or to taste pineapple?'... We really don't have any idea *at all* about how to tell that story. Suppose we use the word *consciousness* to refer to this qualitative aspect of our mental life. Then I think we have to admit that from the point of view of the physicalist, consciousness remains a pretty big mystery.[9]

---

[6]   Laura Seymour, 'The Feasting Table as the Gateway to Hell on the Early Modern Stage and Page', *Renaissance Studies* 34.3 (2020), 392–411, p. 15; Christian Lange, *Paradise and Hell in Islamic Traditions* (Cambridge, 2016), pp. 60–1.

[7]   Thomas Aquinas, *Summa Theologiae*, trans. Fathers of the English Dominican Province (New York, 1948), vol. 5, Suppl. Q.70 Art 1. (p. 2825). The quotation about clinging 'keenly' is from *De Ecclesiasticis Dogmatibus* xvi, attributed formerly to St Augustine, currently to Gennadius of Massilia.

[8]   Aquinas, pp. 2827–8.

[9]   Shelly Kagan, *death* (New Haven, 2012), pp. 38–9.

Strikingly, something as everyday as smelling coffee or tasting pineapple is the one thing that stymies Kagan's physicalist argument that we have no souls and do not survive death.[10] Smell and taste are not to be explained away and so implicate him in questions of the afterlife. For those encountering the afterlife of hell in the Renaissance texts under discussion, taste proves to be part of being ensouled. Tastes are *qualia* rising beyond the physical to encompass moral questions of greed, social conscience (for example, Dekker introduces a gluttonous Prodigal who mocked the poor while alive), or thankfulness for God's gifts. Through repetitive actions, food urgently desired but never enjoyed, and banquets that incite us to flee, the myth of Tantalus is sunkenly at work in Marlowe, Dekker, and Milton's texts. Food in these authors' hells stimulates the appetite even as it repels the taste, combining Tantalus's desired feast with the feast that even he would flee.

Marlowe – Bitter Mixing

Marlowe's 'perjur'd wight' Sigismond is condemned to eat 'Zoacum' in hell. The reference leads back to the Zaqqūm tree described in the Qur'an as having devils' heads for fruit. The Qur'an mentions Zaqqūm several times; for instance, Surah 37. The damned consume Zaqqūm, which burns their insides, and try to slake their thirst with scalding water (a hellish drink that appears several times in the Qur'an and hadith).[11] Marlowe's usage combines classical and biblical influences with early modern source materials on Islam and Turkey to present Zoacum as confusingly both delightfully abundant and disgusting. This dual attraction and repulsion necessarily evokes the rhythm of Tantalus's torment.

Orcanes, the Muslim king of Natolia, had agreed a truce and mutual defence alliance with Sigismond, the Christian ruler of Hungary. Each swears fidelity by their respective religion. However, when they perceive Orcanes's military strength to be weaker than their own, the Christian forces treacherously attack him. If Marlowe read the Qur'an, he may be drawing on the specific condemnation of this in Surah 16:92. Orcanes denounces the falsehood of Sigismond and his allies, and hedges his bets by invoking both Christ, whom he assumes will seek revenge on Sigismond

---

[10]   Kagan, *death*, p. 41.
[11]   Lange, *Paradise and Hell*, p. 137. See, for instance, Surah 38:57. For an English translation of the Qur'an, see *The Koran*, trans. N. J. Dawood, (London, 1956).

for breaking his Christian oath, and 'Mahomet' (a common early modern English spelling of Muhammad, whom Marlowe misrepresents Muslims as worshipping). Orcanes then re-enters the battle and conquers Sigismond. Orcanes envisages Sigismond in a version of hell derived from the Qur'an, mixed with a potential biblical reference to armies or nations becoming animals' prey (Isaiah 18:6). Additional classical references to the flower-goddess Flora, and to Tartarus as the underworld, create an example of what Steve Mentz calls a typical Marlowan confluence of 'models of Latin poetry' and 'Turkish cultural influence'.[12] In terms of characterisation, Orcanes's interrelation of these different strands of imagery reflects his strategically broadened religious allegiances, and a belief that 'Christ or Mahomet hath bene my friend'.[13] In terms of authorial decisions, though, Marlowe seems to be drawing on whichever religious or mythological sources help him to present the most terrible Renaissance hell. 'Tartarian streames' suggest water, not fire. Placed in combination with the 'banefull' fruit tree, these 'streames' strongly suggest Tantalus's torments. The 'Turkish cultural influence', however, means that even if Orcanes manages to break from the Tantalus-frame and drink the Tartarian streams, he cannot enjoy them: they 'scald', like foods in the Qur'anic hell.

> Now shall his barbarous body be a pray
> To beasts and foules, and al the winds shall breath
> Through shady leaues of euery sencelesse tree,
> Murmures and hisses for his hainous sin.
> Now scaldes his soule in the Tartarian streames,
> And feeds vpon the banefull tree of hell,
> That *zoacum*, that fruit of bytternesse,
> That in the midst of fire is ingraft,
> Yet flourisheth as *Flora* in her pride,
> With apples like the heads of damned Feends.[14]

Orcanes distinguishes Sigismond's body from his soul. Animals destroy the former; the latter is consigned to hell. Nevertheless, Orcanes describes the soul's torment in sensory terms. It can be scalded and it must feed on 'bitter' 'zoacum'. 'Scald' usually refers to the effect of hot liquid or steam, though it can relate to any heat (including fire). As it can also mean to become

---

[12] Steve Mentz, 'Marlowe's Mediterranean and Counter-Epic Forms of Oceanic Hybridity', in *Travel and Drama in Early Modern England*, ed. Claire Jowitt and David McInnis (Cambridge, 2018), pp. 55–71 (p. 55).

[13] Christopher Marlowe, *Tamburlaine the Great* (London, 1590), G5v.

[14] Marlowe, *Tamburlaine*, G5v.

sore, raw, and inflamed, there is a suggestion here of a skin-like soul. The meaning of 'bitter' extends beyond brute physicality to encompass moral and emotional meanings: Sigismond's sorrow and his food are both bitter. In the early modern era, as today, the fact that gustatory vocabulary like 'bitter' and 'sweet' can also refer to emotional states enables taste to blur the boundary between body and soul. Indeed, some recent psychological research suggests that sweet or bitter tastes can evoke sweet or bitter mental states, and that particular mental states can alter how food tastes, because taste and odour are produced not only by the chemical composition of food but through a combination of memory, emotion, and moral and rational judgements.[15] When Marlowe's Bad Angel asks Faustus to 'taste' hell, he means it literally and also in the sense of 'exploring' or 'experiencing'.[16] Marlowe does not stage hell in *Tamburlaine*, but his *copia* lets us 'taste' the punishment Orcanes envisages Sigismond enduring, and the emphasis on sensory perception lends immediacy to his description. Orcanes frames Sigismond's soul as having (quasi-)corporeal experiences even when separated from his body. Zoacum's cephalomorphic fruits, which Marlowe further aligns with Edenic 'apples', might bite back at Sigismond. Marlowe's sentence develops dismayingly: we reach first for alluring 'Flora', but Flora disappears to leave Orcanes caught in a mutually cannibalistic kiss with demon-faced food.

John Michael Archer places Marlowe's work within a group of early modern English plays that he says misrepresent Islam, represent it 'tendentiously', or fail to represent it. Archer describes Orcanes's triumph-speech as one of a 'series of scenes' that 'seem to have sprung from an abortive encounter with some traces of Islamic thought in medieval and early modern learning'.[17] As Gillian Woods explains, Marlowe's desire to mock Christianity may have shaped his treatment of Islam. She suggests that, when Tamburlaine burns the Qur'an, Marlowe deliberately evokes similarities between Islam and Christianity in order to imply anti-Christian blasphemies that he could not stage explicitly.[18] If so, Marlowe's deliberately

---

[15]   For instance, Kendall Erskine et al, 'The Bitter Truth About Morality', *PLoS One* 7.7 (2012), e41159. See Pamela Dalton, 'There's Something in the Air', in *Olfactory Cognition*, ed. Gesualdo Zucco et al (Amsterdam, 2012), pp. 25–38 (p. 31).

[16]   Christopher Marlowe, *The Tragicall History of the Life and Death of Doctor Faustus* (London, 1616), H2r-v (B text).

[17]   John Michael Archer, 'Islam and *Tamburlaine's* World Picture', in *A Companion to the Global Renaissance*, ed. Jyotsna Singh (Hoboken, 2007), pp. 63–81 (pp. 72–3).

[18]   Gillian Woods, 'Marlowe and Religion', in *Christopher Marlowe in Context*, ed. Emily Bartels and Emma Smith (Cambridge, 2013), pp. 222–31 (p. 228).

retractable evocation of similarity between Islam and Christianity intersects with the ways in which Tamburlaine is racialised, evoking 'markers
of Eurocentric similarity' through his pale skin but demonstrating 'affect'
and 'actions' which challenge this similarity and weaken any boundaries
between 'paleness' and 'barbarousness'.[19]

Archer sees Marlowe's 'Zoacum' lines as 'direct quotation' from the
Qur'an.[20] However, even when readers in Western Christendom used the
available translations of the Qur'an, their experience was often not 'direct'
but mediated by pro-Christian, anti-Islamic polemic. If Marlowe did read
the Qur'an, it would have been in Latin, as the first complete English translation of the Qur'an was not available until 1649. Such Latin translations
strove for linguistic accuracy but, as Thomas Burman explains, this was gen-
erally motivated by the desire to ground anti-Islamic arguments in accurate
knowledge of the tenets of Islam, with paratextual material directing such
polemic and guiding the assumedly Christian reader towards a sense of
shock.[21] It is unlikely that Marlowe is referring directly to a Latin Qur'an.
He seems to have gained his knowledge of Zaqqūm second-hand, primarily from German historian Philippus Lonicerus's description of 'Zoacum' in
Chronicorum Turcicorum (1578). Marlowe includes a conspicuous adjectival
addition: his Zoacum 'flourisheth' in hell. In the original Arabic, Zaqqūm
grows in, or comes out of, hell's nethermost part. Medieval and early modern
Latin Qur'ans preserve this idea, simply describing Zaqqūm (variant spellings
include 'azacum', 'ezetus', 'ezecum', 'Azachon') as 'coming out' ('emittens', or
'egreditur') of hellfire. This includes Robert of Ketton's translation, which

---

[19]   Sydnee Wagner, 'New Directions: Towards a Racialized Tamburlaine', in
Tamburlaine: A Critical Reader, ed. David McInnis (London, 2020), pp. 129–46
(p. 137).

[20]   Archer confuses Marlowe's potential Qur'anic sources, conflating Robert of
Ketton (twelfth-century translator of the Qur'an into Latin) with Robert of Chester
(near-contemporary translator of Arabic algebraic works into Latin). Produced under
a wider pro-Christian project guided by Peter the Venerable, Ketton's paraphrastic
translation, hostilely named *Lex Mahumet Pseudoprophetae*, was first published by
Theodor Bibliander in 1543 as *Machumetis saracenorum principis eiusque successorum
vitae, doctrina ac ipse alcoran* (Basel, 1543). Ketton's was the most-read Qur'an version
among European Christians; Thomas Burman notes that Ketton was probably aided
by a Muslim translator, Muhammad, whose identity and contribution are not exten-
sively recorded or credited, *Reading the Qur'an in Latin Christendom* (Philadelphia,
2014), p. 15. See also Gregory Miller, 'Theodor Bibliander's *Machumetis saracenorum
principis eiusque successorum vitae, doctrina ac ipse alcoran* (1543) as the Sixteenth-
century "Encyclopedia" of Islam', *Islam and Christian–Muslim Relations* 24.2 (2013),
241–54.

[21]   Burman, *Reading the Qur'an*, pp. 14–15 and pp. 60–2.

Archer suggests Marlowe may have read in an edition that was bequeathed to his Cambridge college, Corpus Christi, in 1575.[22] When interpreted as 'to grow successfully' or even 'to thrive', 'flourisheth' fits with the Qur'an's suggestion that Zaqqūm grows perpetually, and is not destroyed by hellfire.[23] But 'flourisheth' can also signify 'to bloom', 'embellish', or 'grow with vigour'. Such positive connotations of abundance are strengthened by Marlowe's mention of 'Flora in her prime' and his contrast between the burgeoning Zoacum and the 'sencelesse tree[s]' on earth. Lonicerus likewise uses 'florere' (to blossom or flourish) in his description of 'Zoacum'. Lonicerus's spelling 'Zoacum' and reference to Islamic hell as 'Tartarus' strengthen the idea that Marlowe referred primarily to this history rather than to Latin translations of the Qur'an.[24] Tartarus originally referred to the Greek and Roman mythological underworld but Lonicerus and Marlowe overlap it with hells envisaged by the religions of Renaissance Europe. The notion of 'direct quotation' obscures Marlowe's *in*direct approach to Zaqqūm through an amalgam of biblical, historical, and classical writings, and his own descriptive extensions of the Zoacum-image. Marlowe's engagement with Lonicerus stimulates literary and imaginative exploration, and allows him to intensify the sensual horrors of the classical underworld by combining them with an obliquely seen version of an Islamic hell.

Marlowe's 'flourish[ing]' tree and its 'apples' are echoed in Giles Fletcher's description of 'Zoacum' as 'alwaies greene and flourishing' and with 'a great abundance of apples' in *The Policy of the Turkish Empire: The First Booke* (1597).[25] These quotations are from Fletcher's third

---

[22] Ketton describes 'ezetus' growing out of hellfire 'ex sua radice gehennae focum emittens', in *Theodor Bibliander: Le Coran en Latine*, ed. Henri Lamarque (Lyon, 2010), p. 136. Egidio da Viterbo, Leo Africanus, and Johannes Gabriel Terrolensis' 1518 translation reads, 'et est quaedam arbor quae egreditur de radice inferni', Katarzyna Starczewska, *Latin Translation of the Qur'an (1518/1621): Commissioned by Egidio da Viterbo. Critical Edition and Case Study* (Wiesbaden, 2018), Surah 37.

[23] I am very grateful to Faisal Alramah for explaining how well various English definitions of 'flourish' fit the Arabic.

[24] Philippus Lonicerus, *Chronicorum Turcicorum* (Frankfurt, 1584), II. Ethel Seaton argues strongly that Marlowe used Lonicerus alongside one-time Turkish captive Giovanni Antonio Menavino's description of 'Zoacum', in 'Fresh Sources for Marlowe', *The Review of English Studies* 5.2 (1929), 385–401. Marlowe's vocabulary echoes Lonicerus's more widely here – for example, 'ingrafted' (fixed in) perhaps reflects Lonicerus's 'infixam'.

[25] Fletcher emphasises Zoacum growing despite hellfire, 'such is the wil of God'. His use of Lonicerus and Menavino's phrase 'Zoacum Agassi' suggests their influence, Giles Fletcher, *The Policy of the Turkish Empire: The First Booke* (London, 1597), T1v–T2r.

chapter, which presents Turkish beliefs about the afterlife within a biased framework that views Western Christian beliefs as overridingly correct. Fletcher makes much of the repetitive nature of eating in the afterlife (for example, heaven's fruits regrowing immediately once eaten), and links this to other repetitions such as the heavenly spouses' daily renewed virginities. Fletcher's emphasis on repetition is not unique. The religious studies scholar Christian Lange describes wider Islamic traditions of body parts burnt away and regrown in hell (deriving from Qur'anic references; for instance, Surah 4:56) as the hellish obverse of paradise's miraculously regrowing fruits and renewing virginities.[26] Milton's angels suggest one interpretation of the repeated need to eat in the afterlife: humans are not self-sustaining but depend on God whether in earth, heaven, or hell, '[f]or know, whatever was created, needs/ To be sustain and fed'.[27] In the snapshot of Sigismond grappling with his sterile meal, Orcanes does not dilate on how Sigismond might be 'sustained' in hell. Milton and Dekker, however, do address the never-ending nature of infernal torments and the difficult-to-imagine damned body which hungers, thirsts, and feels pain for eternity without being totally destroyed. In so doing, they foreground another aspect of the buried Tantalus myth: eternal repetition.

Dekker – Simulation

Quid famem infixam intimis
agitas medullis?[28]

(Why do you stir up the hunger fixed in my inner marrow?)

Tantalus's torment plays on his ability to imagine himself gaining satisfactory nourishment. This is what motivates him to reach for the fruits and water. Dekker's *If It Be Not Good* stages just such a tantalised emotional state in especially excruciating detail. Where Marlowe combines various cultural influences, Dekker applies the New Testament story of Dives and Lazarus, localised for a London audience and foregrounded alongside horrifying events from recent cultural memory, to bring his hell emotively home. Marlowe does not stage the Zoacum tree; the audience sees only Sigismond's corpse as Orcanes describes the experiences due to Sigismond's

---

[26]   Lange, *Paradise and Hell,* p. 130.
[27]   John Milton, *Paradise Lost* (1674) V.413–14, in *The Riverside Milton,* ed. Roy Flannigan (Boston, 1998),
[28]   Seneca, *Thyestes,* lines 97–8.

soul. Dekker, however, does stage the soul, and thereby makes visible the torments of hell. His play spends time on the enactment of his perjured characters' cravings for specific beverages. Their imaginative desires are stirred by devils to painful peaks, but the drinks themselves are never provided. Instead, Dekker's damned are vengefully served molten gold, snake venom, and blood: drinks befitting their corrupted state.

The early Islamic commentator Ibn Sina suggested that damned souls might be tormented solely by the 'similitudes' imprinted in their imaginations.[29] Positioning our ability to imagine or 'simulate' food's taste and texture as crucial to our experience of eating, cognitive science has recently enabled us to illuminate the theatrical power of this misery. Esther Papies, Lawrence Barsalou, and Dorottya Rusz draw on 'simulation theory' to explain how, in the absence of physical stimuli, the brain can flesh out an experience of taste using stored 'situated memories' of foods and drinks. These memories can be activated by contextual cues 'responsive to state and trait individual differences' 'such as visual and sensory features (for example, appearance, taste, texture of a food or drink), contextual features (for example, time, place, other people present), motor actions (for example, cutting, grasping, chewing), current states (for example, hunger, pleasure, health goals), and other information'. For instance, an image of cake 'can lead to a vivid simulation...of its sweet taste and creamy texture', the movements involved in lifting one's fork, and feelings of 'reward' consequent on eating.[30] Modern scholarship's rooting of cognition in the kinetic body and neuronal brain is not strictly equivalent to Aquinas's idea that the soul 'clings keenly to its senses and wits' when death separates it from the body. Nevertheless, such cognitive studies show how everyday experiences of hungering imaginatively after food can help us to understand the urgent desires of the damned. Early modern writers implicitly acknowledge that if damned souls lacked the faculties of memory (of past pain, of lost pleasures) and imagination (of future pain, of craved-for pleasures), hell's power would diminish. Dekker encourages audiences to draw on memories and contextual cues to appreciate hell's gustatory torments. He simultaneously represents souls tormented by their own memories of food and drink, and by cues that arouse hunger and thirst. This means that readers, audiences, and characters on stage have structurally similar

---

[29]   Peter Heath, *Allegory and Philosophy in Avicenna (Ibn Sînâ)* (Philadelphia, 1992), p. 69.

[30]   Esther Papies, Lawrence Barsalou, and Dorottya Rusz, 'Understanding Desire for Food and Drink', *Current Directions in Psychological Science* 29.2 (2020), 193–8, p. 194.

yet individuated experiences of a personal hell, each tailored according to specific prior experiences, memories, and imaginative capacities.[31]

Dekker asks us to taste hell. He evokes these types of simulated taste-based torment as a means to attract audiences already familiar with the plays of Kyd and Marlowe, and to outdo these predecessors. *If It Be Not Good* revolves around diabolic infiltration of various institutions (counting-house, monastery, court). At the end of the play, hell is revealed. The devils Ruffman, Shacklesoul, and Lurchall are depicted tormenting real-life figures from Dekker's era, selected to accord with Dekker's anti-Catholic 'humour', alongside fictional characters. The French Catholic regicide François Ravaillac (1578–1610) and the English Catholic would-be regicide Guy Fawkes (spelt 'Faulx', perhaps to emphasise his falseness; 1570–1606) burn alongside a generic Prodigal and the fictional cheating merchant-usurer Barterville.[32] The devils are also awaiting Moll Frith (a real person who had already been turned into a literary character in Dekker and Middleton's 1611 *The Roaring Girl*). Dekker's sudden introduction of historical figures into a previously fictional, folkloric narrative accompanies a shift to particularly astounding infernal stage-effects. Dekker sets the scene spectacularly with a stage direction that contrasts the devils' delighted energy ('leaping in great ioy') with the immobility of their victims 'standing in their torments'.

> *The play ending, as they goe off, from vnder the ground in seuerall places, rise vp spirits, to them enter, leaping in great ioy, Rufman, Shackle soule, and Lurchall, discouering behind a curten, Rauillac, Guy Faulx, Barteruile, a Prodigall, standing in their torments.*[33]

The damned are 'stuck' in several ways, not least in their fixation on thirst. All the damned call urgently for 'drinck' but Barterville also complains of being 'heart-burnt'. This combines, as is characteristic of him, bathos (he feels a touch of heart-burn after his life's excesses) with eschatology (his heart roasts in hellfire).

---

[31]   On the solipsism of theatrical taste, see Lucy Munro, 'Staging Taste', in *The Senses in Early Modern England, 1558–1660*, ed. Simon Smith, Jacqueline Watson, and Amy Kenny (Manchester, 2015), pp. 19–38.

[32]   Ravaillac had a vision asking him to convince Henri IV to convert Huguenots to Catholicism. Unable to meet with Henri, and fearing Henri would declare war on the pope, Ravaillac killed Henri in 1610.

[33]   Thomas Dekker, *If It Be Not Good, The Diuel Is In It* (London, 1612), L3r. Subsequent references to this edition are given parenthetically.

Barterville:	Whooh: hot, hot, hot,-drinck,-I am heart-burnt.
Prodigall:	One drop, a bit.
Faulx:	Now, now, now.
Barterville:	I am perbold, I am stewd, I am sod in a kettle of brimstone, pottage. – it scaldes, – it scaldes, – it scaldes, – it scaldes – whooh
Diuels:	Ha ha ha:
Prodigall:	But one halfe crom, a little little drop, a bit [...]
Barterville:	Zounds drinke, shall I choake in mine Inne? drinck.
Omnes:	Drinck, drinck, oh! one drop, one drop, to coole vs.
Ruffman:	So many tapsters in hell, and none fill drinck here:
Omnes:	Ball no more, you shall be liquord [*Exeunt*] [...]
Barterville:	Some sacke [...]
	Let the sacke be mulld [...]
	Man is an asse, if he sit broyling thus ith glasse house. [...]
	Without drinke: two links of my chaine for a three halfe peny bottle of mother consciences Ale: drinke.
Omnes:	One drop of puddle water to coole vs. (L3r-v)

Like the biblical Dives, Dekker's damned call for the merest water-drop but are denied. Dives, the rich man who mocked a pauper, experiences a drastic reversal of fortune in the afterlife. His eternal punishment in hell revolves around a lack of refreshing drink: 'he cried and said, Father Abraham, have mercy on me, and send Lazarus, that he may dip the tip of his finger in water, and cool my tongue; for I am tormented in this flame'. Abraham replies that this is impossible (Luke 16:23–6). In *Dekker his Dreame* (1620), the description of a dream-journey into hell, Dekker again evokes Dives and Lazarus, and recalls *If It Be Not Good*'s language of 'crums', 'one drop' of water, and (as we shall see) devils offering gall in place of refreshment:

They that for Table-crums refus'd to buy
And (for their soules) hoord vp Eternity,
Here offred worlds of Treasure, but to get
One drop of Water: (O hels infinite Heate!)
Yet not a drop was sufferd once to fall:
To quench their thirst, Diuels held out caps of Gall.[34]

Like Barterville who, true to his name, attempts to barter his way out of hell with his wealth, the damned in Dekker's dream 'offred worlds of *Treasure*' for '[o]ne drop of *Water*' but are denied.

---

[34]   Thomas Dekker, *Dekker his Dreame* (London, 1620), E3v.

The Dives and Lazarus story held particularly emotive power for early modern preachers and theologians, possibly because thirst is such a commonly understood distress that it can bring hell within our imagination's grasp. In *A Pleasant and Profitable Treatise of Hell* (anonymously, and here faithfully, translated into English in 1668 from the 1632 Latin text), the Jesuit Drexel devotes a chapter to hunger and thirst in hell. This includes a recounting of the Dives and Lazarus story. Drexel helps his readers appreciate the damned's painful thirst by harnessing, and thus demonstrating the misery-making power of, earthly experiences. He urges us to consider experiences we can remember or even induce ('make...tryal thereof'), like licking salt until we are deeply thirsty, or experiencing certain illnesses. He says

> ...while the damned lived they seem to have licked nothing but salt, so rageing is their thirst in hell. How horrible a torment thirst is, it is hard for any one to express, unless he have made some certain tryal thereof: In this particular we may well credit the sick, who are frequently so tortured with thirst, that they esteem it the very dregs of their distempered cup, or their greatest disease.[35]

Jeremias Drexel's curious image of the 'distempered cup' figures thirst itself as a kind of drink: having drained this anti-drink to the 'dregs', the sick person is left even thirstier. Decades earlier, Dekker stages hell with unavailable cups of water, howling Drunkards, and constant cries of thirst. Dekker's devils do pledge Faulx with an 'infernal boule' of liquor, but, like Drexel's 'distempered cup', the drink 'choake[s]' rather than satisfies Faulx (L4r).

Papies et al. consider the 'new potentially problematic desires' generated by our ability to simulate a vivid experience of food and drink in a discussion that is shaped by broader concerns with calorific foods and obesity.[36] Barterville's desires are problematic in a different way: triggered by hell's heat, they will never be satisfied. Dekker's humour partly stems from the fact that, though Barterville's thirst is clearly rooted in hell's parching environment, his desire for specific alcoholic drinks is not what Papies et al. would describe as 'congruent' with its context. Barterville behaves as though he is 'in mine Inne', not a lake of eternal fire. He orders 'some Sacke' and stipulates amid other sinners' wails, 'let the sacke be mulld'. Later, he requests ale, while the others, more desperately, crave stagnant

[35]   Jeremias Drexel, *A Pleasant and Profitable Treatise of Hell*, trans. Anon (London, 1668), E7v.
[36]   Papies et al, p. 194.

puddles. When the devils promise, '[y]ou shall be liquord', the phrase's meaning is not totally clear, but they are certainly not offering the damned their craved-for drinks. As the damned are stewing as if in 'potage' (mushy soup, porridge, or stew), the devils are perhaps offering to add more boiling liquor to their 'kettle' or to boil them until they liquefy. Alternatively, they may be promising to bring unappetising drinks which (as we shall see) only exacerbate the damned souls' thirst. Experimental psychologist Egon Peter Köster suggests taste and smell 'make us feel at home in our world'.[37] Peopled with London characters, Dekker's local hell torments Barterville with *dis*location from familiar contexts, twisting the tastes he used to find homely. Barterville expresses earthly desires and would have the tastes he remembers transposed into hell. This creates unsatisfying simulations that torment him.

The devils' treacherous promise of drink further torments the damned. Barterville calls for 'lemon water' (a refreshing drink made from water and sliced lemons), 'ruby water' (possibly a restorative medicinal draught), and 'postern water' (probably spring water).[38] However, the 'lymon' water the devils offer to Barterville and his fellow sinners turns out to be molten gold, and the other drinks served are hot blood stabbed from the sinner's own breast, and (as in Dekker's 1620 *Dreame*) poisonous snakes to 'suck'.

Enter Shackle soule with a burning torch, and a long knife, Lurchall with a handfull of Snakes, A third spirit with a ladle full of molten gold, All three make a stand, laughing.

---

[37]   Egon Peter Köster, 'The Specific Characteristics of the Sense of Smell', in *Olfaction, Taste and Cognition*, ed. Catherine Rouby et al (Cambridge, 2002), pp. 27–44 (p. 27).

[38]   Rarely mentioned in print, ruby water may have been made from rubies grated into, or placed in or over, simmering water. In 1609, midwife Justine Siegmund pronounces it a common obstetric remedy for haemorrhage, *The Court Midwife*, ed. and trans. Lynne Tatlock (Chicago, 2005), pp. 182, 187. 'Carbuncle water' (carbuncles being any red stones, including rubies) is indicated for various ailments including fever and weakness; for example, Ysbrand van Diemerbroeck, *The Anatomy of Human Bodies*, trans. William Salmon (London, 1694), K1r-v. 'Postern water' is an ingredient in some cordials, including in Elizabeth Jacobs' manuscript treatise 'for the Ricketts', *The Early Modern English Version of Elizabeth Jacobs Physicall and Chirugicall Receipts*, ed. Miriam Criado-Peña (Newcastle, 2018), p. 55. Cyrus Hoy and Fredson Bowers' gloss to the Dekker text suggests it derives from Tower Hill's 'postern spring', *Introduction, Notes, and Commentaries* (Cambridge, 1980), vol. 1, p. 122.

Omnes: Leaue howling and be dambd.
Shacklesoul: Heres drinke for thee royall villaine.
                                    [*Stabs Rauillac*]
Rauaillac: Oh!
Shacklesoul: Ist not good!
                For bloud th'ast thirsted, and thy drinke is bloud.
                Strikes it so cold to thy heart? heres that shall warme thee
                                    [*Agen*]
Rauaiilac: Damnation, furies, fire-brandes –
                                    [*Hand burn't off*]
Omnes: Ha, ha, ha.
Prodigall: One drop of moisture, but one crum.
Lurchall: Art hungry, eate this adder: dry? Sucke this Snake.
Prodigall: Sucke and be dambd thy selfe: Ile starue first. Away
Barteruille: Is not this all waters? Ruby water, some Ruby water,
                Or els a bottle of posterne water to saue charges, or els a
                Thimble-full of lymon water, to coole my stomatch the ru
Spir[it?]:   By is swilld vp all, heres lymon, downe with't.
Barteruille: Foh, the great diuell or els some Aquauite woman has made
                water, It scalds me. (L3r-v)

In referencing the play's title, '[i]st not good!', Dekker revels in his success
at bringing Kyd's description of hell theatrically to life. Alternating stasis
and movement, Dekker has nearly reconciled two elements that are difficult to imagine simultaneously: a damned soul's eternal fixity and its eternal
torment. Now it is the devils' turn to 'make a stand', posing with their instruments and drawing attention to them. Verbally, visually, gesturally, they *offer*
drinks in order to increase the damned's thirst. The phrase 'here's drink for
thee' and the brandished ladle will set off particularly strong simulations of
imminently satisfied thirst in the damned's minds. This is in keeping with
recent psychophysiological research: Papies et al. found that a picture of an
apple pie with the fork towards the viewer's hands as if offering imminent
satisfaction evokes particularly strong simulations. Papies et al. link this to
higher 'purchase intentions', inadvertently recalling Renaissance prodigals'
attempts to buy their way to better treatment in Hell.[39] Simultaneously, the
stage-ladle suggests that something is awry as this prop is associated in contemporary plays like Marlowe's *The Jew of Malta* (1590) and *The Tragœdy of
Rollo* (potentially co-written by John Fletcher and Ben Jonson with revisions
by Phillip Massinger, c. 1617) with poisonings, and jokes about the prover-

---

[39]   Papies et al, p. 196.

bial long spoon needed when dining with the devil.[40] The speech-prefixes are slightly jumbled at this point, but the line '[t]he ruby is swilld vp all, here's lymon downe with't' should probably be attributed to a 'Spirit' as Barterville is marked as replying at 'Foh...' In carefully referencing the 'ruby' and 'lemon' water Barterville so wants, the devils underscore the fact that he is not getting them. To 'swill' could be to stir, drench, drink greedily. 'The ruby is swilled up' might mean the ruby water is stirred up and ready, or that the ruby is drenched in water, or alternatively be paraphrased as the ruby water has all been guzzled, so have some lemon instead. What is certain is that the devils describe ruby water being prepared or drunk. This strongly arouses Barterville's desires for specific drinks, proportionally worsening his unquenched thirst. When the devils proffer 'lymon', Barterville plausibly starts mentally to simulate the taste of lemony water in preparation for drinking it, only for his actual experiences to be cruelly different. The drink's scalding nature further torments him: he speculates that he is drinking the devil's urine or alcoholic urine of a woman who makes or drinks 'aquavitae' (ardent distilled spirits, ironically meaning 'water of life').

As an apposite punishment, the devils offer money-loving Barterville all the gold he wants by pouring it boiling down his throat, with a lake of boiling gold as additional drink. Again, they arouse Barterville's thirst with vocabulary that suggests abundant, quenching drink ('runnes', 'slake'):

Minos:	Throwe him head-long into our boyling-Lake,
	Where molten Golde runnes.
Lurchall:	His thirst it cannot slake,
	Seas could not quench his dropsie (M3r)

'Dropsie' here perhaps signifies excessive desire for water and/or the ability to store huge amounts of fluid, like Donne's 'hydroptique earth', rather than being an accurate medical term.[41] The devils frame their response to Ravaillac's thirst as equally fitting. They invite Ravaillac to drink his own blood because as a murderer he is metaphorically blood-thirsty.[42] Similarly, they tell the greedy Prodigall to 'feed on' that which

---

[40]   Christopher Marlowe, *The Famous Tragedy of The Rich Jew of Malta* (London, 1633), F4r; John Fletcher [Ben Jonson, Phillip Massinger], *The Tragœdy of Rollo* (Oxford, 1640), D1r.

[41]   John Donne, 'Nocturnal on St Lucy's Day', in *Poems by J. D.* (London, 1633), Bb2r.

[42]   The Gunpowder conspirators' trial calls execution 'a Reward due to Traitors, whose Hearts be hardened: For that it is Physic of State and Government, to let out corrupt Blood from the Heart', 'The Trials of Robert Winter [etc]...1606', in R.

offers no nourishment: 'beggaries' basket' (M1v). If 'feed' is used in the sense of 'taking in' or 'experiencing', the Prodigall 'feeds' on the experience of being hungry. His body, 'falne away' (made thin) reflects his spiritual condition, 'falne away/ From heaven' (M1v). Dekker makes thirst both the dominant torment in hell and the governing metaphor for sin. Evil desires on earth are figured as 'thirsts' (for gold, for blood) and punished through desire for drink – provoked to fever pitch and unsatisfied – in hell. Though Faulx speaks of 'souls', he and his fellow sinners' torment relies on sensory vocabulary and the physicality of the stage. Blood, weapons, golden liquid, and the focus on actors' body parts, such as Ravaillac's hand 'burnt off', create a corporeal, spectacular hell.[43] Indeed, informed his soul will be tortured, Barterville remarks, 'I never had any soule to speake on' (M2v). The remark is hilarious in its dismissiveness but also, in its Christian context, shockingly blasphemous. Dekker's final scene may be seen as proving Barterville wrong, but Dekker also confronts the difficulty of staging immaterial souls by grounding the imaginative acts in material vocabulary and stage-effects.

In order for their punishment to make sense, and to seem justified to theatre audiences, a soul in hell must be significantly similar to the person they were when they lived and sinned on earth. Ideally, they remember their sins, and understand they are being punished as the one who committed these sins. Christian philosopher Dean Zimmerman suggests applying 'the I-rule', whereby 'I' refers to 'a conscious agent and so a thing with mental states'; the duration for which we can continuously say 'I' is the duration for which we continue to exist after death.[44] When those in hell say 'I', this should be recognisably similar to the 'I' they were on earth. Dekker makes his damned souls conspicuously continuous with their earthly selves through the emphasis on their continued desire for food and drink based on memories of earthly life, and their continued ability to taste and feel. Dekker achieves further continuity not only by making the damned's hellish punishments fit their earthly crimes, but also by showing them

Bagshaw et al, *Cobbett's Complete Collection of State Trials* (London, 1809), vol. 2, p. 184. Thyestes's son's blood is a differently unquenching, wicked drink, dribbling Tantalus-like from his lips (Seneca *Thyestes*, line 985).

[43]   On early modern theatrical practices surrounding stage-blood and dismembering, see Lucy Munro, 'They Eat Each Others Arms', in *Shakespeare's Theatres and the Effects of Performance*, ed. Farah Karim-Cooper and Tiffany Stern (London, 2013), pp. 73–93.

[44]   Dean Zimmerman, 'Personal Identity and the Survival of Death', in *The Oxford Handbook of Philosophy of Death*, ed. Ben Bradley et al. (Oxford, 2013), pp. 97–154 (pp. 104–5).

fixating on those crimes. Dekker's damned are statically trapped by their earthly identities, 'standing in their torments'. The consistency of Barterville's 'I' is used for humorous effect: in hell, he behaves as thirstily and avariciously as he did on earth, seemingly oblivious to the enormity of his situation. In the midst of cries of thirst, Faulx harps on gunpowder and the buildings he could destroy '[t]owers, towers, towers, towers, pinnacles & towers, battlements and pynnacles, steeples, abbeys, churches and old chimnyes', and Ravaillac cries 'ile confesse nothing' even though devils tear him 'peece meal' (M1r-L3r). Dekker may be drawing on R. E.'s 1610 translation of a French account of Ravaillac's torture and execution, which repeats the phrase, 'torne to peeces' and empha-sises Ravaillac's refusal to repent. This is in contrast to contemporary reports of his confession and absolution by a priest. R. E.'s account may also be the source of Dekker's character having his hand burnt off. It relates that the knife Ravaillac used to assassinate Henri was chained to his right hand. Then, when he was tortured,

> flaming with fier and Brimstone, wherin the knife, his right hand, and halfe the arme adioyning to it, was in most terrible manner consumed, yet nothing at all would he confesse, but yelled out with such horrible cryes euen as it had beene a Diuell, or some tormented soule in hel: And surely if Hells tortures might be felt on earth, it was approued in this mans punishment.[45]

In the severity of his tortures, 'Diuell'-like cries and specifically hellish pun-ishments of 'fire and Brimstone', Ravaillac experiences hell on earth. R. E.'s text and Dekker's stage become spaces where hell manifests on earth and earthly tortures inspire infernal torments. Ravaillac seems caught in such a space, perpetually trapped in his tortured body, even after death.

By discovering hell 'behind a curten', Dekker plays with the convention found in revenge tragedies, including *The Spanish Tragedy*, of ending a play by drawing back a curtain to reveal horrifying tableaux of dead bodies. The critics Sarah Dustagheer and Philip Bird write that associations with the cur-tains which covered paintings in early modern galleries turn this curtained-off stage-space into a place of memory and stillness.[46] Perhaps taking his cue from the B-text of *Doctor Faustus*, Dekker prefers to reveal a dynamic scene. He replaces the object-like corpse-tableau with a vigorous performance of the

---

[45]   R. E., *The terrible and deserued death of Francis Rauilliack* (London, 1610), B1r.
[46]   Sarah Dustagheer and Philip Bird, '"*Strikes Open a Curtain Where Appears a Body*": Discovering Death in Stage Directions', in *Stage Directions and Shakespearean Theatre*, Sarah Dustagheer and Gillian Woods, eds (London, 2018), pp. 213–37.

inability to die that comes after death. Instead of revenge tragedy's memorial-like corpse, Dekker makes memories of delicious drink into instruments of torture. Dustagheer and Bird track how the dead bodies revealed in revenge tragedy can raise questions about representation and the separation of body and soul.[47] Dekker has already staged an answer with a hell that cycles Tantalus-like between stillness and movement. His damned are continuous with their past selves, unable to progress and improve; defined by their worst deeds, they are condemned to repeat them. Nathalie Rivere de Carles designates onstage curtains as a means of 'dramatic punctuation in a continuous performance'.[48] Dekker certainly uses his curtain to announce an innovative response to the Senecan challenge to depict 'something worse than' eternal hunger and thirst. However, he does so using revenge-tragedy conventions, not least because his inclusion of Faulx and Ravaillac indicates both divine and politico-religious revenge.

Milton – Corrupted Taste

Dekker's devils speak sarcastically; when they state 'here's lymon' the point is that the liquid they proffer is *not* lemon water, but something horrible *per se*. In *Paradise Lost* Book X, visual cues also provoke Milton's devils to desire specific foods, without satisfaction. Milton raises new questions about the damned's experience of taste. His devils are offered seemingly appealing fruit that then tastes horrific to them. This is not necessarily a problem with the fruit but, potentially, with the devils themselves: their tastebuds and minds are so corrupt that they register all food, however delicious, as disgusting. Some Christian writers interpret the Dives and Lazarus story to mean that seeing heaven's pleasures exacerbates the damned's torments while by contrast the blessed rejoice at seeing the damned's pain.[49] To behold Eden's innocent 'pleasures' was a torment for Milton's Satan:

> [...]; and the more I see
> Pleasures about me, so much more I feel
> Torment within me, as from the hateful siege
> Of contraries; all good to me becomes
> Bane, [...] [50]

---

[47]   Dustagheer and Bird, '*Strikes Open a Curtain*', p. 236.
[48]   Nathalie Rivere de Carles, 'Performing Materiality: Curtains on the Early Modern Stage', in Karim-Cooper and Stern, *Shakespeare's Theatres*, pp. 51–70 (p. 55).
[49]   For instance, Aquinas, *Summa*, III. Suppl. 94.1–3.
[50]   *Riverside Milton*, *PL* IX.119–23.

Like Marlowe's 'banefull' Zoacum, Satan evokes several meanings of 'bane': good is Satan's deadly enemy, the cause of his ruin, and poisonous to him. More specifically, Satan is plausibly saying he cannot enjoy good things because his corrupted being converts them into poison ('bane').

This reading is strengthened by the passage where Milton's devils are transformed to serpents and gorge on fruits resembling the 'alluring fruit' of Eden's forbidden tree.[51] These hellish fruits manifest to accompany the devils' transformation, tormenting them in their new form. Though visually appetising, the fruits taste like the apples of Sodom, where 'their grapes are grapes of gall, their clusters are bitter' (Deuteronomy 32:32). Milton's grove, like Dekker's devils who 'leap' then 'make a stand', combines forebodingly alluring stasis with threatening movement. Milton's snake-devils veer correspondingly from 'fix'd' fascination to desperate movement towards the fruits. This dynamic evokes Tantalus's eternal dance with the tree that torments him. The tree stays still and lets Tantalus approach it, moving away at the last minute. If Tantalus forces himself to stand motionless, knowing it useless to try and reach the fruits, the tree moves towards him, provoking him to repeat his grasping gestures.[52]

> There stood
> A Grove hard by, sprung up with this thir change,
> His will who reigns above, to aggravate
> Thir penance, laden with Fruit like that
> Which grew in Paradise, the bait of *Eve*
> Us'd by the Tempter: on that prospect strange
> Thir earnest eyes they fix'd, imagining
> For one forbidden Tree a multitude
> Now ris'n, to work them furder woe or shame;
> Yet parcht with scalding thurst and hunger fierce,
> Though to delude them sent, could not abstain,
> But on they rould in heaps, and up the Trees
> Climbing, sat thicker than the snakie locks
> That curld *Megæra*: greedily they pluck'd
> The Frutage fair to sight, like that which grew
> Neer that bituminous Lake where *Sodom* flam'd;
> This more delusive, not the touch, but taste
> Deceav'd; they fondly thinking to allay
> Their appetite with gust, instead of Fruit
> Chewd bitter Ashes, which th' offended taste

[51]   *Riverside Milton, PL* IX.588.
[52]   Seneca, *Thyestes*, lines 155–75.

With spattering noise rejected: oft they assayd,
Hunger and thirst constraining, drugd as oft,
With hatefullest disrelish writh'd their jaws
With soot and cinders fill'd; so oft they fell
Into the same illusion, not as Man
Whom they triumph'd, once lapst.[53]

Unlike Dekker's devils' 'great ioy', Milton's serpents are subject to hell's torments. Again, hell is a place of terrible repetition, where 'constrain[ed]' by appetite, the serpents cycle between gorging 'greedily' and rejecting the disgusting fruit, again and again ('not as Man' who only fell 'once'), and they will repeat this transformation annually '[t]o dash thir pride' (X.575). 'Gust' can mean 'relish' but also potentially mere 'wind'. This renders it ambiguous as to whether the bad taste stems from the fruits themselves or the serpents' corrupted bodies. There are two potential readings of this line. In one, the serpents stupidly and indulgently ('fondly') seek to relish the fruits, when they physically cannot. In the other, the serpents fondly attempt to assuage their hunger with fruits that are *per se* unsatisfying, and consist only of insubstantial wind. Like Faulx and Ravaillac, Milton's Satan is both defined and tormented by a repetitive version of his evil act: the temptation of mankind. Marlowe and Fletcher's description of 'Zoacum' as specifically an Eden-like 'apple' tree may stem from similar reasoning: if sin is forbidden fruit, then eating a disgusting version of this fruit is fitting punishment for the transgression. The serpents' sin or 'offence' manifests in 'offended taste'. This evokes both food that is offensive to the taste (i.e., disgusting) and the idea that taste offends, or is offended against.

The serpents undergo cognitive confusion. The actual taste of the fruits is completely different to what is suggested by the appealing feel and appearance – 'fair to sight' they 'not the touch but taste/ Deceaved'. Food's texture and visual appearance cues us to expect particular tastes. To draw, like Drexel, on earthly experiences, anyone who has lost their sense of taste or had it distorted (for example, with flu) will know how odd and even unpleasant the texture of usually delicious foods becomes. For the devils, the effect is utterly repulsive. The offensive taste causes them cognitively to reprocess the fruits' texture to 'soot' (fine particles caused by combustion), 'cinders' (useless residues of combustible substances), and 'ashes' (the powdery remains after combustion). 'Soot', 'ashes', and 'cinders' describe three similar but not precisely identical substances. This suggests that the serpents focus sophisticatedly on the various shades of repulsiveness in their food: sommeliers of the charred and bitter. Perhaps they literally have consumed objects that look and feel like fruit but are really made of ash. Given that good things are 'bane' to Satan, it may also be that these truly are delicious fruits and that it is because the devils' taste is so corrupted that they taste horrendous. Satan's corrupted brain might read the fruit's crunchiness and flaky texture as ash, soot, and cinders, accompanying it with a real or simulated repulsive taste. The *Oxford English Dictionary* references 'soot' as an alternative seventeenth-century spelling and pronunciation of 'sweet(ly)', and this drives home the confusion.[54] In a fascinating, as-yet-unpublished paper, the graduate students Naoya Zushi, Midori Ogawa, and Saho Ayabe-Kanamura find that negative emotions reduce our ability to enjoy delicious tastes. Fear and anxiety reduced their participants' ability to taste a drink's sweetness. Study participants who had watched a horror film excerpt perceived their drink to be less sweet compared to participants who had watched a comedy or scenery-based film.[55] The studies that Zushi et al. draw on, as well as work in behavioural medicine by scholars like Mustafa al'Absi, all suggest that stress and anxiety reduce our ability to appreciate sweet tastes and heighten our susceptibility to sourness.[56] There is no more stressful place than hell.

Milton's choice of 'constraining' is surely ironic: the devils are constrained to be unconstrained, in that they will be unable to control their hunger and thirst. This evokes the sin of Adam and Eve, who were '[f]or one restraint, Lords of the World besides'; that 'restraint' was the prohibition on eating from the Tree of Knowledge.[57] Unlike Dekker's comically recognisable damned individuals, Milton relates gluttonous loss of self-control with loss of (anthropomorphic) identity. This echoes broader representations in infernal literature of the damned's animalistic gluttony obliterating their previous (rational, human) identity.[58] Flung about by a storm whose filthy rain mixes with their bodies, the gluttons in Dante's *Inferno* (Canto 6) cannot control their own movements because they

---

[54]   'soot, adj. and n.2'. *OED Online*. August 2020. Oxford University Press. https://ezproxy-prd.bodleian.ox.ac.uk:2446/view/Entry/184697?rskey=ALR iPn&result=2&isAdvanced=false (accessed 25 August 2020).

[55]   Naoya Zushi et al, 'Fear Reduces Perceived Sweetness: Changes in the Perception of Taste due to Emotional State', *Advance*, Preprint (2019).

[56]   Mustafa al'Absi et al, 'Exposure to Acute Stress is Associated with Attenuated Sweet Taste', *Psychophysiology* 49.1 (2012), 96–103.

[57]   *Riverside Milton, PL* I.32.

[58]   Aziz al-Azmeh, 'Rhetoric for the Senses: A Consideration of Muslim Paradise Narratives', *Journal of Arabic Literature* 26.3 (1995), 215–31, p. 220; Lange, *Paradise and Hell*, p. 151.

lacked self-control during life. Zushi et al. link anxiety to the inability to perceive sweetness and to a 'lack of self control'. Their participants who felt anxious while watching horror films consumed more ice cream and juice but reported that the ice cream and juice tasted less sweet. Zushi et al. suggest that these factors were connected: an inability fully to taste the craved-for sweetness led their anxious movie-watchers to eat and drink ever more in search of satisfaction. The self-control of the blessed in heaven enables them to appreciate sweet tastes: Milton's angels' 'keen dispatch/ Of real hunger'.[59] But, as Drexel writes, in hell, '[n]o sweetness can be of force to mitigate this hunger, or temper the bitterness of this Gall'.[60] Perhaps, then, Milton's Sodom fruits would taste sweet to good angels, but the bingeing serpents are too distressed and un-self-controlled to taste anything but ash. If whether an apple is 'soot' (sweet) or 'soot' (bitter, burnt powder) depends on our moral status, this interestingly twists the Tantalus myth. Milton's devils are unsatisfied not because the fruit flees them but because their own sense of taste is corrupted. For Milton, whether meals in the afterlife are enjoyable or terrible may depend less on whether the meal is offensive *per se*, and more on whether the eater has offended with, or against, the sense of taste.

Conclusions

Drexel says we barely understand earthly hunger, thus how can we understand hell? 'This hunger which we behold with our eyes, we are not sufficiently capable of, and how then shall we understand that most rageing and eternal Famine in Hell? [...] Everlasting hunger is unexplicable, everlasting thirst intolerable'.[61] Literary texts help us use memory and imagination to simulate hellish eating, sometimes with the aid of physical action. The damned we have encountered in the early modern texts under discussion have intense senses of taste, or at least can imagine specific tastes. They keenly feel their deprivation. This leads to what might seem to us, who are 'not sufficiently capable of' hell, inconsistencies. Despite biblical warnings that hell 'utterly destroys' (*apollumi*, Matthew 10:28) soul and body, Dekker's damned continue to exist even though 'torn to peeces', starved, dehydrated, stabbed, burnt, choked. Hell is supposedly a place of eternal despair and destruction, yet Marlowe's Zoacum 'flourisheth'.

59   *Riverside Milton, PL* V.436–7.
60   Drexel, *Treatise of Hell*, E6v.
61   Drexel, *Treatise of Hell*, E6r-v.

Such perdurability-in-destruction is a difficult state of being to convey. Faulx poses it as a question, and the play leaves the answer open: '[w]herefore is thy soule/ Made sensible of tortures which (each minute)/ Kill thee ten thousand times, yet canst not dye?' (L3r). Ravaillac and Faulx do not look inwards to reflect fruitfully on their own states. They prefer instead to question each other. Acutely aware that their souls are 'sensible' (able to perceive through senses and/or emotions), they are examples of the damned who (as in Revelations 9:6) desire death, though death flees from them. Though we sit more comfortably than Faulx and Ravaillac, the particularities of taste in these three Renaissance texts unsettle our understanding of hell. This leaves us reaching hungrily for, and yet repulsed by, ever new answers to Seneca's question.

Works Cited

al'Absi, Mustafa, et al, 'Exposure to Acute Stress is Associated with Attenuated Sweet Taste', *Psychophysiology* 49.1 (2012), 96–103

al-Azmeh, Aziz, 'Rhetoric for the Senses: A Consideration of Muslim Paradise Narratives', *Journal of Arabic Literature* 26.3 (1995), 215–31

Alighieri, Dante, *La Divina Commedia* (Milan, 2000)

Aquinas, Thomas, *Summa Theologiae*, 5 vols, trans. Fathers of the English Dominican Province (New York, 1948)

Archer, John Michael, 'Islam and *Tamburlaine's* World Picture', in *A Companion to the Global Renaissance*, ed. Jyotsna Singh (Hoboken, 2007), 63–81

Bagshaw, R., et al, *Cobbett's Complete Collection of State Trials*, 34 vols (London, 1809)

Burman, Thomas, *Reading the Qur'an in Latin Christendom* (Philadelphia, 2014)

Criado-Peña, Miriam, ed., *The Early Modern English Version of Elizabeth Jacobs Physicall and Chirugicall Receipts* (Newcastle, 2018)

Dalton, Pamela, 'There's Something in the Air', in *Olfactory Cognition*, ed. Gesualdo Zucco et al (Amsterdam, 2012), 25–38

Dawood, N. J., trans., *The Koran* (London, 1956)

de Carles, Nathalie Rivere, 'Performing Materiality: Curtains on the Early Modern Stage', in *Shakespeare's Theatres and the Effects of Performance*, ed. Farah Karim-Cooper and Tiffany Stern (London, 2013), 51–70

Dekker, Thomas, *Dekker His Dreame* (London, 1620)

—————, *If It Be Not Good, The Diuel Is In It A New Play* (London, 1612)

van Diemerbroeck, Ysbrand, *The Anatomy of Human Bodies*, trans. William Salmon (London, 1694)

Donne, John, *Poems by J. D.* (London, 1633)

Drexel, Jeremias, *A Pleasant and Profitable Treatise of Hell*, trans. Anon (London, 1668)

Dustagheer, Sarah, and Philip Bird, "*Strikes Open a Curtain Where Appears a Body*": Discovering Death in Stage Directions', in *Stage Directions and Shakespearean Theatre*, ed. Sarah Dustagheer and Gillian Woods (London, 2018), 213–37

E., R., *The terrible and deserued death of Francis Rauilliack* (London, 1610)

Erskine, Kendell, et al, 'The Bitter Truth About Morality: Virtue, Not Vice, Makes A Bland Beverage Taste Nice', *PLoS One* 7.7 (2012), e41159

Fletcher, Giles, *The Policy of the Turkish Empire: The First Booke* (London, 1597)

Fletcher, John [Ben Jonson and Phillip Massinger], *The Tragœdy of Rollo Duke of Normandy* (Oxford, 1640)

Heath, Peter, *Allegory and Philosophy in Avicenna (Ibn Sînâ)* (Philadelphia, 1992)

Heywood, Jasper, *The Seconde Tragedie of Seneca Intituled Thyestes* (London, 1560)

Hill, Eugene, 'Senecan and Vergilian Perspectives in *The Spanish Tragedy*', *English Literary Renaissance* 15.2 (1985), 143–65

Holy Bible, King James Version (London, 1611)

Hoy, Cyrus, and Fredson Bowers, *Introduction, Notes, and Commentaries to Texts in The Dramatic Works of Thomas Dekker*, 4 vols (Cambridge, 1980)

Kagan, Shelly, *death* (New Haven, 2012)

Köster, Egon Peter, 'The Specific Characteristics of the Sense of Smell', in *Olfaction, Taste and Cognition*, ed. Catherine Rouby et al (Cambridge, 2002), 27–44

Kyd, Thomas, *The Spanish Tragedie* (London, 1592)

Lamarque, Henri, ed., *Theodor Bibliander: Le Coran en Latine* (Lyon, 2010)

Lange, Christian, *Paradise and Hell in Islamic Traditions* (Cambridge, 2016)

Lonicerus, Philippus, *Chronicorum Turcicorum* (Frankfurt, 1584)

Machumetis saracenorum principis eiusque successorum vitae, doctrina ac ipse alcoran (Basel, 1543)

Marlowe, Christopher, *The Famous Tragedy of The Rich Jew of Malta* (London, 1633)

–––––, *Tamburlaine the Great* (London, 1590)

–––––, *The Tragicall History of the Life and Death of Doctor Faustus* (London, 1616)

Mentz, Steve, 'Marlowe's Mediterranean and Counter-Epic Forms of Oceanic Hybridity', in *Travel and Drama in Early Modern England*, ed. Claire Jowitt and David McInnis (Cambridge, 2018), 55–71

Miller, Gregory, 'Theodor Bibliander's *Machumetis saracenorum principis eiusque successorum vitae, doctrina ac ipse alcoran* (1543) as the Sixteenth-century "Encyclopedia" of Islam', *Islam and Christian–Muslim Relations* 24.2 (2013), 241–54

Milton, John, *The Riverside Milton*, ed. Roy Flanagan (New York, 1998)

Munro, Lucy, 'Staging Taste', in *The Senses in Early Modern England, 1558–1660*, ed. Simon Smith, Jacqueline Watson, and Amy Kenny (Manchester, 2015), 19–38

––––, 'They Eat Each Others Arms', in *Shakespeare's Theatres and the Effects of Performance*, ed. Farah Karim-Cooper and Tiffany Stern (London, 2013), 73–93

Papies, Esther, Lawrence Barsalou, and Dorottya Rusz, 'Understanding Desire for Food and Drink: A Grounded-Cognition Approach', *Current Directions in Psychological Science* 29.2 (2020), 193–8

Seaton, Ethel, 'Fresh Sources for Marlowe', *The Review of English Studies* 5.2 (1929), 385–401

Seneca, Lucius Annaeus, *Seneca's Thyestes*, ed. R. J. Tarrant (Oxford, 1985)

Seymour, Laura, 'The Feasting Table as the Gateway to Hell on the Early Modern Stage and Page', *Renaissance Studies* 34.3 (2020), 392–411

Siegmund, Justine, *The Court Midwife*, ed. and trans. Lynne Tatlock (Chicago, 2005)

Starczewska, Katarzyna, *Latin Translation of the Qur'an (1518/1621): Commissioned by Egidio da Viterbo. Critical Edition and Case Study* (Wiesbaden, 2018)

Wagner, Sydnee, 'New Directions: Towards a Racialized Tamburlaine', in *Tamburlaine: A Critical Reader*, ed. David McInnis (London, 2020), 129–46

Woods, Gillian, 'Marlowe and Religion', in *Christopher Marlowe in Context*, ed. Emily Bartels and Emma Smith (Cambridge, 2013), 222–31

Zimmerman, Dean, 'Personal Identity and the Survival of Death', in *The Oxford Handbook of Philosophy of Death*, ed. Ben Bradley et al (Oxford, 2013), 97–154

Zushi, Naoya, Midori Ogawa, and Saho Ayabe-Kanamura, 'Fear Reduces Perceived Sweetness: Changes in the Perception of Taste due to Emotional State', *Advance*, Preprint (2019). https://doi.org/10.31124/advance.9923630

Hell's Kitchen:
Underworlds in Leonora Carrington's Down Below *and* The Hearing Trumpet

HANNAH SILVERBLANK

This chapter escorts the reader to the underworlds fashioned by the surrealist writer and painter, Leonora Carrington (1917–2011). Carrington is known primarily for her career as an English painter, who joined the surrealists in Paris in the late 1930s and later emigrated to Mexico. Here, the focus will be on Carrington's 1944 memoir *Down Below* and her comic novel, *The Hearing Trumpet*, written in 1950 but not published until 1976.[1] Carrington's protagonists in these literary works serve as archetypal visions of the artist herself, as maiden and crone respectively. These personae seek and gain access to underworld realms through painterly maps, alchemical symbolism, and mysterious towers. Carrington's imagining of hell as a salvific space of refuge, which is accessed through a mysterious tower, connects these two texts to the theme of underworld journeys in her wider corpus of work.[2] In a 1952 interview, André Breton, surrealism's most prominent theorist, said: 'Leonora Carrington, in life as in art, has never tried to see any way but through magic.'[3] Carrington's magical hermeneutic is visible in her painterly conjuring of enchanted worlds, and legible in her literary works. She attained an almost mystical status in the eyes of fellow surrealists, who saw her as a visionary who had accessed occult realms of the psyche during her institutionalisation at a hospital for the mentally ill in Santander, Spain, in the early 1940s.

---

[1]   Susan Aberth, *Leonora Carrington: Surrealism, Alchemy and Art* (Aldershot, 2004), p. 60.

[2]   Underworlds appear in several of Carrington's other writings. On symbolic death in 'Little Francis' and *Down Below*, see Kristoffer Noheden, 'Leonora Carrington, Surrealism, and Initiation: Symbolic Death and Rebirth in Little Francis and *Down Below*', *Correspondences* 2.1 (2014), 35–65. On the political stakes of the surrealist project and its fugitive instincts, see Jonathan P. Eburne, *Surrealism and the Art of Crime* (Ithaca and London, 2008), esp. 'Ch. 7: Persecution Mania', pp. 215–43.

[3]   André Breton et al, *Conversations: The Autobiography of Surrealism*, trans. M. Polizzotti (New York, 1993), p. 252.

Before her time in the institution, Carrington made her name as a young and rebellious artist who had rejected her family's ambition that she agree to a socially advantageous marriage.[4] She left her family in England to study art as a young woman, and, in 1937, she met a painter whose work attracted her: Max Ernst. They became lovers and moved into an apartment together in Paris later that year. In 1938 they relocated to a dilapidated farmhouse in St. Martin d'Ardèche. The two transformed the house into a collaborative oasis, filling it with sculptures, painting, and unique architectural features. In the following year the French government declared the German and politically controversial Ernst an enemy alien, and interned him at a camp in Largentière. Carrington was able to provide Ernst with painting supplies, and her lobbying on his behalf with influential Parisian contacts eventually secured his release from Largentière.

However, in 1940, Ernst was interned again, at a more distant camp. Carrington was now unable to access government channels to sue for Ernst's freedom. Alone in rural France, in deep distress about Ernst's status and the horrors of Nazism, she began to experience paranoid visions. Concerned about her safety and by the threat of the encroaching Nazis, some of her friends collected her from St. Martin d'Ardèche and drove her to Spain with them. *Down Below* opens just after Ernst's internment, and details Carrington's trip to Spain, where her psychological state became increasingly destabilised. The memoir's primary focus is on her experiences in the asylum where she was placed, in Santander, Spain. The narration concludes shortly after her cousin helps secure her release from there. After this, Carrington had to dodge her family's attempt to place her in another asylum, and she fled to Mexico, which became her permanent home.

Infernal towers become sites of obsessive interest for Carrington's institutionalised protagonists in her memoir and novel, functioning as architectural and symbolic gateways to escape from institutional cages. In *Down Below,* the 23-year-old Carrington is forcibly placed in an asylum in Spain; in *The Hearing Trumpet,* the 92-year-old Marian Leatherby is reluctantly relocated from her family home to Lightsome Hall, a home for senile ladies, also in Spain. In both texts, a journey toward an underworld realm is used to express psychological and therapeutic themes. This *katabasis* becomes a means to an initiatory form of *gnosis*, where repressed and esoteric knowledge is gained, based on personal experience. It is this form of fugitive initiation which unifies Carrington's hellscapes as realms of escape from institutional cages for her unruly maiden, mother, and crone.

---

[4]   Aberth, *Leonora Carrington*, pp. 11–23.

Carrington's Gnostic Journey with Pierre Mabille

Carrington's account of her institutionalisation was first orally delivered as a memoir called 'Down Below' in 1943, when the 26-year-old told her story in French to Jeanne Mégnen, the wife of the doctor, influential Surrealist writer, and editorial director of the famous art review *Minotaure*, Pierre Mabille. The dictation was done in the abandoned Russian Embassy in Mexico City, in which Carrington was camping with other European refugees.[5]

In its present published form, *Down Below* is organised into five chapters, each of which is titled with the date on which Carrington records and thinks about stages in her institutionalisation.[6] The memoir's opening paragraph is addressed to Mabille, introducing the text as a dialogue with, and creative adaptation of, his work as a physician.

> Exactly three years ago, I was interned in Dr Morales's sanatorium in Santander, Spain, Dr Pardo, of Madrid, and the British Consul having pronounced me incurably insane. Since I fortuitously met you, whom I consider the most clear-sighted of all, I began gathering a week ago the threads which might have led me across the initial border of Knowledge. I must live through that experience all over again, because, by doing so, I believe that I may be of use to you, just as I believe that you will be of help in my journey beyond that frontier by keeping me lucid and by enabling me to put on and to take off at will the mask which will be my shield against the hostility of Conformism.[7]

Carrington thinks of the process of healing as a therapeutic collaboration with Mabille, in which there will be an esoteric journey, using mythological narrative, through and beyond her traumatic memories of institutionalisation. As Jonathan Eburne notes, the composition of the memoir provokes Carrington's 'return to ... hermetic systems she devised in order to explore the significance of paranoiac thinking as something more than just

---

[5] Marina Warner, 'Introduction', in Leonora Carrington, *Down Below* (New York, 2017), pp. vii–xxxvii (pp. xxiv–xxvi).

[6] In the 1980s, Carrington (and editor Marina Warner) revised the 1943 French dictation of the lost but reanimated 1942 English text, along with the English translation first published in 1944 in *VVV* No. 4. See Leonora Carrington, *The House of Fear: Notes from Down Below*, intro. Marina Warner, trans. Kathrine Talbot and Marina Warner (New York, 1988). The text from this edition remains the basis for Carrington, *Down Below* (New York, 2017).

[7] Carrington, *Down Below*, p. 3.

delusion'.[8] Carrington proposes to retrace the steps of her journey through her exploration of iconographic and 'hermetic systems' in conjunction with narration of her psychical symptoms. The occasion of writing provides the opportunity for Carrington to generate new life even in the macabre isolation of the institution.

In *Down Below*, Carrington recounts the other-worldly visions she experienced while receiving shock therapy treatments administered against her will in the asylum.[9] She had been diagnosed with 'marginal psychosis' and treated with seizure-inducing treatments of a drug called Cardiazol. She recalls extensive periods in which she was physically restrained on her bed, and left there in her own excrement.[10] Carrington experiences a sudden and jarring fall from the liberated paradise of her own design into torturous infernos of the psyche and the institution.

Carrington frames the act of telling her experience as a process of re-experience which, through its ritualistic repetition, may engender new or formerly repressed knowledge for herself as well as her reader. She is reluctant to 'live through that experience all over again', conveying a sense of exhaustion and trepidation about its yet-unwritten contents. Yet she is emboldened by the promise that her narrative journey 'may be of use to' Mabille and her reader, and that she might go 'beyond that frontier' with the aid of a magical symbol ('the mask') and a psychopomp (a guide to the underworld, here, Mabille).[11] In this sense, Carrington's paranoid journeys in *Down Below* work toward the hermetic *gnosis*, an epiphanic initiation which is reached through imagined infernal spaces understood belatedly, via the pathways of writing.[12]

The memoir shows how Mabille used, in his psychoanalytic practice, his theories about mythic narratives and esoteric experience as therapeutic tools for both individual and collective transformation. The introduction to his book on myth, *The Mirror of the Marvellous*, suggests the structure of the narrative journeying which Leonora pursues in *Down Below* (as does Marian, in *The Hearing Trumpet*). He calls it 'a collection of maps, going from the map of passionate feelings to the celestial planisphere, by way of

8   Eburne, *Surrealism*, p. 228.
9   For more details, see Warner, 'Introduction', pp. xix–xxi.
10   Aberth, *Surrealism, Alchemy and Art*, p. 26.
11   Carrington, *Down Below*, p. 3.
12   On 'ecological gnosis' in *The Hearing Trumpet*, see Noheden, 'The Grail and the Bees: Leonora Carrington's Quest for Human-Animal Coexistence', in *Beyond Given Knowledge: Investigation, Quest and Exploration in Modernism and the Avant-Gardes*, ed. Harri Veivo et al (Berlin, 2017), pp. 239–52.

the diagrams left by pirates to show the location of their buried treasure'.[13] In *The Mirror*, Mabille collects myths from a wide variety of eras, cultures, languages, and genres, which he imagines as useful 'diagrams' for individual and psychological engagement.[14]

Mabille's preoccupation with the interplay between myth, 'maps', and the psyche resonates with the cartographical symbols used by *Down Below*.[15] Moreover, the images of 'maps', 'the celestial planisphere', 'diagrams,' 'buried treasure' are joined by the architectural spaces of the 'castle' and 'tower'. According to Mabille, most of the mythological works featured in *The Mirror*

> describe in detail ways into the castle, which is paradoxical since it's only possible to read them after having already gone through ordeals and succeeded in penetrating the castle walls. Still, it's true that one can only really benefit by hearing what one already knows and has totally recreated through personal experience ... Guests only for a moment ourselves in the mysterious castle, we will come around to giving our own account of our journey and our stay. Then we, too, will have provided new evidence regarding the marvelous.[16]

This is not knowledge easy to come by: Mabille calls his 'collection of maps' 'admittedly enigmatic plans', which 'permit the discovery of a mysterious castle, not far from the well-traveled paths, hidden by undergrowth and thickets.'[17]

As Kristoffer Noheden and Gloria Orenstein note, Carrington's works are preoccupied with the process of initiation as a means to new kinds of knowledge.[18] While Mabille and Carrington both conceptualise the castle as a space of self-knowledge and transformation, Carrington reframes it as a portal to the underworld. Across her literary works and

---

[13] Pierre Mabille, *The Mirror of the Marvellous: The Classic Surrealist Work on Myth*, trans. J. Gladding (Rochester, VT, 1998), p. 1.

[14] On Mabille's criteria for mythic selection, see *The Mirror of the Marvellous*, p. 3f.

[15] Ella Mudie, 'The Map of Down Below: Leonora Carrington's Liminal Cartography', *English Language Notes* 52.1 (2014), 145–54.

[16] Mabille, *The Mirror of the Marvellous*, p. 3.

[17] Mabille, *The Mirror of the Marvellous*, p. 3.

[18] Noheden, 'Leonora Carrington, Surrealism, and Initiation'; Noheden, 'The Grail and the Bees'; Gloria Orenstein, 'Down the Rabbit Hole: an Art of Shamanic Initiations and Mythic Rebirth', in *Wonderland: The Surrealist Adventures of Women Artists in Mexico and the United States*, ed. Ilene Susan Fort et al (Los Angeles, 2012), pp. 172–83.

her paintings, Carrington situates the underworld as a space of initiatory and epistemological potential. In *Down Below*, she reports that there is, in the asylum's grounds, a pavilion called Down Below (in Spanish, *abajo*) with chthonic associations, which might alleviate her sense of social isolation and her antagonistic relationships.[19] The memoir's protagonist, Leonora, says that

> [it] seemed impossible to communicate with the outside world; I wondered who would help someone, dressed in a bed sheet and a pencil, to get to Madrid.
>
> I had heard about several pavilions; the largest one was very luxurious, like a hotel, with telephones and unbarred windows; it was called Abajo (Down Below), and people lived there very happily.[20]

In her vision, Down Below promises more freedom and greater means to communicate with the outside world. Yet these are the circumstances in which she then takes a voyage to an imagined hell.[21]

Leonora begins to envision the process of arriving in Down Below as a gnostic journey: '[t]o reach that paradise, it was necessary to resort to mysterious means which I believed were the divination of the Whole Truth.'[22] Despite this hope, she perceives that her health presents a barrier to her accessing Down Below, an idea reinforced when she meets a woman named Angelita from Down Below. Angelita, whose name situates her both as 'messenger' (via its Greek etymology) and ironically celestial inhabitant of an underworld, tells Leonora that people do in fact live happily in Down Below, but that Leonora herself 'is not well enough to go there.'[23]

Carrington plots her 'enigmatic plans' in a private language of esoteric symbolism. For instance, she 'gave an alchemical life to the objects according to their position and their contents. (My face cream Night, in the black-lidded jar, contained the lemon, which was an antidote to the seizure induced by Cardiazol.)'[24] By arranging and infusing the objects

---

[19]   Noheden, 'Leonora Carrington, Surrealism, and Initiation', p. 58, takes *Down Below* to represent a kind of 'mythological underworld'; Warner, 'Introduction', p. xxiv, says that the name 'echoes mythological and literary descents into hell' and reframes the inferno as 'an actual safe space, a sanctuary within the grounds of the asylum.'

[20]   Carrington, *Down Below*, p. 35.

[21]   Carrington, *Down Below*, pp. 28–31.

[22]   Carrington, *Down Below*, p. 35. On the *gnosis* in this passage, see Noheden, 'Leonora Carrington, Surrealism, and Initiation'.

[23]   Carrington, *Down Below*, p. 38.

[24]   Carrington, *Down Below*, p. 46f.

which surround her with talismanic meaning, Leonora performs the roles of sculptor, alchemist, and initiate within a system of meaning she superimposes upon the space of the asylum and her journey toward escape. Yet her symbolist language finds no apt reader in the medical community at the asylum, nor does her lemon fully protect her from the jarring experiences of Cardiazol injections. She is neither able to find an interlocutor who can understand her symbolic meanings, nor can she easily parse the message of the symbols surrounding her.

Leonora begins to believe that one of her doctors, Don Luis, has gone mad. She recalls that she saw him clutching a box with excrement in it, and postulates that he may have swapped souls with his dog. As she ponders this, she imagines that the hospital staff are ritually preparing and purifying her for a 'triumphal entry' into the coveted Down Below. The thought of her sacred procession to Down Below makes her 'happy', despite her corporeal condition: strapped into her bed, with no indication from her doctors and nurses that she will go Down Below. However, the solace provided by this imagined initiation is soon undercut, replaced with an alternative and unchosen descent:

> [a] new era began with the most terrible and blackest day in my life. How can I write this when I'm afraid to think about it? I am in terrible anguish, yet I cannot continue living alone with such a memory ... I know that once I have written it down, I shall be delivered. But shall I be able to express with mere words the horror of that day?[25]

Carrington once again draws attention to the retraumatising aspect of writing her memoir. She strives for an epiphany of 'Knowledge' which might be shared with others, in order to free her from the unbearable isolation of her trauma: she 'cannot continue living alone with such a memory.'

This 'memory' is excised into a harrowing account of her physical and psychological symptoms in response to forced injections of Cardiazol, a violent hellscape of drug-induced, epileptic, and objectified alienation. Leonora's room is entered by a stranger with a briefcase, doctors, nurses, and attendants. When she tries to assert some control over the terms of their engagement, both by trying to limit the number of people in her room, and by announcing her hopes to move to Down Below, her doctor ignores her and injects her with Cardiazol. This triggers a dizzying drop into an underworld of psychosomatic symptoms.[26]

25   Carrington, *Down Below*, p. 39.
26   Carrington, *Down Below*, p. 13f. Jonathan Eburne argues that the trauma of

All of a sudden, José, Santos, Mercedes, Asegurado, and Piadosa were in my room. Each one of them got hold of a portion of my body and I saw the centre of all eyes fixed upon me in a ghastly stare. Don Luis's eyes were tearing my brain apart and I was sinking down into a well ... very far ... The bottom of that well was the stopping of my mind for all eternity in the essence of utter anguish.[27]

This experience of descent is followed by a reversal in motion, a sickening and vertiginous return to the 'surface'.

With a convulsion of my vital centre, I came up to the surface so quickly I had vertigo. Once more I saw the staring, ghastly eyes, and I howled: 'I don't want ... I don't want this unclean force. I would like to set you free but I won't be able to do so, because this astronomical force will destroy me if I don't crush you all ... all ... all. I must destroy you together with the whole world, because it is growing ... it is growing, and the universe is not big enough for such a need of destruction. I am growing. I am growing ... and I am afraid, because nothing will be left to destroy.'

And I would sink again into panic, as if my prayer had been heard. Have you an idea now of what the Great Epileptic Ailment is like?[28]

Carrington's description of her 'pitiably hideous' convulsions provides access to the nauseating jerks and pulls which the drug induces in her, in which she 'grimaced and [her] grimaces were repeated all over [her] body.'[29] She recalls herself howling in unheeded agony, while being, without consent, dragged into a dark underworld and then jerked back to the surface. When she asks her reader, 'Have you an idea now of what the Great Epileptic Ailment is like?' she reiterates one purpose of the memoir: to share the knowledge gained through her experience on her psychic 'journey'.

When Carrington's access to the building Down Below is eventually granted, it seems to underwhelm her. She prepares excitedly for her arrival, thinking herself 'destined to bring Knowledge.'[30] In addition, she thinks of Down Below as a site of social reconnection, having 'spent too much time putting up with the solitude of my own knowledge.'[31] But when she finally

these episodes refers to their resemblance to Carrington's rape by Spanish soldiers in Madrid, shortly before her institutionalisation, *Surrealism*, p. 224.
[27]   Carrington, *Down Below*, p. 40.
[28]   Carrington, *Down Below*, p. 40.
[29]   Carrington, *Down Below*, p. 40.
[30]   Carrington, *Down Below*, p. 47.
[31]   Carrington, *Down Below*, p. 47.

arrives in Down Below, the place does not turn out to be the transformative hellscape she had hoped it would be.

> There were three storeys: in each a door was open. I could see in the rooms, on the night tables, other solar systems as perfect and complete as my own. '*Jerusalem knew already!*' They had penetrated the mystery at the same time as I. On the third floor, I came upon a small ogival door; it was closed; I knew that if I opened it, I would be in the centre of the world. I opened it and saw a spiral staircase; I went up and found myself in a tower, a circular room lighted by five bull's-eye windows ... I took the great disorder which reigned on this table for the handiwork of God and of His Son: disorder among the various objects that were there, disorder in the cogs of the human machinery which, immobilized, kept the world in anguish, war, want, and ignorance.[32]

The hermetic knowledge which Leonora has been developing through sculptural arrangements of her food and possessions has already been accessed by this space and its unnamed inhabitants. The author does not specify the identity attached to the pronoun 'They', who 'penetrated the mystery' alongside her.

Carrington proceeds to open windows and create specifically hermetic, alchemical arrangements of 'cosmic objects', but the results of her sculptural work are never understood as revelatory. Down Below turns out to provide no access to the transformative initiation or sharing of knowledge that Carrington imagined. When she is finally granted a room of her own in Down Below, she reports that '[t]he room was just as I had seen it, only smaller, and the painted ceiling was in fact flat, not vaulted; I entered there without emotion, almost with a sense of disappointment.'[33] Her association of Down Below with liberation and knowledge is then undermined when she receives another Cardiazol injection after moving into Down Below. It is only through the process of writing and retracing her time in Santander that Carrington is able to fully internalise, think with, and build knowledge from the alchemical imagery and hermetic mapping that she pursues while institutionalised.

---

[32] Carrington, *Down Below*, p. 47.
[33] Carrington, *Down Below*, pp. 57–8.

The Hearing Trumpet:
Hell as Witch's Kitchen, Digestive System, and Womb

However, the isolated, paranoid hellscapes of *Down Below* are transformed in *The Hearing Trumpet* into spaces of collective transformation. In the infernal tower of *The Hearing Trumpet*, the protagonist,
Marian Leatherby, gains initiation into a goddess cult, a coven, and
gnosis, transforming the kinds of surreptitious intuition and sympathetic
symbolism which failed Leonora in *Down Below*. These differences in
Carrington's treatment of the salvific power of hell are partly an effect
of genre: a memoir of a period of trauma (which she later described as
a period of possession) and a comic utopian novel. While *The Hearing
Trumpet* was being written, Carrington's relationship with fellow expatriates Remedios Varo and Kati Horna fostered her interest in magical
and esoteric themes.[34]

Marian is a toothless, nonagenarian grandmother, with a beard and
a magical trumpet that serves as an assistive hearing device. When rele-
gated by her family to Lightsome Hall, Marian is cut off from her friend
Carmella, her hen, and her cats. Yet, she unexpectedly finds herself connected to a new network of mystical crones covertly engaged in goddess
worship. Marian goes through a *katabasis* which is, eventually, facilitated
through these women, who provide her with information about what interests her: a portrait of the Abbess of Santa Barbara de Tartarus, a castle from
which she has never seen anyone enter or leave, feminist retellings of myth,
and the worship of the goddess of many names and faces. These women
who serve as Marian's neighbours and spiritual guides live in buildings of
far-fetched, fantastic design ('[p]ixielike dwellings shaped like toadstools,
Swiss chalets, railway carriages, ... something shaped like a boot, another
like ... an outside Egyptian mummy').[35]

The narrative's comic sensibility, and surprising perspectives, situate
Marion as an elderly Alice in Wonderland figure from the start:

[t]he fact that I have no teeth and never could wear dentures does not in
any way discomfort me, I don't have to bite anybody and there are all sorts
of soft edible foods easy to procure and digestible to the stomach. Mashed
vegetables, chocolate and bread dipped in warm water make the base of my

---

[34]   See Whitney Chadwick, *Women Artists and the Surrealist Movement* (Boston,
1985), pp. 181–218. See also Stefan van Raay et al, *Surreal Friends: Leonora
Carrington, Remedios Varo and Kati Horna* (Surrey, 2010).
[35]   Carrington, *The Hearing Trumpet* (Boston, 1996), p. 29.

simple diet. I never eat meat as I think it is wrong to deprive animals of their life when they are so difficult to chew anyway.[36]

Her underworld descent takes the form of a voluntary downward tumble into a cauldron of infernal vegetable soup (a rather soggy twist on Alice's rabbit hole, hybridising mundanity with surrealism). In this broth of the self, Marian is forced to confront, answer, and eat her own doubles. From the broth she comes to a new kind of knowledge and community.

As residents at Lightsome Hall collectively resist the teachings of its director, Dr Gambit, Marian experiences growing affinities with them. Through her imaginative preoccupation with a portrait of a mysterious winking nun she embarks on a journey of *gnosis* and initiation.[37] A fellow resident of Lightsome Hall, Christabel Burns, notices Marian's interest in the portrait, and offers her a manuscript which tells of a repressed mytho-history surrounding the Holy Grail and the winking nun. Marian's interest in this nun, the 'Abbess of Santa Barbara de Tartarus', leads her on a journey of rebellion and eventually a ritual of death, self-consumption, and rebirth into an ecologically topsy-turvy world. In a new ice age, Marian experiences a liberatory blending of identities with various heretical and divine characters, including the winking abbess.

The patriarchal and paranoiac character of Carrington's social relationships in *Down Below* is still present in *The Hearing Trumpet*, but the infernal journey in *The Hearing Trumpet* is made with a host of varied companions and fellow goddess-worshippers. In *Down Below*, Catherine (a friend of Leonora's) makes an amateur analysis of Leonora's psychic state:

> Catherine, who had been for a long time under the care of psychoanalysts, persuaded me that my attitude betrayed an unconscious desire to get rid for the second time of my father: Max, whom I had to eliminate if I wanted to

---

[36]   Carrington, *The Hearing Trumpet*, p. 3. Natalya Lusty, *Surrealism, Feminism, Psychoanalysis* (Burlington, VT, 2007) regards the narrator in Carrington's short story, 'The Debutante', as having 'Alice's own practical but absurd powers of reasoning in both *Through the Looking Glass* and *Alice's Adventures in Wonderland*', p. 26. On the theme of 'wonderland' in American surrealist painting, see Fort et al, *In Wonderland: The Surrealist Adventures of Women Artists in Mexico and the United States* (Los Angeles, 2012).

[37]   Victoria Ferentinou, 'The Quest for the Goddess: Matriarchy, Surrealism and Gender Politics in the Work of Ithell Colquhoun and Leonora Carrington', in *Surrealism, Occultism and Politics*, ed. Tessel M. Bauduin, Victoria Ferentinou, and Daniel Zaman (New York and London, 2018), pp. 173–93 (p. 185f).

live ... I think she was mistaken when she said I was torturing myself. I think that she interpreted me fragmentarily, which is worse than not to interpret at all.[38]

Once Carrington is confined in the asylum nothing more is heard of Catherine. By contrast, in *The Hearing Trumpet*, Carmella (a character based on Carrington's real-life best friend Remedios Varo) takes on the role of whimsical yet resourceful companion to Marian. She provides the hearing trumpet (which lets Marian find out about her family's plan to send her to Lightsome Hall), and rescues Marian's chaotic and hungry coven when they escape the Hall near the novel's end. Likewise, Christabel Burns acts as internal psychopomp on Marian's journey into hell. Catherine is the inadequate friend who leads Leonora toward the institution; Carmella and Christabel do the opposite.

Another contrast between the memoir and the novel emerges in their representations of food and hunger. At Lightsome Hall, food is highly coveted and regulated, so as to create a tantalising atmosphere for its residents, who eventually attempt to reassert their power through a coordinated hunger strike. The kitchen of *The Hearing Trumpet* is a space of magical collaboration which facilitates surreptitious rebellion against the patriarchal agenda of the Hall. Marian ponders:

> [t]he person who controls the distribution of food has almost unlimited power in a society such as ours. Mrs Gambit's despotic rule of the kitchen seemed an unfair advantage. I wondered if it would not be possible to organize a small mutiny.[39]

Much of the novel's anxiety revolves around the procuring, preparation, and eating of food. Marian is frequently shamed by Dr Gambit for her overeating of cauliflower, which he cites as a moral failing, or sin, which she must do 'The Work' in order to correct.[40] He admonishes Marian that

---

[38] Carrington, *Down Below*, p. 5f. On the failure of Catherine's analysis, see Eburne, *Surrealism*, p. 221f.

[39] Carrington, *The Hearing Trumpet*, p. 58.

[40] Carrington's Dr Gambit is a parody of George Gurdjieff, whose system of self-development in *The Fourth Way* is often called 'The Work'. For a recent analysis of the political significance of Carrington's parody of Gurdjieff, see Ricki O'Rawe, '"Should we try to Self Remember while playing Snakes and Ladders?": Dr Gambit as Gurdjieff in Leonora Carrington's *The Hearing Trumpet* (1950)', *Religion and the Arts* 21 (2017), 189–208.

As long as we are victims of Habit we are slaves to Vice. I advise you to begin by giving up cauliflower. I notice you have an inordinate appetite for this vegetable, your reigning passion, in fact, Greed.[41]

In this way, Carrington aligns the space of the institution with the kind of hellscape in which the sinner must be punished in correspondence with their sin, and superimposes multiple hells within the narrative.[42]

The alchemical nature of the symbols and iconography forged by Leonora in the text of *Down Below* have no real kitchen space in which to manifest themselves, and no fellow cooks or eaters with whom to engage in kitchen-craft. By contrast a plethora of fellow eaters and cooks accompany Marian in *The Hearing Trumpet*. Although Marian is regularly hungry, and jealous of anyone she perceives to be eating more than herself, she participates in the hunger strike in solidarity with her fellow coven members, against the teachings of Dr Gambit and his programme, the Well of Light Brotherhood. By contrast, in *Down Below* Leonora has an anorexic and symbolic relationship with food, which she arranges into personal patterns and esoteric sculptures. She understands her stomach as a mirror or material realisation of Madrid itself, which must be kept pure. The way in which these two characters conceptualise their stomachs as political sites corresponds to what they find in their respective underworlds. It is, for instance, during a teatime assembly, as she tries to tune out Dr Gambit's droning lecture, that Marian feels a sense of recognition and deep curiosity to know more about the portrait of the winking abbess.

> The face of the nun in the oil painting was so curiously lighted that she seemed to be winking, although that was hardly possible. She must have had one blind eye and the painter had rendered her infirmity realistically. However the idea that she was winking persisted, she was winking at me with a most disconcerting mixture of mockery and malevolence.[43]

The theme of bifurcated vision also appears in the opening of one of the chapters of *Down Below*, in an admission that her testimony relies on fiction to give meaning, and speaks of how an 'egg' creates *gnosis* via its hybridity of the 'macrocosm and the microcosm': it, she comments, is a kind of 'crystal' ball.

---

[41]   Carrington, *The Hearing Trumpet*, p. 58.
[42]   This approach to food and appetite can be contextualised against Carrington's own positive use of kitchen space in Mexico, especially alongside her friend Remedios Varo. See Orenstein, 'Down the Rabbit Hole', pp. 175–77.
[43]   Carrington, *The Hearing Trumpet*, p. 36f.

I am afraid I am going to drift into fiction, truthful but incomplete, for lack of some details which I cannot conjure up today and which might have enlightened us. This morning, the idea of the egg came again to my mind and I thought that I could use it as a crystal to look at Madrid in those days of July and August 1940—for why should it not enclose my own experiences as well as the past and future history of the Universe? The egg is the macrocosm and the microcosm, the dividing line between the Big and the Small which makes it impossible to see the whole. To possess a telescope without its other essential half—the microscope—seems to me a symbol of the darkest incomprehension. The task of the right eye is to peer into the telescope, while the left eye peers into the microscope.[44]

This bifurcated vision reflects Carrington's own proclivity for bilateral drawing and writing, for which she was chastised in school.[45] Marian reflects on the obscure nature of her attraction to the winking abbess' portrait.

Really it was strange how often the leering abbess occupied my thoughts. I even gave her a name, keeping it strictly to myself. I called her Dona Rosalinda Alvarez della Cueva, a nice long name, Spanish style. She was abbess, I imagined, of a huge Baroque convent on a lonely and barren mountain in Castile. The convent was called El Convento de Santa Barbara de Tartarus, the bearded patroness of Limbo said to play with unbaptised children in this nether region. How all these fancies occurred to me I do not know, but they kept me amused, especially during sleepless nights. Old people do not sleep much.[46]

The infernal nature of this abbess appears twice in the name given to her by Marian, which alludes to the chthonic (*cueva*, or 'cave') and to the Greek mythological underworld (Tartarus). The 'Barbarus' part of the Abbess's name connects her to Marian in so far as they are both 'bearded', and hence androgynous.[47]

In the underworld, Marian meets the Abbess and the Queen Bee. Before this encounter, Marian has already experienced a sense of attraction to bees: her 'preferred' site on the facility is the 'bee pond', and she reflects on how

[44]   Carrington, *Down Below*, p. 19.
[45]   Aberth, *Surrealism, Alchemy and Art*, p. 12. See also Marian's discussion of her travels with her mother, in Carrington, *The Hearing Trumpet*, pp. 83–5. Warner addresses the 'unmatched eyes' in Carrington's paintings and the theme's correspondence to Carrington's fragmented selfhood, *Down Below*, pp. xxviii–xxix.
[46]   Carrington, *The Hearing Trumpet*, p. 53.
[47]   On androgyny in the alchemical context, see Alexander Roob, *The Hermetic Museum: Alchemy & Mysticism* (Köln, 2020), pp. 370–7.

'[t]his secluded spot was the haunt of thousands of honey bees that zimmed all through the warm days at their business. I could sit amongst the bees for hours on end and feel happy.'[48] Bees buzz through the novel with great industry, drawing Marian into affinity with the other residents, as co-members of a 'hive'. Their presence anticipates Marian's eventual fusion with an infernal 'Queen Bee' and with the Abbess. Though until that meeting the mystical significance of bees eludes Marian's conscious understanding ('why [the bees] pleased me so I cannot tell'), they are well-known alchemical symbols of the wish to rise to knowledge.[49]

Alexander Roob notes how bees are used to express theosophy in alchemical writings:

[l]ike bees attracted by the scent of the rose, the lovers of Theo-Sophia stream by from all directions to climb the seven steps of the 'mystic ladder', through 'the gate of eternal wisdom'. This gate, narrow (*angustus*) but sublime (*augustus*) is ... 'the force of light' and 'the eternal centre of life' ... open everywhere in the darkness of this world as 'a little seed'.[50]

In *The Hearing Trumpet*, bees, steps, ladders, gates, centre-points appear in Marian's journey into hell and back again. Intellectual understanding of these themes and images is subordinated to sympathetic response: it is Marian's vague but powerful attraction to the portrait of the winking nun and the bee pond which serves to point her to the 'gate' of the life force, the hellmouth tower of Lightsome Hall.

Curious about the tower and its possible occupants, Marian queries her sage co-resident Christabel Burns. Christabel demurs, "'I am not allowed to tell you ... That is something you have to find out for yourself. There are three riddles you have to answer before you are allowed to enter the tower.'"[51] Like Angelita in *Down Below*, Christabel points out that Marian is not ready to access the Knowledge she covets. Yet Christabel then provides Marian with various tools, puzzles, and experiences to make a journey to the underworld possible.

The first riddle that Christabel poses to Marian is

"I wear a white cap on my head and my tail
All seasons my caps I wear without fail

---

48   Carrington, *The Hearing Trumpet*, p. 40.
49   Carrington, *The Hearing Trumpet*, p. 40.
50   Roob, *Hermetic Museum*, p. 272.
51   Carrington, *The Hearing Trumpet*, p. 151.

Around my fat belly my girdle is hot
I move round and round tho' legs I have not."[52]

Marian deduces her way through reasoning to the first riddle's solution, 'the earth', with relative ease. Christabel then poses the second riddle.

"I never move as you whirl round and round
I sit and I watch you with never a sound
If you tilt far enough caps become belt
New caps are made the old caps will melt
Though legless your whirling will then appear lame
I seem to move but I don't, what's my name?"[53]

This second riddle poses more of a challenge to Marian, who eventually solves it with the hermeneutic assistance of the 'planisphere', a piece of alchemical technology brought to her by her friend Carmella. It is the planisphere which enables Marian to see the riddle from a different cosmic perspective, and find the answer, 'the pole star'.

The third riddle eludes Marian's understanding until she undertakes some experiential travel with the help of Christabel Burns and the other elderly inhabitants of Lightsome Hall.

"One of you turns while the other will sit
And though the caps change they always will fit
Once in the life of a mountain or rock
I fly like a bird though bird I am not
When you get new caps my prison will break
The watchers who slept will now be awake
And over their land I will fly once again
Who is my mother? What is my name?"[54]

Only when Marian reaches the tower with her friends does she find the solution to the third riddle, which allows her ingress to the tower. The tower is thus the incentive to solving the riddles as well as a catalyst to recognition of their significance. The tower, however, appears to be collapsing:

Rifts appeared in the snow, the house groaned as if in pain, and we heard objects falling … That portion of the building suddenly glowed red as if it

---

[52]   Carrington, *The Hearing Trumpet*, p. 151.
[53]   Carrington, *The Hearing Trumpet*, p. 151.
[54]   Carrington, *The Hearing Trumpet*, p. 151f.

was on fire. The great stone tower swayed from side to side, then the air was rent with the wound of a mighty crackling and the walls split open like a broken egg. One tongue of flame shot out from the crack like a spear, and a winged creature that might have been a bird emerged. It paused momentarily on the brim of the shattered tower and we witnessed for a second an extraordinary creature. It shone with a bright light coming from its own body, the body of a human being entirely covered with glittering feathers and armless. Six great wings sprouted from its body and quivered ready for flight. Then with a shrill long laugh it leapt into the air and flew north, till it was lost to our sight.[55]

The winged bird-like figure is the answer to the second half of the final riddle, '[w]hat is my name?', and Marian recognises it as 'Sephira', the identity of the first person in the third riddle, a Cabalist symbol of the ten aspects of the 'Tree of Life'.[56]

With this part of the enigma realised, Marian tells Christabel that she still cannot answer the part of the final riddle which asks, '[w]ho is my mother?'[57] Christabel says she must proceed further toward the tower to find out more. Experiential *gnosis* proves essential to the process of unfolding the riddles' meaning. Marian continues her approach to the tower, from which 'tufts of smoke' and the 'strong smell of sulphur and brimstone' emerge. Marian still does not realise that she is facing a hellgate, but instead assumes the tower might be on fire from the inside.[58] When she reaches the tower's interior, she is faced with a choice of how to continue her journey:

"Up or Down?" asked Christabel as we found ourselves inside. A winding staircase led up to the top of the tower. Part of the steps had crumbled away and through the great crack in the wall the night sky was visible now, moving with gathering clouds. At our feet yawned an opening where steps faded into darkness below ...

"Down," I replied at last, because of the warm wind that blew from within the earth. Falling into a crematorium was still better than freezing to death on top of the tower. I would have turned back, but curiosity went deeper than fear.[59]

---

[55]   Carrington, *The Hearing Trumpet*, p. 167f.
[56]   David Godwin, *Godwin's Cabalistic Encyclopedia* (Woodbury, M. N., 2020), p. xiv.
[57]   Carrington, *The Hearing Trumpet*, p. 152.
[58]   Carrington, *The Hearing Trumpet*, p. 168.
[59]   Carrington, *The Hearing Trumpet*, p. 135f.

Like Carroll's Alice, it is curiosity which impels Marian to this under-world descent.

'Up or Down?', like the alchemical motto 'as above, so below', appears in Carrington's paintings, which show bi-directional growth in celestial and chthonic spheres.[60] The choice of ascent or descent is presented as physically intuitive rather than intellectually guided, and Marian's animal instincts toward warmth and comfort push her to go down: the warmth of the underworld rather than the arctic earth and sky. Lightsome Hall is as a kind of celestial, patriarchal realm of tantalising cruelty. Marian's choice of 'Down' is part of a quest for chthonic nourishment: '[a]s I reached the bottom of the steps I could smell sulfur and brimstone. The cavern was as warm as a kitchen.'[61]

Carrington's hell serves as a kind of gnostic mirror, where the pro-tagonist journeys and meets herself refracted into various faces. She first encounters her own double, with an ageless and uncanny visage, in the alchemical kitchen: '[b]eside the flames sat a woman stirring a great iron cauldron ... When we faced each other I felt my heart give a convul-sive leap and stop. The woman who stood before me was myself.'[62] After Marian and her double ponder what she might have found at the top of the tower ('Santa Clauses', her double suggests with a cackle), Marian becomes unsure which figure is her 'real' self. She allows her double to decide the matter.

When I was well within range she suddenly jabbed the pointed knife into my backside and with a scream of pain I leapt right into the boiling soup and stiffened in a moment of intense agony with my companions in distress, one carrot and two onions.

A mighty rumbling followed by crashes and there I was standing outside the pot stirring the soup in which I could see my own meat, feet up, boiling away as merrily as any joint of beef. I added a pinch of salt and some pep-percorns then ladled out a measure into my granite dish. The soup was not as good as a bouillabaisse but it was a good ordinary stew, very adequate for the cold weather.[63]

---

[60]   For the alchemical significance of this motto, see the 'Emerald Tablet' in Heinrich Khunrath, *Amphitheatrum sapientiae aeternae* (Hamburg?, 1595). Such bi-directional growth is evident in Carrington's painting, *Maja del tarot (Double Portrait of María Félix)*, 1965.

[61]   Carrington, *The Hearing Trumpet*, p. 172.

[62]   Carrington, *The Hearing Trumpet*, p. 172.

[63]   Carrington, *The Hearing Trumpet*, p. 176.

The reader learns what happened, but not why Marian kills, cooks, seasons, and eats herself, nor what it felt like to experience her own death from both within and without. The experiential initiation has been simultaneously described and obscured, shrouding the *gnosis* from the uninitiated. This reinforces Carrington's mystic stance as a bringer of knowledge, as well as an initiate who obscures crucial aspects of her occult *gnosis*.

When Marian sips the broth of herself, she does so in Hell's 'womb', which is also figured as a kitchen space. She then takes herself into her own digestive tract, in a way that blends the gastrological with the maternal. Marian is both digesting herself and giving birth to a new self. She is united with Queen Bee and the Abbess through an 'obsidian mirror' (an object associated with the cults of the Egyptian goddess Isis, as well as the Great Goddess).

> From a speculative point of view I wondered which of us I was. Knowing that I had a piece of polished obsidian somewhere in the cavern I looked around, intending to use it as a mirror. Yes, there it was, hanging in its usual corner near the bat's nest. I looked into the mirror.[64]

Although this is Marian's first visit to the tower, she knows the space and its contents: the 'a piece of polished obsidian somewhere', hanging 'in its usual corner near the bat's nest'. She has access to unexplained knowledge perhaps through her identification with the chthonic figures, with whom she is about to blend.

> First I saw the face of the Abbess of Santa Barbara de Tartarus grinning at me sardonically. She faded and then I saw the huge eyes and feelers of the Queen Bee who winked and transformed herself into my own face, which looked slightly less ravaged, owing probably to the dark surface of the obsidian.
>
> Holding the mirror at arm's length I seemed to see a three-faced female whose eyes winked alternatively. One of the faces was black, one red, one white, and they belonged to the Abbess, the Queen Bee and myself. This of course might have been an optical illusion.
>
> I felt very well and refreshed after the hot broth, and somehow deeply relieved, just as I felt long ago after I had the last of my teeth out.[65]

Marian uses a tool of Isis to see that she has become a Hecate-like triple goddess, whose various heads belong to herself, the Abbess, and the Queen

[64]   Carrington, *The Hearing Trumpet*, p. 176.
[65]   Carrington, *The Hearing Trumpet*, p. 176.

Bee. She links her own visage and her narrative into the proliferation of faces attached to the mother goddess, and she takes on the triplicity of the Great Goddess. She assumes the triple alchemical colouration of black, white, and red, which, as Victoria Ferentinou has pointed out, 'recalls Graves's triple Goddess, who is "woman in her divine character"'.[66] Through this mirror, hell becomes not only a 'kitchen', but also a 'womb': '"This is Hell ... But Hell is merely a form of terminology. Really this is the Womb of the World whence all things come."'[67]

Conclusion: Infernal Identification with the Goddess and the Hive

A major distinction between the transformative power of Carrington's *katabases* across these two works is the presence or absence of women and animals with whom Carrington can find transformative affinity. Marian's access to the underworld and the goddess is enabled through her relationships with fellow women. The presence of the goddess is what catalyses the salvific channels of surrealism's splendour to spill into topsy-turvy utopia. The earth's poles shift in order to bring Marian the environment which she had imagined for her own old age. The dangerous over-identification and dissolution of self that Leonora experiences in *Down Below* is replaced with a salvific sublimation of Marian's identity into shared hermetic and occult experience with her friends and the mystical figures that inspire her.

Across both of these literary works, Carrington situates semi-autobiographical figurations of the maiden, the mother, and the crone in dehumanising institutional cages. She conceptualises escape from these mundane hells on earth through journeys into transformative underworld realms. Reading these texts in dialogue allows us to recognise the blocks facing Carrington's alchemical, paranoid, intuitive practice of proto-art therapy in the asylum. Similar cartographies and mythological journeys are present in both texts, but with radically different atmospheres and outcomes.

Down Below revolves around the world of paranoid failure and delusion, a world that is later re-experienced in the process of its composition and multiple re-writings, and transformed, through the alchemy of psychoanalytical symbolism, into something that reconnects Carrington into a community of fellow European expatriates. We might therefore read Carrington's collaboration with Mabille as a step on the journey toward balancing her microcosmic knowledge of paranoia with a macro-

---

[66]   Ferentinou, 'Quest for the Goddess', p. 186.
[67]   Carrington, *The Hearing Trumpet*, p. 172.

cosmic expression of the narrative. *The Hearing Trumpet* features aspects of *Down Below*'s underworld journey and pushes them further, within the context of collective salvation and *gnosis*. The quest of the isolated maiden in *Down Below* permeates the steps of the crone-like Marian's journey in *The Hearing Trumpet*. In hell, Marian sees her own ageless double, a figure that transcends and blends the triplicity of the maiden, mother, and crone, and who embodies her own union with the Triple Goddess. In place of the alienating surplus of identities that Leonora desires to strip away in *Down Below*, *The Hearing Trumpet* provides a multitude of sympathetic identities that link Marian into a cackling, dancing band of triumphant revellers who share in the transformative power of the infernal descent.

Works Cited

Aberth, Susan, *Leonora Carrington: Surrealism, Alchemy and Art* (Aldershot, 2004)

Breton, Andre, et al, *Conversations: The Autobiography of Surrealism*, trans. M. Polizzotti (New York, 1993)

Carrington, Leonora, *Down Below*, intro. Marina Warner (New York, 2017)

—————, *The Hearing Trumpet* (Boston, 1996)

—————, *The House of Fear: Notes from Down Below*, intro. Marina Warner, trans. Kathrine Talbot and Marina Warner (New York, 1988)

Chadwick, Whitney, *Women Artists and the Surrealist Movement* (Boston, 1985)

Eburne, Jonathan P., *Surrealism and the Art of Crime* (Ithaca and London, 2008)

Ferentinou, Victoria, 'The Quest for the Goddess: Matriarchy, Surrealism and Gender Politics in the Work of Ithell Colquhoun and Leonora Carrington', in *Surrealism, Occultism and Politics*, ed. Tessel M. Bauduin, Victoria Ferentinou, and Daniel Zaman (New York and London, 2018), 173–93

Fort, Ilene Susan, Teresa Arcq, and Terri Geis, *In Wonderland: The Surrealist Adventures of Women Artists in Mexico and the United States* (Los Angeles, 2012)

Godwin, David, *Godwin's Cabalistic Encyclopedia* (Woodbury, MN, 2020)

Khunrath, Heinrich, *Amphitheatrum sapientiae aeternae* (Hamburg?, 1595)

Lusty, Natalya, *Surrealism, Feminism, Psychoanalysis* (Burlington, VT, 2007)

Mabille, Pierre, *The Mirror of the Marvellous: The Classic Surrealist Work on Myth*, trans. J. Gladding (Rochester, VT, 1998)

Mudie, Ella, 'The Map of Down Below: Leonora Carrington's Liminal

Cartography', *English Language Notes* 52.1 (2014), 145–54

Noheden, Kristoffer, 'Leonora Carrington, Surrealism, and Initiation: Symbolic Death and Rebirth in Little Francis and *Down Below*', *Correspondences* 2.1 (2014), 35–65

Noheden, Kristoffer, 'The Grail and the Bees: Leonora Carrington's Quest for Human-Animal Coexistence', in *Beyond Given Knowledge: Investigation, Quest and Exploration in Modernism and the Avant-Gardes*, ed. Harri Veivo et al (Berlin, 2017), 239–52

O'Rawe, Ricki, '"Should we try to Self Remember while playing Snakes and Ladders?": Dr Gambit as Gurdjieff in Leonora Carrington's *The Hearing Trumpet* (1950)', *Religion and the Arts* 21 (2017), 189–208

Orenstein, Gloria, 'Down the Rabbit Hole: An Art of Shamanic Initiations and Mythic Rebirth', in *Wonderland: The Surrealist Adventures of Women Artists in Mexico and the United States*, ed. Ilene Susan Fort et al (Los Angeles, 2012), 172–83

van Raay, Stefan, et al, *Surreal Friends: Leonora Carrington, Remedios Varo and Kati Horna* (Surrey, 2010)

Roob, Alexander, *The Hermetic Museum: Alchemy & Mysticism* (Köln, 2020)

Samuel Beckett's Not I

MARGARET KEAN INTERVIEWS LISA DWAN

The actor Lisa Dwan has won international acclaim for her dramatisation of Samuel Beckett's late works. She first performed Not I *in 2005 at the Battersea Arts Centre, London. In 2013, she produced and began to tour a solo show,* The Beckett Trilogy, *which brought together three Beckett pieces:* Not I *(1972),* Footfalls *(1976), and* Rockaby *(1981). In* Not I, *a spotlit disembodied mouth appears to float high above the otherwise darkened stage, firing out a jarringly discontinuous monologue.* Footfalls *shows May, pacing back and forth outside what we take to be her dying mother's room, in dialogue with a voice we cannot see.* Rockaby *features a solitary aging woman sat, fading, in a wooden rocking chair while the pre-recorded voice of the actor speaks of her past and the rocking chair rocks of its own accord.*

MK You are recognised internationally for your performances of Samuel Beckett's tortured voices, in particular the monologue *Not I*, and your one-woman show *The Beckett Trilogy* (Royal Court, 2014), where you brought together *Not I*, *Footfalls*, and *Rockaby*. How did this specialism come about?

LD The very first Beckett piece I encountered was on TV, when I was twelve. I came into the living room and saw this haunted man's face as he walks into a room, shuts the door, closes the curtains, sits on the bed, and hears a voice, relentless, viper-like, speaking to him of death, guilt, and pain. The voice seems to be coming from behind his eyes; he keeps trying to shut them to shut out the sound but cannot [*Eh Joe*, 1966, where a lonely man is taunted by the voice of a women he knew]. Years later, I remember a fellow actor describing to me *Not I*, where the actor's head is tied in place but the mouth appears to roam or oscillate across the auditorium creating an optical illusion to accompany monologue which is both very difficult to memorise and bruisingly hard to endure as a listener. It was only in 2005, with an audition for *Not I* unexpectedly scheduled for the following day at Battersea Arts Centre, that I sat down alone to read the script. I found myself tapping along very quickly. The text seemed almost like sheet music: three lines, dot dot dot. Two lines, dot dot dot. 'Ba ba...bababa ba ba ba...out...into this world... this world...tiny little thing...before its time...in a godfor-...what?..girl?'

MK You keyed into the part almost immediately, despite its dislocatory form?

LD It seemed like its rhythm was holding me rigid, but there were all these little explosions (for instance, those written in bold, like '**ha!**'), a cacophony in the rhythm. I had to rely on my own vocabulary to deal with the text. As a dyslexic and as a trained dancer I use rhythm and instinct. So I thought it would be fun to deal with phrases like 'the machine / so disconnected', by turning me into the machine, 'so dis-con-ect-ed'. If you look at the parallels between *Not I*, *Footfalls*, and *Rockaby*, Beckett locks us in through the rhythm. In *Not I* it is a machine gun, allegro rhythm that is impossible to escape; *Footfalls* is the slow, painful, relentless pacing of the nine footfalls; *Rockaby* has a rocking chair. What I tried to imagine when I was doing *Rockaby* was a heart monitor.

MK You have the perfect skill set for late Beckett: physical stamina (which in your case comes from a training in ballet), exceptional memory retrieval, precision in the articulation of a part, even at great speed, and an intuitive comprehension of the wit and quirks in the text.

LD I use the musical rhythms in the text to aid performance, but for *Not I* my memory of the physical script also helps me keep focus. In performance you have to deal with your own inner Not I, a force which could so easily pull you out of kilter. So I visualise the page of my own copy of the text: I know every stain and tear on the page, intimately. I know where I am on that page and that is how I orientate myself in performance. When it feels like I'm taking flight, I cling onto the memory of those words on the page, and this helps me keep my place despite the strain of performance.

MK *Not I* is one of the most disorientating theatre experiences there is: the audience is held in pitch-black darkness while an outlandish mouth bombards them with speech. The play makes extreme technical demands on its performer. This is a lengthy and complex monologue to be spoken at the speed of thought while the actor is immobilised backstage, blindfolded and fixed into a harness, with the blacked-out stage spotlighting just her lips and mouth, suspended in space and seemingly disembodied. Do you use these constraints to enhance the performance?

LD I don't use them to enhance the performance, I am enhanced because of those constraints. One of the joys of being a ballet dancer is that you get to be a rat, or a snowflake, or part of a women's group that dance angry men to death. You get to inhabit these archetypal roles. However, my early career moved from ballet into TV because I fulfilled certain narratives in other people's imagination: the blonde, and the bitch, and the psycho, and the girlfriend, and the whore (I've no more whores left in me!). But I have a weird voice with a colossal range. I only learnt that through Beckett. Beckett has no interest in me or my body, but invites me to be a voice that is neither woman nor man nor child, but a creature which is all these things, and perhaps even already dead. So I'll happily put on a blindfold, and tie my head onto a plank of wood: sure it is uncomfortable, but it is also the most liberated of positions.

MK Is bringing such honesty to a performance terrifying?

LD As a practitioner you have to be in contact with truth, and Beckett digs down towards a truth by paring away to the 'it' of it all. Billie Whitelaw checked me when she heard me using an artificial non-expressive monotone in my performance because I had heard that Beckett didn't want his actors acting. "What are you doing?" she asked. "That's artifice, that has to go."

Here's a story: I was asked to perform *Not I* in the Marble Arch caves in County Fermanagh, one of the longest cave systems in Europe. The set had to be brought down by boat; I had to come down by boat; the audience would enter, twenty-seven of them in a boat. They find me tied to a wall, in the head-board, blindfolded, in black makeup, with a light shone on me. I'm dirty, cold, damp, and my legs are completely numb because I've been down there the whole day. I can't see, hear, or move, totally disorientated – and it was one of the greatest performances of *Not I* that I ever did in all of fifteen years of performing it! Something came into my performance there. A voice came into me there like I was dead, and I was rocking to and fro, as though I was roaming. My voice must have dropped two octaves – I had never known that my body could make those sounds.

MK A Dante-esque production, actively blocked from any rapport with your audience! How did you connect with them?

LD Performing *Not I* is like being in a séance. I could smell the perfume, the cigarettes, the expectation in the audience, and feel it if someone got lost. I used to get panic attacks – and so would the audience. They would leave the auditorium in a panic and I would know, even though I couldn't see it happening.

MK Perhaps the audience may be willing you to stop? They may not want to be where you have taken them, even though that's why they came to the theatre. There is a defensive medieval view that the damned should be rejected precisely to avoid sharing their experience, their perspective, and there is something in *Not I* that seems to confront a similar fear of vulnerability.

LD As one of my friends said, 'Beckett is a very cruel writer. It might be OK for him to express the world that way, but the rest of us need our delusions.' Yet Beckett does represent our defiance. Mouth in *Not I* scrambles for alternative ways to tell her story; in *Footfalls*, a challenge by May to beat the tormented narrative by developing her own ghostly story, despite the efforts of her mental 'thuggee', Miss Winter; while in *Rockaby*, the character reaches out for another 'living soul'. Hell is too definite a destination for Beckett, whose characters can still change outcomes – perhaps they live in Purgatory.

MK Or the place of the unborn child, Limbo?

LD Beckett attended a lecture which Jung gave when he was in London, which dealt in part with the creature which is not quite born. The audience questioned Jung: were they themselves born or not? (And the answer? They weren't quite there!) Beckett talks about this in *Texts for Nothing*, working out from *The Unnamable* to the thirteen 'afterwords' of *The Unnamable*, on a trajectory to *Not I*. In *Texts for Nothing 5* Beckett sarcastically refers to Limbo: 'sweet thing theology' he says. And in *Footfalls* the dominant mother voice speaks of the child who is not quite there: 'dreadfully un-'. The nine footsteps in *Footfalls* (changed from seven), refer both to the nine circles of hell and to the nine-month gestation in the life cycle.

MK When you put the three short plays, *Not I*, *Footfalls*, and *Rockaby* together in one performance, did you make the decision on which order they should be in solely for practical reasons, such as the makeup and the set?

LD Yes. Fortuitously the order in which they were performed gave a satisfying cycle: Mouth makes those sounds at the beginning, with a birth sound ('...out...into this world'), then there was the painful mother–daughter adolescence, and then there was rocking toward the end of life.

MK '[T]ime she stopped.' It must be difficult to return to everyday parts, after such *katabatic* descents. Such a narrative form provides the opportunity to return to society with greater wisdom, but the experience sets you apart and who can you find to listen?

LD We are all conditioned to be frightened of the hell of loneliness, and to look away. At a recent talk I gave on feminism, misogyny, and Me Too, one person tried to shame me with the comment that "You strike me as quite a lonely person." The whole audience groaned! I replied: "I have licked the ground of loneliness. I have toured the world on my own and licked the ground and I am not frightened of it. Therefore, I am liberated from the threat of loneliness. Because the truth is that we are all going down alone. You are going to have to die alone. I am going to have to die alone, to confront my maker or makers or whatever it is, alone. And I feel OK with that today. And that means I am not going to rush into some decision to distract myself from that impending truth. I've licked it; I've eyeballed it; I'm OK with it."

Works Cited

Samuel Beckett: The Complete Dramatic Works (London, 1986)
Samuel Beckett: Texts for nothing and other shorter prose, 1950–1976 (London, 2010)
Samuel Beckett: The unnameable (London, 2009)

PART III

Mind the Gap:
Telling the Tale

Terra tremens:
Katabasis *in Seamus Heaney's*
District and Circle *(2006)*

RACHEL FALCONER

In his address to the Royal College of Surgeons in Ireland, in 2001, Seamus Heaney spoke about the sense of dislocation and fear experienced by many in the wake of the bombings of the World Trade Center in New York City. There was, he said, a 'feeling that a crack had run through the foundations of the world, that the roof was blown off, that the border between the imaginable and the possible had been eradicated.'[1] His artistic response was to undertake a translation of Horace's *Odes I*, 34, a poem that describes the speaker's shock on hearing Jupiter, the god of thunder, drive his chariot across a clear sky. Re-read in the aftermath of the terrorist attacks, Horace's Ode spoke to him in a new way, 'about *terra tremens,* the opposite of *terra firma.* About the tremor that runs down to earth's foundations when thunder is heard and about the tremor of fear that shakes the very being of the individual who hears it' (*WT* 13–14).

A similar tremor of fear is captured in the five-sonnet sequence 'District and Circle', which Heaney expanded from two existing sonnets, in the weeks after the bombing of the London Underground on 7 July 2005. The semi-autobiographical poem reflects back on the summer of 1962, when a young Heaney commuted to work at the London Passport Office on the Tube.[2] In the expanded sequence, Heaney's dreamy descent into the Underground takes on echoes of Aeneas's descent into Hades, and the appearance of his father's ghost triggers a crucial turning point in his journey. This expanded version becomes the title poem in Heaney's 2006 collection, *District and Circle,* a volume that meditates on the current state of our fragile, mortal earth, our '*terra tremens'*.[3]

---

[1]   Seamus Heaney, 'The Whole Thing: On the Good of Poetry' (lecture delivered in Dublin, 5 November 2001), in *The Recorder: Journal of the American Irish Historical Society* (2002), 5–20 (p. 7). Hereafter *WT*, and cited parenthetically by page number.
[2]   Seamus Heaney, *Stepping Stones: Interviews with Seamus Heaney*, ed. Dennis O'Driscoll (London, 2008), p. 410.
[3]   Heaney, 'District and Circle', in *District and Circle* (London, 2006),

The roof has blown off the known world not only because of international terrorism, but also because of global-scale, human-induced climate
change. Ours is perhaps the first generation to come to know the human
mind as capable of destroying the earth's ecosystem.[4] A sense of threat to
the natural environment runs through *District and Circle* in poems such as
'Höfn', 'Moyulla', 'The Birch Grove', 'On the Spot', and 'The Tollund Man
in Springtime.' These dark pastoral poems are embedded within a broader
narrative arc in the volume as a whole of a mythical descent to the underworld and return.

As collected and arranged in *District and Circle,* Heaney's millennial
poems fall broadly into the tripartite shape of a *katabatic* journey, beginning with the disruption of ordinary reality by a cataclysmic event, then
a descent into the mythic underworld that is triggered by the shock of
disruption, and finally, a return to the altered, material world. The narrative arc is traversed in several individual poems, but it also provides an
overarching structure to the collection: the Horatian ode, 'Anything Can
Happen', marks the opening phase (dislocation of normal reality, orientation towards Dis, or Hades), 'District and Circle' enacts the poet's Virgilian
descent, and 'The Tollund Man in Springtime' effects a regenerative return
from the underworld.

Katabasis in Our Time

In his lecture to the Royal College of Surgeons, Heaney observed how 'religious language sprang naturally to the lips of leaders' in the aftermath of
9/11, as 'talk of good and evil fulfilled a need and gave an order to the
threatening chaos' (*WT* 7). The righteous militarism of US and UK governments in the early 2000s brought back for Heaney the 'high rhetoric' of the
First World War: 'high rhetoric in high places,' with their 'high certainty
about God on our side, high flags and high patriotism' (*WT* 8). Modern
war poetry, rather than rejecting the religious notion of Hell, explores how
this concept in the twentieth and twenty-first centuries is materialised in
actual hells on earth.[5] But the descent journey into the underworld and

---

pp. 17–19. Subsequent page references for the poems in this volume are cited
parenthetically.

[4]   See, for instance, Bill McKibben, *The End of Nature* (New York, 1989); Bruno
Latour, 'The End of Nature', in *Politics of Nature,* trans. Catherine Porter (Cambridge,
MA, 2004), 25–31.

[5]   For the actualisation of Hell in modern history, see George Steiner, *In Bluebeard's
Castle* (London, 1971), p. 47.

back also offers a way of structuring, giving shape, coherence, and a means of resistance to infernal experience. By deploying the classical *topos* of *katabasis,* poets draw upon, in Heaney's phrase, one of the richest deposits of the civilisation (*WT* 9). Classical *katabasis,* the narrative of the descent journey into Hades, is one of the oldest and most enduring 'deposits' of Western literature, encompassing some of our most ancient stories, from the *Epic of Gilgamesh* and Homer's *Odyssey XI* to Virgil's *Aeneid VI* and Dante's *Inferno*.[6]

'No lyric has ever stopped a tank,' Heaney readily conceded.[7] And no lyric has ever dismantled an oil tank standing three storeys tall in Alberta's tar sands, either.[8] But art can provide space for reflection and an imaginative shift to the point of view of the 'stranger'. In an essay on translating Horace's ode, Heaney describes how two American friends, on holiday in Florence at the time of the 9/11 attacks, turned to Renaissance art to work through their shock and grief.[9] Drawing on the language of medicine, Heaney explains that they were seeking the power of art for 'its capacity to distinguish itself from us and our needs and at the same time to make ourselves and our needs distinct and contemplatable'.[10] The art gave them a chance to step away from their immediate emotional reaction to the news from New York. As Heaney writes in *Stepping Stones,* art 'creates a pause in the action, a freeze-frame moment of concentration'.[11]

In Heaney's translation of Horace, sympathy and detachment are distributed in equal measure. Again, the translation has attracted some critical censure, both for its detachment and its hint of sympathy for the perpetrators of the 9/11 attack. But Heaney draws on Horace precisely to detach

[6]   Raymond Clark, *Catabasis: Vergil and the Wisdom Tradition* (Amsterdam, 1979), defines *katabasis* as 'a Journey of the Dead made by a living person in the flesh who returns to our world to tell the tale' (p. 34). Generically, its aim is the recovery of wisdom lost or concealed in the past. See Rachel Falconer, *Hell in Contemporary Literature: Western Descent Narratives since 1945* (Edinburgh, 2005); Erik Martiny, 'Modern Versions of Nostos and Katabasis: A Survey of Homeric Hypertexts in Recent Anglophone Poetry', *Anglia* 127.3 (2009), 469–79; and Michael Thurston, *The Underworld in Twentieth-Century Poetry: From Pound and Eliot to Heaney and Walcott* (Basingstoke, 2009).

[7]   Seamus Heaney, *The Government of the Tongue* (London, 1988), p. 107; and Heaney, *Stepping Stones*, p. 407.

[8]   On Alberta, Canada's tar sands, see Jim Robbins, 'The Dilbit Hits the Fan' (*Places*, Oct 2015).

[9]   Seamus Heaney, 'Reality and Justice: on Translating Horace', *Irish Pages* I.2 (2002/2003), 50–3.

[10]   Heaney, 'Reality and Justice', *Irish Pages*, p. 50.

[11]   Heaney, *Stepping Stones*, pp. 382–3.

himself from taking sides. As Heaney foresaw, the 'fallout' would be a redu-
plication of the violence elsewhere:

> the irruption of death into the Manhattan morning produced not only world-
> darkening grief for the multitudes of victims' families and friends, but it also
> had the effect of darkening the future with the prospect of deadly retaliations.
> Stealth bombers pummeling the vastnesses of Afghanistan, shock and awe
> loosed from the night skies over Iraq, they all seem part of the deadly fallout
> from the thunder cart in Horace's clear blue afternoon.[12]

Heaney's loose translation of Horace's *Odes I*, 34 was first published as
'Horace and the Thunder' in *The Irish Times,* 17 November 2001. In the
same month, he read the poem in public on two formal occasions, in Urbino
and Dublin. It subsequently appeared (in slightly differing versions) in *The
Times Literary Supplement,* as well as a multilingual volume produced for
Amnesty International, and a range of other journals in Ireland and abroad,
before reaching its final publication in *District and Circle*.[13] The translation
itself makes no explicit reference to the bombing of the World Trade Center
but, in at least two lectures and two publications, the poem is described as
having been composed explicitly in response to 9/11. The poem's detached
obliquity, and the pointedly explicit nature of Heaney's prose commentary,
are two complementary aspects of Heaney's ethically driven response to the
international outbreak of violence at the start of the millennium.

---

[12]   Seamus Heaney, *Anything Can Happen, a Poem and Essay by Seamus Heaney
with Translations in Support of Art for Amnesty* (Dublin, 2004), p. 18.
[13]   Heaney's translation of Horace *Odes I*, 34 is published in (at least) ten places:
(1) Quoted in 'The Whole Thing', p. 20; (2) 'Horace and the Thunder' in *The Irish
Times* (17 November 2001), Weekend 10; (3) Quoted in 'Towers, Trees, Terrors, a
rêverie in Urbino' (lecture delivered in Urbino, 23 November 2001), in *In forma di
parole. Seamus Heaney poeta dotto, a cura di Gabriella Morisco* 23.2 (2007), 145–56,
p. 156; (4) 'Horace and the Thunder' (New York, 2002); (5) 'Horace and Thunder'
[sic] in *The Times Literary Supplement* (18 January 2002), p. 40; (6) 'Horace and the
Thunder' published together with 'Reality and Justice: On Translating Horace, Odes
I, 34', *Translation Ireland* (Spring 2002), 8–11; (7) 'Horace and the Thunder, After
Horace, Odes, I, 34' published together with 'Reality and Justice', *Irish Pages*, 50–3;
(8) 'Anything Can Happen, *after Horace, Odes, I, 34*' in *Anything Can Happen*, p.
11; (9) 'Horace and the Thunder' in *A Shiver* (Thame, 2005); (10) 'Anything Can
Happen', in *District and Circle*, p. 13.

'Anything Can Happen'

Heaney's title, *District and Circle,* indicates how his 2006 collection aims to embrace global concerns as well as reaffirm ties to his own childhood 'district' in Co. Derry. Reflecting the trajectories of the London Tube's District and Circle lines, referred to in the title poem, Heaney's *katabatic* journey both circles back in time and projects forward into the millennial present. In terms of poetic form, the cultural 'deposit' being forwarded and transformed in *District and Circle* is the sonnet, in both Shakespearean and Petrarchan varieties. The echo of Shakespeare in 'A Shiver' is underlined with the near-rhyming couplet at the end, but elsewhere, as in 'District and Circle', Heaney uses the Petrarchan sonnet, with its ninth line *volta,* to map the trajectory of a mythic descent and return.

The first ten poems of the collection, six of which had been published earlier in a pamphlet entitled *A Shiver* (2005), make up the opening movement, or the first of three acts. Most of these poems are set in Heaney's childhood around the family farm at Mossbawn. Although based on the daily life of a rural community, they are still 'coloured by a darkened understanding' of war and therefore 'capable of bearing the brunt of present realities'.[14] In 'Anahorish 1944', Heaney recalls the arrival of American troops in tanks and jeeps, headed for the war in Normandy. Before the soldiers arrive, the community is already ringing with the 'untranscendent music' (*DC* 51) of turnip-snedders, sledgehammers, and blacksmiths' anvils.

The title poem from the earlier pamphlet, *A Shiver* (2005), appears in the first section of *District and Circle*. It provides a nuanced connection between the dark pastoral recollections of Mossbawn, and the Horatian Ode. Heaney recalls a childhood memory of learning to use a sledgehammer:

> The way you had to stand to swing the sledge,
> Your two knees locked, your lower back shock-fast
> As shields in a *testudo,* ... (*DC* 5)

The 'you' being addressed here is not only the poet's childhood self but anyone who has dealt a violent blow, from the ancient Romans implied in the '*testudo*' (a military 'tortoise' formation) to contemporary terrorists and heads of state. He compares the 'gathered force' of the hammer blow to 'a long-nursed rage / About to be let fly' (*DC* 5). In his essay on Horace,

---

[14]   Heaney, *Literary Papers, 1963–2010*, The National Library, Dublin, 1.xvii.10 ('PBS Bulletin', 28 February 2006).

he links this rage to the question posed in Shakespeare's Sonnet 65: 'How with this rage shall beauty hold a plea, / Whose action is no stronger than a flower?'[15] In 'A Shiver', he anticipates Jupiter's thunder, in the weighty blow of the sledgehammer:

> does it do you good
> To have known it in your bones, directable,
> Withholdable at will,
> A first blow that could make air of a wall,
> A last one so unanswerably landed
> The staked earth quailed and shivered in the handle? (*DC* 5)

While in the Horace translation, Heaney withholds any sense of agency or blame for violence, here the addressee is directly accosted with responsibility: 'does it do you good / To have known it ... ?' If this question accuses the perpetrators of violence, it is also self-directed as an ethical challenge to his own art: what good does it do to have known poetry? Or as Czesław Miłosz puts it, still more accusingly, 'what is poetry which does not save / Nations or people?'[16] In *District and Circle,* this dark pastoral limbo is interrupted by the eruption of violence in Horace's *Odes I,* 34.

When Heaney first returned to the Latin poem, just after 9/11, he was immediately struck by the 'uncanny soothsaying force' of Horace's lines.[17] The tone of Heaney's translation heightens the sense of Horace as a familiar acquaintance, and he starts up a conversation without preamble or ceremony:

> Anything can happen. You know how Jupiter
> Will mostly wait for clouds to gather head
> Before he hurls the lightning? Well, just now
> He galloped his thunder cart ... (*DC* 13)

This translation corresponds loosely to Horace's second stanza:

> ... namque Diespiter
> igni corusco nubile diuidens
> plerumque, per purum tonantis
> egit equos uolucremque currum, [...] (*Odes I,* 34, ll. 5–8)

---

[15]   *The Norton Shakespeare*, ed. Stephen Greenblatt et al, (New York, 1997), pp. 1944–5

[16]   Czesław Miłosz, *The Collected Poems: 1931–1987* (New York, 1988), p. 66.

[17]   Heaney, *Anything Can Happen*, p. 15. Rpt. Heaney, 'Reality and Justice', *Irish Pages*, p. 51.

In his essay, 'Reality and Justice', Heaney reprints an unnamed prose translation as the basis for a comparison with his own verse translation:

> For the father of the sky, who mostly cleaves the clouds with a gleaming flash, has driven through the undimmed firmament his thundering steeds and flying car.[18]

Heaney's opening stanza is more colloquial than Horace's, with a relaxed, second-person address ('you know ... well, just now') and a Kavanagh-like, prosaic 'cart', for Horace's formal 'currus'. From this informal beginning, Heaney's poem then shifts into a more elevated style for the middle two stanzas, describing Jupiter's thunderclap and Fortune's eagle-like swoop down on its victims. The fourth stanza concludes in terse, chiseled, end-stopped sentences, with no first- or second-person address, or indeed any mention of human presence at all. It is this newly alien, infernal reality which necessitates the poet's journey into the underworld.

While he preserves the four-quatrain structure of the Latin ode, Heaney drops Horace's first stanza and adds a fourth of his own invention. In Horace's poem, the urbane poet is jolted out of his free-wheeling attitude to the gods by a sharp reminder of their infinite powers. The Latin first stanza describes the poet's return to proper religious observance. Heaney's decision to cut this first stanza unmoors the ode from its religious context. Whatever moral we draw from Heaney's poem, it cannot be the terroristic one that the gods exact vengeance on non-believers. God, or Jupiter, is also conspicuously absent from Heaney's rendering of lines 12–13, 'ualet ima summis // mutare ... deus' ('the god has power to change the highest things to/for the lowest'), as 'anything can happen'.[19] In the poem's final version, this theologically neutral phrase appears twice, in the first and eighth lines, and is also adopted as the title. *Anything Can Happen* was also chosen as the title of a collection of twenty-three translations of Heaney's poem, put together for Amnesty International in 2004, where the translations are paired in the 'languages of conflict' – for example, in pairs of English and Irish, German and Russian, and Hebrew and Arabic translations.[20] The familiar expression thus comes to denote a collective artistic decision to voice both sides of these longstanding, military conflicts, with god and divine right belonging to neither side.

18   Heaney, 'Reality and Justice', *Irish Pages*, p. 51.
19   The prose translation is Heaney's, from 'Reality and Justice', *Irish Pages*, p. 52.
20   Heaney, *Anything Can Happen*, pp. 19, 44.

In his second stanza, corresponding to Horace's third, Heaney introduces three slight changes of emphasis which draw the poem into the orbit of 9/11 and its aftermath. Both poets declare that Jupiter's thunder shakes the earth and the underworld (Heaney suppresses the more obscure reference to Taenarus but retains Styx as synecdoche for Hades). Horace says it even shakes 'Atlanteus ... finis' (line 11), a compressed phrase suggesting the Pillars of Hercules, at the western end of the Mediterranean and eastern limit of the Atlantic.[21] In Heaney's version, this becomes 'the Atlantic shore itself', where New York's World Trade Center stood. Secondly, Heaney changes the verb 'concutitur' ('is rocked') from passive, simple present to active, historical past ('shook'), so that the event of Jupiter's thunderous arrival comes to stand for a specific, world-altering catastrophe: 'his thunder cart ... shook the earth ... Styx ... the Atlantic shore itself' (lines 4–7). Although he then switches back to Horace's simple present tense, to generalise about what can happen, anytime, a modern reader now has a particular disaster in mind. And this is reinforced in the final 2006 text, where Heaney changes 'things' to 'towers' in his eighth line. All earlier versions of the poem had read, 'Anything can happen, the tallest things / Be overturned' (a free rendering of 'valet ima summis / mutare ... deus'). But reading the poem in the aftermath of 9/11, few would miss the allusion to New York City's Twin Towers in Heaney's 'tallest towers ... overturned'.

The third stanza (Horace's fourth) contains the correspondences that Heaney found uncanny in their close fit between the original Latin and the 2001 context. Here is Horace's fourth and final stanza, and the prose translation, followed by Heaney's version:

> ... Valet ima summis //
> mutare et insignem attenuat deus,
> obscura promens; hinc apicem rapax
> Fortuna cum stridore acuto
> sustulit, hic posuisse gaudet. (*Odes I,* 34, lines 12–16)

> (To change the highest for the lowest, the god has power; he makes mean the man of high estate, bringing what is hidden into light: Fortune, like a predator, flaps up and bears away the crest from one, then sets it down with relish on another.)

---

[21]   S. J. Harrison, 'Heaney as Translator: Horace and Virgil', in *Seamus Heaney and the Classics*, ed. Harrison, et al (Oxford, 2019), pp. 244–62 (p. 251).

Anything can happen, the tallest towers //
Be overturned, those in high places daunted,
Those overlooked regarded. Stropped-beak Fortune
Swoops, making the air gasp, tearing the crest off one,
Setting it down bleeding on the next.[22]

Heaney finds an 'eerie correspondence' between Horace's image of the highest brought low, and the 'dreamy, deadly images of the Twin Towers'. And there is 'an equally unnerving fit' between the 'conventional wisdom of the Latin "obscura promens" (bringing the disregarded to notice)' and the '*realpolitik* of the terrorist assault'. For Heaney, this assault not only produced 'world-darkening grief for the multitudes of victims' families and friends' but also it brought 'to new prominence the plight of the Palestinians and much else in and about the Arab world'.[23] In his 2001 version, published in *The Irish Times,* Heaney translates 'obscura promens' as 'those overlooked esteemed', though later this line is slightly toned down, from being 'esteemed' to being 'regarded'. Even in the latter version, few voices in the western media took such an even-handed stance to the attacks, especially as early as 2001.

Horace's 'rapax Fortuna' draws on the Roman legend that an eagle crowned the head of the future king Tarquin the Elder.[24] For Heaney, 'rapax Fortuna ... becomes an image for the impulse to attack or to retaliate,' referring, unless I am mistaken, to the violent attack of the terrorists, as well as the recriminations by the US government that were to follow.[25] The shift from the simple past tense of 'It shook the earth' to the present of 'Anything can happen' and 'Fortune swoops' contributes to the sense that a single act of violence has set in motion a recurring cycle of attack and retaliation. Heaney's poem thus studiously avoids attributing human agency to the violence, and while this has disturbed some readers, I see it as one of the poem's strengths. By keeping his gaze steadily on the victims of violence, he withholds any oxygen of publicity to the perpetrators, who in this poem have lost their human faces entirely. Along with the Roman eagle, Heaney's phrase, 'Stropped-beak Fortune' alludes to his friend Ted Hughes's poem, 'Crow's Song of Himself', in which 'Crow stropped his beak and started in on the two thieves'.[26] In Hughes's series of Crow poems, the bird inhabits

---

22   Heaney, 'Reality and Justice', *Irish Pages,* p. 52.
23   All quotes are from Heaney, 'Reality and Justice', *Irish Pages,* p. 52.
24   See Harrison, 'Heaney as Translator', p. 251.
25   Heaney, 'Reality and Justice', *Irish Pages,* p. 53.
26   With thanks to Neil Roberts for this reference.

a degraded, polluted world, what Heaney sums up as 'the Crow-cursed universe' lacking the possibility of grace.[27] So although Heaney withholds blame from either side, the violent blow itself is given the face of a predatory bird, associated with godlessness and empire.[28]

Horace's poem ends with the raptor Fortune's stoop, but Heaney adds another quatrain, dense with classical allusion. And here, not only is human agency excluded, but the consequences of the violence are registered on the vast geological rather than human scale:

> Ground gives. The heaven's weight
> Lifts up off Atlas like a kettle-lid.
> Capstones shift, nothing resettles right.
> Telluric ash and fire-spores boil away. (*DC* 13)

The one reference to the man-made environment is the 'kettle-lid', a decidedly human-scale, quotidian object that seems out of place in the volcanic movement of the rest of the quatrain. The lifting of Atlas's burden (the sky, in classical mythology) may also trigger a positive counter-image for Biblically schooled readers. When Heaney explains how 'the shaken earth called up an image of the lifted roof', he calls attention to the same motif in the New Testament story of a roof being lifted off, at Capernaum, so that a paralysed man could be lowered inside, to be healed by Jesus.[29]

But the allusions to Virgil in the last three lines are more ominous. Atlas being relieved of his burden of sky is an image that recurs five times in the *Aeneid,* as Stephen Harrison notes.[30] In *Aeneid IV,* Mercury alights on thunder-crowned Mount Atlas on his way to commanding Aeneas to leave Carthage (Ae.IV.247f.). And in *Aeneid VI,* Anchises mentions Mount Atlas as the outer limit of Augustus Caesar's expanding empire (Ae.VI.792–97).[31] In both cases, the allusion to Atlas is associated with Rome's aggressive imperial ambitions, which in Heaney's poem take on

---

[27]   Heaney, 'On Ted Hughes's "Littleblood"', *Finders Keepers* (London, 2002), p. 409.

[28]   See Hughes's tyrannical 'Hawk Roosting': 'I kill where I please because it is all mine. /... My manners are tearing off heads – / The allotment of death', *Collected Poems* (London, 2005), p. 69.

[29]   Heaney, 'Reality and Justice', *Irish Pages,* p. 53. Matthew (9:1–8), Mark (2:1–12), and Luke (5:17–26). Cf. Heaney's poem 'Miracle' in *Human Chain* (London, 2012), p. 17.

[30]   Harrison, 'Heaney as Translator', p. 252.

[31]   See *Vergili Opera,* ed. R. A. B. Mynors, 2 vols (Oxford, 1980), vol. 2, p. 183f and 252.

an additional association with the US government's 'high rhetoric' in the wake of the 9/11 attacks. If the ash and smouldering fire-spores recall the 'dreamy, deadly images' of the crumbled twin towers, there is already a counter-movement implied in the mention of ground giving and 'telluric ash' boiling. The rare adjective 'telluric' means 'of the earth', from the Latin, *tellus*, and if the ground gives, the portals of the underworld could well be opening already. Heaney's neologism 'fire-spores' seems very closely related to Virgil's 'semina flammae' ('seeds of flame').[32] In Book VI, just before Aeneas undertakes his descent, his ships land at Cumae, and the Trojan youths leap ashore to seek the 'semina flammae' hidden in the flinty rock (Ae.IV.6). 'Ground gives' before Aeneas, when he follows the Sibyl into her cave and down to the shores of the Styx.

Some readers might find this density of classical allusion inappropriate in a poem written designedly in response to a contemporary political atrocity. But we might also appreciate this indirection as one of the poem's strengths. The translation can help distance us from our immediate, emotional reactions, by structuring and formalising sound, introducing complex layers of associations, and arresting the leap to judgment. Heaney's 'Anything Can Happen' develops what T. S. Eliot described as the capacity for abstract feeling, by directing those feelings back into the depths of Roman history.[33] In the case of Horace's ode, the theme of political violence is further screened by the projection of historical reality into myth. Imagining a terrorist assault as the swoop of a predatory mythical beast can have the virtue of delaying or deflecting the all-too-understandable instinct to seek out individual names and faces with the purpose of killing them in revenge.

In 'Towers, Trees, Terrors', a lecture delivered in Urbino, Heaney ponders the significance of the Latin *urbs* ('city') as a concept of community existing in writers' imaginations long before the era of international terrorism. He remembers how, reading Livy at school,

> the noun *urbs*, feminine and radiant, gleamed constantly at the centre of the historian's narrative. That narrative was mostly concerned with matters military and masculine, but every now and then Livy would refer to Rome simply as the *urbs*, and for a moment the city turned from being the site of government and imperium to being a mixture of *alma mater* and muse.[34]

---

[32]   Harrison agrees with this conjecture, 'Heaney as Translator' p. 252.

[33]   T. S. Eliot, 'Tradition and the Practice of Poetry' (Lecture delivered at University College, Dublin, 1936), *The Southern Review* 21.4 (1985), 873–88, see p. 883.

[34]   Heaney, 'Towers, Trees, Terrors', pp. 148–9.

Contrastingly, Horace's famously urbane voice makes no mention of the *urbs* in *Odes I*, 34. And in Heaney's adaptation, only the late addition of the word 'towers' references the city of New York. The two towers which Heaney describes in his lecture are medieval ruins, located respectively in the Apennines, near Urbino, and in the West of Ireland; both are 'set in lonely countryside'.[35] Walking towards Urbino, W. B. Yeats had discovered the Apennine tower 'amid a visionary, fantastic, impossible scenery', a vision that inspired his own purchase of a lonely, Irish tower, where he produced two great collections of poetry, *The Tower* and *The Winding Stair*.[36] Arguably, then, Heaney muses on these twinned towers as poetic and visionary alternatives to the decimated towers of the World Trade Center. Put simply, the *urbs* is being re-imagined from the margins, from a vantage point outside history. The visionary city is 'feminine and radiant' rather than 'military and masculine', and it is accessed through reverie, or the waking dream-world of poetry.

In *District and Circle*, the entire earth has suffered a mortal blow, from the Atlantic shore to underearth and heaven's lid. This damage extends well beyond the world of human political conflict. Thus, 'Höfn' gives us a glimpse of polar ice caps melting and glaciers on the move, where the awakening of this '[u]ndead grey-gristed earth-pelt, aeon-scruff' foreshadows the end of human culture and 'every warm, mouthwatering word of mouth.' (*DC* 53). In 'Moyulla', Heaney returns to his personal Helicon, the River Moyola which flows near the grounds of the family farm at Mossbawn. But here the 'clear vowels' of the river's name have 'suffered muddying' (the 'o' darkening to 'u' in 'Moyulla') because the river itself is 'Milk-fevered' and 'Froth at the mouth / of the discharge pipe' (*DC* 58–9).[37] In the twenty-first century, the Earth has 'felt the wound' of human presence, and 'sighing through all her works, g[ives] signs of woe'.[38]

The cataclysmic overturn of the 'military and masculine' *urbs,* and the mortal wounding of Earth, compel the poet to undertake his dreamy descent into the underworld. The collection explores a wide variety of traditions relating to the underworld, but the ethical imperative driving this

---

[35]   Heaney, 'Towers, Trees, Terrors', pp. 148–9.

[36]   Heaney, 'Towers, Trees, Terrors', pp. 147, 148.

[37]   'I wanted the darkening of the vowel from 'ola' to 'ulla' to suggest the darkening of the ecological climate, the pollution of the river over time' (Heaney, *Stepping Stones*, p. 406).

[38]   After the fall of Eve, 'Earth felt the wound, and nature from her seat / Sighing through all her works gave signs of woe / That all was lost.' John Milton, *Paradise Lost*, ed. Alastair Fowler, 2nd edn (Harlow, 1998), IX.782–84.

poetic exploration of different cultural underworlds is most clearly discernable in the title poem of the collection, 'District and Circle'.

'District and Circle'

In this five-sonnet sequence, the poet's recollection of a habitual commute on the London Underground takes on the dimensions of a Virgilian *katabasis*. A busker with whom he exchanges glances at the entrance of the station becomes a sibylline gatekeeper, while the approaching train rumbles and growls like a three-headed Cerberus (lines 4–8, 19–20). The poet steps onto the train amid a crowd of commuters from whom he feels separate and estranged, like Aeneas amongst the dead souls when he steps onto Charon's barge (lines 31–5, 42–50). Then, as the train ferries him under the streets of London, he catches a glimpse of his father's face in his own reflection, as if like Aeneas he were greeting his dead father in the underworld (line 58). The sonnet sequence thus jolts backward in time as the poet descends into the underground.

The first and final stanzas of 'District and Circle' were originally composed as part of a sequence of poems about the Tollund Man, one of the Iron Age bodies unearthed from peat bogs who had featured in Heaney's *Wintering Out* (1972).[39] Heaney then extracted the two stanzas to create a diptych of two sonnets, entitled 'District and Circle', which described the Iron Age revenant, travelling between Earls Court and St James's Park, on the two Tube lines that serve those stations.[40] Formally, each sonnet in the diptych had a distinct *volta* or turn, between the eighth and ninth line, as is characteristic of the Petrarchan sonnet. With this two-stanza poem, Heaney had, then, already forged a connection between the mid-poem *volta* of a Petrarchan sonnet and the doubling-back movement of a *katabatic* descent and return.[41] The Tollund Man rises from the underworld to confront 'a world of surveillance cameras and closed-circuit TV, of greenhouse gases and acid rain'.[42] Although the diptych was not then overtly autobiographical, Heaney was already exploring the sense of a disconnect

[39]   Heaney, *Stepping Stones*, p. 410; Heaney, 'One Poet in Search of a Title', *The Times* (25 March 2006); Seamus Heaney, 'The Tollund Man', in *Wintering Out* (London, 1972), pp. 36–7.
[40]   Heaney, *Stepping Stones*, p. 410.
[41]   See Meg Tyler on Heaney's use of the sonnet in 'District and Circle', in '"The Whole of Me A-Patter"', in *The Soul Exceeds its Circumstances*, ed. Eugene O'Brien (Notre Dame, 2016), pp. 129–48 (p. 135f).
[42]   Heaney, 'Poet in Search'.

from his Northern Irish identity when, in the summer of 1962, he worked
for the Passport Office in London. The title of the diptych signified Heaney's
'inclination to favour a chosen region and keep coming back to it', and eventually he adopted it as the working title of the collection in progress.[43] This
account of the poem's genesis reveals the close link between the autobiographical, five-sonnet 'District and Circle' and 'The Tollund Man in Springtime',
which introduces the final section of the 2006 volume.

The London Underground was bombed on 7 July 2005, as part of four
coordinated suicide attacks which killed fifty-two people, and injured more
than seven hundred others. Heaney's poetic response to this terrorist atrocity
was once again both deliberate and obliquely veiled, as had been his decision to translate Horace's ode. In the months following 7/7, he expanded
'District and Circle' into a five-sonnet sequence. His decision to incorporate
the original diptych was a way of 'keep[ing] faith with the London lines'
while the added sections allowed for a 'deeper dwelling with the motif' of
the descent journey.[44] While his original introduction of the poem for the
Poetry Book Society mentioned the circumstances of 7 July, Heaney later
faxed another version with the reference removed. Rather than making the
poem sound 'occasional/ topical', he wanted to locate its inspiration in 'the
oddness/ oldness of the memories'.[45] The three additional sonnets were 'not
particularly to do with the atrocity', Heaney later wrote, but were composed
with the awareness that a poem about the underground would now 'have
to bear additional scrutiny'.[46] The first-person voice has shifted from the
Tollund Man to an autobiographical speaker in the longer version.[47] But the
first-person speaker also functions as an everyman figure, channelling emotions any traveller journeying across London on the Tube today might feel,
given our collective knowledge of how the Circle Line had once been transformed into a circle of Hell, and might be again.

If the poem conveys this mixture of private and collective unease, it also
offers redress in the form of the poet's, and potentially the reader's, transformation of consciousness in the course of his journey underground. 'District
and Circle' conveys the dream-like quality of the repeated, daily commute

---

43   Heaney, 'Poet in Search'.
44   Heaney, 'Poet in Search'.
45   Heaney, *Literary Papers*, 1.xvii.4 (letter to Chris Holifield, 28 February 2006).
46   Heaney, *Stepping Stones*, p. 410.
47   Heaney, *Stepping Stones*, p. 410. An earlier draft of the poem is still more pointedly autobiographical; Heaney remembers being rebuked by his London supervisor
at the Passport Office: '"Slow coach on the Green Line, were you, Paddy?/ Out with
the navvies last Night?"', Heaney, *Literary Papers* I.xvii.2.

underground; an early draft of the poem contains the line, 'As if I had entered not a train but knowledge.'[48] But the classical echoes amplify that experience, aligning the poet in his ordinary journey with Aeneas, as he prepares to face the terrors of the underworld.[49]

In 'Anything Can Happen', there is one main tense shift from habitual action to a singular event. By contrast, in 'District and Circle', the tense sequencing is extremely complex and elastic, underlining the oneiric atmosphere of the poem. As I have discussed elsewhere, such disordering of time is a generic feature of *katabatic* narratives.[50] In the first sonnet, the poet's enigmatic exchange of nods with a sibylline busker seems to be a habitual, even ritual, practice: note the 'would' in 'I'd trigger and untrigger a hot coin' (line 10). In the second, third and fourth stanzas of 'District and Circle', the verb tenses shift into the simple past: 'I missed the light' (line 22), 'I re-entered the safety of numbers' (line 30), 'I reached to grab' (line 43). And here the dream time crystalises into the narrative of a single, singular journey, whose mythic goal is the recovery of loss, or discovery of secret, otherworldly wisdom. At the same time, though, a series of participial verbs continue to imply repeated action: 'newcomers / Jostling and purling ... then succumbing' (lines 33, 35), and the poet 'waiting', 'Stepping', 'Listening', 'craning' (lines 39, 42, 49, 59). So that the whole journey seems suspended between eternal recurrence and the 'now-or-never whelm' of a cataclysmic event (line 40).

The poet asks himself: '[h]ad I betrayed or not, myself or him?' (line 36). This seems like a question to be posed once, if enigmatically. But it turns out to be a habitual self-accusation: '[a]lways new to me, always familiar, / This unrepentant, now repentant turn / As I stood waiting' (lines 37–9). This guilty thought being described as a 'turn', along with the 'turned' (doubled and reversed) adjective 'unrepentant/repentant', alerts us to the disturbances that occur at the sonnet's *volta* here, and in every sonnet in the sequence. In the third sonnet, the key question, 'Had I betrayed or not', comes slightly too soon, curtailing the second quatrain and hastening the sestet, so that the sonnet falls one short of fourteen lines. In the first sonnet, lines eight and nine are short lines, which again disturbs the *volta* from octet to sestet. And in the final sonnet, the disturbance comes early, with short lines disrupting the transition between quatrains in the octet. Then the poem ends abruptly, with a final line of three syllables, a compound adjective thrown free of the sestet, both grammatically and visually

48   Heaney, *Literary Papers*, 1.xvii.2.
49   Heaney, *Stepping Stones*, p. 410.
50   See Falconer, *Hell in Contemporary Literature*, pp. 42–62.

on the page. All of these rhythmic stutters in the sonnet form contribute to the impression of a disordered, dream-like temporality, now cyclical and regular, now accelerated and discontinuous.

Traditional *katabatic* journeys may be protracted or quick, may involve multiple encounters with underworld shades or none, but they nearly always feature a threshold crossing, a ground-zero trial, and a re-ascent to light. As in his earlier collection *Seeing Things* (1991), Heaney associates Aeneas's crossing of the Styx on Charon's barge with his own personal memories of being stopped at loyalist checkpoints in Northern Ireland.[51] Here the motif is developed further, revealing stronger tensions between the poet and the souls crowding the shore. The poet at first stands aloof from the jostling crowd at the platform, 'Street-loud, then succumbing to herd-quiet' (line 35). At this point, there is no 'we', no self-identification with the 'human chain' (line 32). He is absorbed in his own thoughts, and an ellipsis in line 35 (indicating the missing line of the octet) separates him from the other commuters. He asks himself, 'Had I betrayed or not, myself or him?'

At a border control in County Derry, a betrayal might involve denying your ties to a particular Catholic or Protestant community. Here the sense of betrayal seems both more personal and more detached. The identity of the 'him', at first obscure, is made clear in the final sonnet, where he sees his father in the glass reflection of the train window. So, one way of construing his inward questioning is to suggest he has 'repentant' feelings of *pietas* towards his father, as well as worries about having betrayed his own Northern Irish Catholic identity in an 'unrepentant' pursuit of poetic vocation. Whether his pious obligations to his father and to himself are one and the same, or in conflict, is unclear from the syntactic structure of the question. But either way, he keeps himself separate from the London crowd as he stands waiting for the train (line 39). For a section of the poem composed months after the July bombings in London, this is notably distanced from the strong feelings of identification and outrage that were then circulating in the British media. As in the Horace translation, Heaney's response to political violence is carefully distanced.

The poet's threshold crossing onto the Tube conflates two scenes from *Aeneid VI*: Aeneas's seizure of the golden bough, and his boarding of Charon's barge. The order of the episodes is reversed, so that the poet steps in with the crowd, 'caught up in the now-or-never whelm / Of one and all' (lines 40–1) like the souls thronging onto Charon's barge. On a literal level, this depicts the poet thrown together with fellow commuters, recollected

---

[51]   For instance, 'And yes, my friend, we too', in Seamus Heaney, *Seeing Things* (London, 1991), p. 94.

from the summer of 1962; but metaphorically, the parallel with *Aeneid VI*
suggests he is also stepping in with the shades of the dead, specifically the
fifty-two people killed in 2005. Once on the train, he reaches for the carriage
strap, in a gesture that resembles Aeneas's clutch for the bough, even as the
train takes on the function of Charon's barge:

> Stepping on to it across the gap,
> On to the carriage metal, I reached to grab
> The stubby black roof-wort and take my stand
> From planted ball of heel to heel of hand
> As sweet traction and heavy down-slump stayed me.
> I was on my way, well girded, yet on edge,
> Spot-rooted, buoyed, aloof, ... (*DC* 18)

The poet's stance, 'well girded, yet on edge ... buoyed, aloof' recalls the many
Virgilian boat scenes in *Seeing Things*, while his 'heavy down-slump' specifically recalls Aeneas's unusual weight in the barge: 'gemuit sub pondere
cumba' ('Under that weight the boat's plied timbers groan').[52] The gesture of
reaching for the overhead strap handle further duplicates Aeneas's snatch at
the golden bough: 'corripit Aeneas extemplo auidus ... que refringit', 'There
and then, / Aeneas took hold of it'.[53] While physically, the gesture merely
steadies the poet in the moving train, metaphorically the poet's Northern
Irish identity is being stayed and affirmed in this transformative, threshold
crossing. This metaphorical significance is suggested by the sudden thicken-
ing of language with consonant clusters, spondaic accents, and Anglo-Saxon
root words, notably in the phrase, 'stúbby bláck roóf-wórt'. 'Wort' is an
archaic word (from the Old English *wyrt*) meaning a plant used in stews or
medicine, but when used in compound nouns, it refers to the second element
in the names of plants (for example, 'figwort', 'woundwort').[54] 'Roof' also has
an Old English origin, from *hrof,* meaning 'ceiling' or 'roof'.[55] One of its etymological meanings is also 'coffin-lid', an apt term for a growth hanging from

---

[52] Ae.VI. 413; translation by Seamus Heaney, *Aeneid Book VI* (London, 2016),
line 553.

[53] Ae.VI. 210; translation by Seamus Heaney, 'The Golden Bough' (lines 126–8),
Translation 22 (1989), 197–201.

[54] "wort, n.1". *OED Online*. December 2020. Oxford University Press. https://
ezproxy-prd.bodleian.ox.ac.uk:2446/view/Entry/230371?rskey=OnQEvj&result=1
(accessed 13 December 2020).

[55] "roof, n.". *OED Online*. December 2020. Oxford University Press. https://
ezproxy-prd.bodleian.ox.ac.uk:2446/view/Entry/167250?rskey=AY51G0&result=1
(accessed 13 December 2020).

the ceiling of the underworld, but perhaps that is pressing Heaney's etymological subtext too far. But the image of a strap handle as an organic ceiling-growth links to the vocabulary of farming that Heaney deploys in the fourth sonnet: he is '[s]pot-rooted' (line 48) by 'sweet traction' (line 46), with 'planted ball of heel' (line 45) and in the fifth sonnet, 'lofted arm a-swivel like a flail' (lines 57). All these words reconnect the poet to his farmer father, and reaffirm him in his rural, County Derry identity.

In the last two sonnets, this personal affirmation broadens out to a more collective redress, offering a visionary connection to the 'feminine and radiant' *urbs* of Livy's prose, and the city of Carthage where Aeneas falls in love with Dido. In a way, this alternative, radiant *urbs* persists as a mirror image of the 'military and masculine' cities of Rome and London. When 'country' language infiltrates the modern, urban space of the Tube train, there is a bridging of two worlds; and the modern, high-speed city comes to seem closer, less '[b]lindsided' (lines 55) to its ancient origins. In the fifth and final sonnet of the sequence, the train hurtles its passengers, including the poet, into the underground network of tunnels. 'So deeper into it' (line 56), the poet tells himself, and by 'it', he means both the District and Circle lines, and the memories of his home district, in rural County Derry. In stance, he is like Aeneas holding the golden bough before him: 'My lofted arm a-swivel like a flail' (line 57). A 'flail' is not only an ancient military weapon but a rod used to flatten crops, so, like the golden bough, it combines links to nature and technology. As with Aeneas, the aim of his journey turns out to be a longed-for meeting with his father's shade. This he glimpses in his own face, reflected in the train window: 'My father's glazed face in my own waning / And craning ...' (lines 58–9). There is, conspicuously, no main verb in this entire last sonnet, so these floating participial verbs contribute to the impression that the poet is here adrift in a dream time cut off from the narrative present.

In themselves, the paired verbs 'waning and craning' capture the two-way trafficking movement of this poem. 'Waning' implies ageing (hence, starting to look like his father), but 'craning' suggests a straining to see ahead, and into the future, like the small boy at the window in Heaney's earlier poem, 'Seeing Things'. More broadly, this glimpse of his father holds the poet still, in a temporal limbo, while at the same time he is being 'hurtled forward' (line 66) by the train; its 'jolt and one-off treble' (line 61) and 'long centrifugal / Haulage of speed' (lines 62–3) become a figure for linear, chronological time itself. Being able to stand still, with 'planted ball of heel', while travelling forward at speed, suggests learning to balance opposing allegiances between Northern Irish rural past, and urban, British present. All the formal and thematic pairings in the poem, from the exchange of nods with the busker and the pairing of verbs throughout (lines 10, 16, 20, 31, etc.), to the end-line near-rhymes, and the sestet's fold-back on the octet, contribute to this notion of finding a balance between opposing tensions, rather than giving way to a single direction of travel. Yet again, what distinguishes this glimpse of the 'father's glazed face' from the recognition scene in 'Seeing Things' ('I saw him face to face, he came to me') is that it is not trapped in the fairy-tale time of romance, but is being hurtled forward in the train, and by implication, in the movement of historical time.[56]

The poet's glimpse of his father's face, in 'District and Circle', establishes a link with the past that is not only personal and patrilinear, but also socially conscious and, perhaps unexpectedly, feminine. Clearly, the major parallel is with Aeneas when he finds Anchises's shade in Elysium. But there is a secondary echo, quite significant in its implications, of Aeneas's famous encounter with the ghost of Dido in the Fields of Mourning. Aeneas recognises her despite the uncertain light, and her 'wavering form' (Heaney's translation) is compared to a rising moon:

> ... Phoenissa recens a uulnere Dido
> errabat silua in magna; quam Troius heros
> ut primum iuxta stetit adgnouitque per umbras
> obscuram, qualem primo qui surgere mense
> aut uidet aut uidisse putat per nubila lunam

(with wound still fresh, Phoenician Dido was wandering in the great forest, and soon as the Trojan hero stood near and knew her, a dim form amid the shadows – even as, in the early month, one sees or fancies he has seen the moon rise amid the clouds)[57] (Ae.VI.450–454)

This is Heaney's translation of the passage:

> ... still nursing her raw wound,
> Dido of Carthage strayed in the great forest.
> As soon as the Trojan came close and made out
> Her dimly wavering form among the shadows,
> He was like one who sees or imagines he has seen
> A new moon rising up among the clouds
> On the first day of the month; ... [58]

---

[56]   Heaney, *Seeing Things*, p. 18.
[57]   H. R. Fairclough trans., *Virgil: Eclogues, Georgics, Aeneid 1–6*, revised by G. P. Goold (Cambridge, MA, 1999), p. 565.
[58]   Heaney, *Aeneid Book VI* (2016), lines 604–10.

Heaney translates 'Phoenissa' as 'of Carthage' to underline the historic rivalry between Carthage and Rome, in which Aeneas and Dido's affair is already implicated from the beginning of the *Aeneid*. When Heaney compares his father's face to a crescent moon, glimpsed in the underworld, the metaphor comes laced with echoes of Aeneas's encounter with Dido. It will be carried forward later in the volume, when the Tollund Man remembers 'moony water' (*DC* 56) from his former life.

The parallel is underlined when, a few lines later, the poet describes himself as 'the only relict / Of all that I belonged to' (lines 65–6). According to the *Oxford English Dictionary*, the primary meaning of 'relict' is 'widow'.[59] Virgil's 'Widow Dido' is a character already at home in English tragedy, from Marlowe's 1593 play, *Dido Queen of Carthage* to Purcell's 1680 opera, *Dido and Aeneas*. The word 'relict' also has a specifically Irish connection, as it appears frequently on gravestones, describing widows of soldiers killed in battle. Hence Steven Matthews credibly suggests that Heaney is aligning himself with the survivors of massacre, and perhaps we could add, the survivors of the London bombings.[60] When the poet describes himself as a 'relict' he is, then, taking on the burden of a communal sense of belonging, one that notably hybridises feminine and masculine ancestries: Dido, Irish war widows, and Aeneas's father, Anchises.

In 'Towers, Trees, Terrors', Heaney praises 'that lovely, elegiac cadence' at the beginning of the *Aeneid*, 'which introduces and swiftly dispenses with the history and destiny of Carthage: *Urbs antiqua fuit* ... '[61] He continues, 'the word *urbs* is sounded very sweetly and very lovingly, but this time sadly because Virgil is telling us that all of its mystery and beauty and essential *urbanitas* is now to pass from Carthage to the new city of Rome'.[62] Heaney finds in the opening lines of the *Aeneid* a powerful evocation of the beauty and mystery of the ancient *urbs*. What makes the evocation of the city typically Virgilian, for Heaney, is the melancholy awareness of its impermanence. The adverbs 'sweetly, lovingly, sadly' also suggest that for Heaney, Carthage represents the lost, 'feminine and radiant' *urbs* that he finds gleaming off the pages of Livy. At the same time, the lost *urbs* gets forwarded in time in the way, for example, Virgil's epic links Troy, Carthage,

[59]   "relict, n.". *OED Online*. December 2020. Oxford University Press. https://ezproxy-prd.bodleian.ox.ac.uk:2446/view/Entry/161914?rskey =uTmo3a&result=1&isAdvanced=false (accessed 13 December 2020).

[60]   Steven Matthews, 'Bucketful by Glistering Bucketful', *Poetry Review* 97:1 (2007), 91–3, p. 93.

[61]   Heaney, 'Towers, Trees, Terrors', p. 149.

[62]   Heaney, 'Towers, Trees, Terrors', p. 149.

and Rome in a shared history. In 'District and Circle', the poet's dreamily free association of his roots and reading play on this shared history to link London, Belfast, and his own abandoned rural district into one and the same human chain.

Descent journeys typically end with the hero's return from the underworld. We might therefore expect to find an upward movement in the final sestet of 'District and Circle'. Heaney subverts this generic expectation by portraying himself as continuing the underground journey:

> And so by night and day to be transported
> Through galleried earth with them, the only relict
> Of all that I belonged to, hurtled forward,
> Reflecting in a window mirror-backed
> By blasted weeping rock-walls.
> Flicker-lit. (DC 19)

The first line above retains the sound of Virgil's 'tandem trans fluuium' (Ae.VI.415), where the description of Aeneas' passage across the Styx also, dreamily, lacks a main verb. If the reflection of his father's face recalls Dido in the lines above, here the poet applies the widow sobriquet to himself: 'the only relict / Of all that I belonged to'. He is, on several levels, taking up the burden of his political and cultural history. Later, in his translation of *Aeneid VI* (2016), Heaney will describe Aeneas and his followers as 'the last relicts' of 'Troy's name and fame' (lines 93, 95), a phrase suggesting that Aeneas is a kind of war widow himself, in that he survives the massacre at Troy, and suffers many years of migratory exile. Heaney identifies with this condition of exile, as is reflected in his choice of 'Relict' as a working title for the poem in one of its early drafts.[63]

Relicts are also religious or sacred objects (*OED* 2a, 3), and in this final sestet, Heaney seems to be imagining himself as just such an object, passively 'hurtled forward' in time. In the penultimate lines, the words 'blasted' and 'weeping', though referring literally to the tunnel walls, also resonate with the memory of bomb blasts and weeping survivors. So that the final adjective '[f] licker-lit' describes the poet-as-relict, 'hurtled forward' by the force of that explosion. But even while describing that experience of fragmentation, the sestet offers resistance to it, in the sense that 'reflecting' and 'mirror-backed' oppose the rush of 'forward' movement. And also, though a solitary 'only relict', the poet is also blasted forward 'with them', the London commuters of his earlier memory as well as the 'herded shades' of the victims of 7/7. This

---

63   Heaney, *Literary* Papers 1.xvii.2, p. 4.

is only the second use of a collective pronoun in the entire poem (he mentions 'we' descending the escalators in line 18), and here it underlines the poet's stance of solidarity, if not identification, with the London travellers.

The poet's own identity remains ambiguous, his apartness implied by the isolation of 'Flicker-lit' as the final line, his memoriousness by the internal rhyme of '[f]licker-lit' with 'Reflecting' and 'relict'. And of course, '[f]licker-lit' itself combines the opposites of darkness and light, or lightness in the dark, like the golden bough gleaming in its hidden grove.[64] Thus if the poet identifies with Aeneas, on a heroically self-willed journey of descent, he also sides with those who suffer fates not of their choosing, and over which they have no control. Indeed, the fragmentation and distillation of an epic narrative (the *katabasis* of *Aeneid VI*) into a five-sonnet lyric sequence seems designed expressly to allow these other relicts of the past to be forwarded in time.

'The Tollund Man in Springtime'

There is no return from the underworld in 'District and Circle', but the *katabasis* there is complemented by the *anabatic* movement of 'The Tollund Man in Springtime' (*DC* 55–7). Formally, within the 2006 collection, this sequence of six, regular sonnets firms up and fills out the five ragged sonnets of the title poem. Thematically, the Tollund Man re-ascends from the under-earth, or rather, the museum case in which his exhumed body has been on display. In *Stepping Stones,* Heaney describes him as 'somebody who had 'gathered ... [his] staying powers'. He gets ... back into the living world by an act of will that is equally an act of imagination.'[65] It is, then, by marrying that epic sense of purpose implied in Heaney's 'act of will' with the lyric gesture towards freedom that the Tollund Man becomes a 'principle of regeneration.'[66] Like 'The Tollund Man' in *Wintering Out,* the revenant here speaks the poem in the first-person, a sign of his function as a detached alter-ego, or 'soul guide', for Heaney himself. 'He functioned as a kind of guardian other, risen out of the Jutland bog', Heaney suggests, adding that 'the convention is to call such a figure a "persona" but in this case he felt more like a transfusion.'[67]

---

[64]   Compare the face of the protagonist, illuminated by a rotating police siren light, at the end of the *banlieue* film, *La Haine* ('Hate', 1995), dir. Mathieu Kassovitz.

[65]   Heaney, *Stepping Stones*, p. 411.

[66]   Heaney, *Stepping Stones*, p. 411.

[67]   Heaney, 'Poet in Search'.

Though less overtly than in 'District and Circle', the Tollund Man's ascension also mirrors and doubles Aeneas's journey through Hades. Questions of faith and betrayal play over in his mind, starting up echoes of Dido at the beginning of the poem: 'Faith placed in me, me faithless as a stone ... I'd hear soft wind / And remember moony water in a rut.' (lines 39, 41–2). On a homelier scale, he wields a local golden bough to ensure his safe passage through the alien world of a modern urban environment:

> Through every check and scan I carried with me
> A bunch of Tollund rushes – roots and all –
> Bagged in their own bog-damp. (*DC* 57)

While in 'District and Circle', the poet feels unease and danger in the London Tube, for the Tollund Man, the modern city is toxic due to environmental pollution:

> I smelled the air, exhaust fumes, silage reek,
> Heard from my heather bed the thickened traffic
> Swarm at a roundabout five fields away
> And transatlantic flights stacked in the blue. (*DC* 56)

The Tollund Man derives his 'staying power' from contact with the earth, or more specifically, a farmer's rural life: 'Cattle out in rain, their knowledgeable / Solid standing and readiness to wait, / These I learned from' (lines 57–59). Led on by this soul-guide, or principle of regeneration, Heaney records that he found himself writing 'poems about glacier melt and river flow, crab apples and fiddlehead ferns, birch groves and alder trees.'[68] The Tollund Man keeps step with Heaney 'in the world of surveillance cameras and closed-circuit TV, of greenhouse gases and acid rain.'[69] Since he and the other 'bog bodies' were most likely sacrificial victims in ancient fertility rituals, the Tollund Man can also stand for victims of political violence, from ancient Irish and Danish history to our own times: his 'contrary' spirit was 'strengthened when they chose to put me down / For their own good' (lines 10–11). His ability to will himself back to life thus gives an upward turn to the idea that '[a]nything can happen', and '[t]hose overlooked [can be] regarded' (*DC* 13). Like Virgil's Aristaeus, he is a figure who survives catastrophe and keeps going.

---

68   Heaney, 'Poet in Search'.
69   Heaney, 'Poet in Search'.

Although the bough-like rushes have disintegrated by the time the Tollund Man is ready to make his ascent, he breathes in their dust and pollen, death, and new life, which afford him magical protection as he crosses into a new urban existence.

> Dust in my palm
> And in my nostrils dust, ...
> / ... As a man would, cutting turf,
> I straightened, spat on my hands, felt benefit
> And spirited myself into the street. (*DC* 57)

Within the volume as a whole, the Tollund Man's *anabasis* thus completes the descent journey initiated in 'District and Circle'. He comes back from the dead not to transcend the actual, historical world, but to live in it as he finds it. There is an ongoing sense of his living in exile: 'in those queues / Of wired, far-faced smilers, I stood off / Bulrush, head in air, far from its lough' (lines 68–70). It is the presence of this alien, dark pastoral figure, with bulrush head, phantom limbs, and snakeskin lidded eyes (line 30) that guarantees the city a measure of natural regeneration at its heart. '[N]either god nor ghost' (line 4), he is the ancient double of the *urbs,* not on the margins but in the midst of us, lost but waiting to be found.

Works Cited

Clark, Raymond, *Catabasis: Vergil and the Wisdom Tradition* (Amsterdam, 1979)

Eliot, Thomas Stearns, 'Tradition and the Practice of Poetry', *The Southern Review* 21.4 (1985), 873–88

Falconer, Rachel, *Hell in Contemporary Literature: Western Descent Narratives since 1945* (Edinburgh, 2005)

La Haine ('Hate', 1995), dir. Mathieu Kassovitz

Harrison, S. J., 'Heaney as Translator: Horace and Virgil', in *Seamus Heaney and the Classics*, ed. Harrison et al (Oxford, 2019), 244–62

Heaney, Seamus, *Aeneid Book VI* (London, 2016)

—————, *Anything Can Happen: a Poem and Essay by Seamus Heaney with Translations in Support of Art for Amnesty* (Dublin, 2004)

—————, *District and Circle* (London, 2006)

—————, 'The Golden Bough', *Translation: the Journal of Literary Translation* XXII (Fall, 1989), 197–201

—————, *The Government of the Tongue: The 1986 T. S. Eliot Memorial*

Lectures and Other Critical Writings (London, 1988)

————, 'Horace and the Thunder' in *The Irish Times* (17 November 2001), Weekend 10

————, 'Horace and the Thunder' (New York, 2002)

————, 'Horace and Thunder' [sic] in *The Times Literary Supplement* (18 January 2002), 40

————, *Human Chain* (London, [2010] 2012)

————, *Finders Keepers: Selected Prose 1971–2001* (London, 2002)

————, *Literary Papers, 1963–2010,* The National Library, Dublin. http://catalogue.nli.ie/Collection/vtls000358500 [accessed 19 December 2018]

————, 'One Poet in Search of a Title', *The Times* (25 March 2006). http://entertainment.timesonline.co.uk/tol/arts_and_entertainment/books/article1082510.ece. [accessed 19 December 2018]

————, 'Reality and Justice: On Translating Horace, Odes I, 34', *Irish Pages* 1.2 (Autumn, Winter, 2002/2003), 50–3

————, 'Reality and Justice: On Translating Horace, Odes I, 34', *Translation Ireland* (Spring 2002), 8–11

————, *Seeing Things* (London, 1991)

————, *A Shiver* (Thame, 2005)

————, *Stepping Stones: Interviews with Seamus Heaney,* ed. Dennis O'Driscoll (London, 2008)

————, 'Towers, Trees, Terrors, a rêverie in Urbino', in *In forma di parole. Seamus Heaney poeta dotto, a cura di Gabriella Morisco* 23.2 (2007), 145–56

————, 'The Whole Thing: On the Good of Poetry', in *The Recorder: Journal of the American Irish Historical Society* (2002), 5–20

————, *Wintering Out* (London, 1972)

Horace, *Opera*, ed. E. C. Wickham (Oxford, 1975)

Hughes, Ted, *Collected Poems* (London, 2005)

Latour, Bruno, 'The End of Nature', in *Politics of Nature,* trans. Catherine Porter (Cambridge, MA, 2004), 25–31

Martiny, Erik, 'Modern Versions of Nostos and Katabasis: A Survey of Homeric Hypertexts in Recent Anglophone Poetry', *Anglia* 127.3 (2009), 469–79

Matthews, Steven, 'Bucketful by Glistering Bucketful', *Poetry Review* 97:1 (2007), 91–93

McKibben, Bill, *The End of Nature* (New York, 1989)

Miłosz, Czesław, *The Collected Poems: 1931–1987* (New York, 1988)

Milton, John, *Paradise Lost*, ed. Alastair Fowler, 2nd edn (Harlow, 1998)

Robbins, Jim, 'The Dilbit Hits the Fan', *Places* (October 2015). https://placesjournal.org/ [accessed 11 November 2020]

Steiner, George, *In Bluebeard's Castle: Some Notes Towards the Re-definition of Culture* (London, 1971)

Thurston, Michael, *The Underworld in Twentieth-Century Poetry: From Pound and Eliot to Heaney and Walcott* (Basingstoke, 2009)

Tyler, Meg, '"The Whole of Me A-Patter"', in *'The Soul Exceeds its Circumstances'*, ed. Eugene O'Brien (Notre Dame, 2016), 129–48

Vergili Opera, ed. R. A. B. Mynors, 2 vols (Oxford, 1980)

Virgil: Eclogues, Georgics, Aeneid 1–6, trans. H. R. Fairclough, revised by G. P. Goold (Cambridge, MA, 1999)

Whirlpools, Black Holes and Vortical Hells in Literature

JONATHAN R. OLSON

On 10 April 2019, the Event Horizon Telescope project published an image based on data collected from eight radio observatories of the supermassive black hole in galaxy Messier 87. In Brussels, at one of five simultaneous press conferences held internationally to announce the event, Heino Falcke introduced the image by invoking the cultural associations of a black hole:

> if you know the story behind that image, you're looking at the region that we've never looked at before, the region we cannot really imagine being there. It feels like really looking at the gates of hell, at the end of space and time; the event horizon; the point of no return. That is awe-inspiring, to me at least, but it's also important for physics.[1]

Within this cultural digression of only twenty-five seconds, Falcke touched on several connotations that the phenomenon of black holes have accrued within a few decades of theoretical discussion and indirect observation: they are unimaginable, a portal to hell, the boundary of the physical universe, and a microcosm of the chronological end of the universe. Falcke's final point is that black holes inspire awe. This locates them in the realm of the sublime. The black hole is one of the more recently recognised species of naturally occurring vortices that comprise a venerable tradition of metaphorical resonance in literary and cinematic texts.[2] The cultural associations listed by Falcke frequently collocate with one another in such texts. This chapter focuses on how these associations combine in texts about one particular type of vortex, the whirlpool. In the later twentieth century, the metaphorical connotations of the whirlpool became applied, virtually

---

[1] 'Breakthrough Discovery in Astronomy: First Ever Image of a Black Hole', video posted by European Commission, 10 April 2017. The transcription is mine, made from the video recording rather than quoted from news reports that lightly edited these remarks, such as Daniel Clery, 'For the First Time, You Can See What a Black Hole Looks Like', *Science*, 10 April 2019, or Leah Crane, 'First Ever Real Image of a Black Hole Revealed', *New Scientist*, 10 April 2019.

[2] Charles D. Minahen has examined the literary lives of many types of vortices in Minahen, *Vortex/t: The Poetics of Turbulence* (University Park, PA, 1992).

wholesale, to the black hole. This chapter limits itself to a series of close readings of literary depictions of whirlpools' connections to the dislocatory depths of hell that anticipate and inform, if not directly inspire, later depictions of black holes.

Charybdis and Hell

Rather than taking the *nekyia* (evocation of the dead) in Book XI of the *Odyssey* as the starting point of an exploration of hell, this chapter considers the series of episodes that occur upon Odysseus' return from the house of Hades. In Book XII, Odysseus and his crew voyage back to Aeaea, where Circe, who had directed Odysseus to Hades at the end of Book X, will now instruct him in how to navigate past the Sirens and either the Planctae or Scylla and Charybdis. Circe anticipates Book XII's formal motif of recapitulation without repetition at the outset, when she greets Odysseus's crew as 'Unhappy men, who went alive to the house of Hades,/ so dying twice, when all the rest of mankind die only/ once' (XII.21–3).[3] Besides foreshadowing the crews' second death within the next four hundred lines, Circe hails not only the sailors but the cyclical form of the ensuing book. In her instructions to Odysseus, Circe describes Charybdis's tidal nature by warning him that 'three times a day she flows it up and three times she sucks it/ terribly down' (XII.105–6). Her character as a whirlpool is made clear by Odysseus's own observations that 'when in turn again she sucked down the sea's salt water,/ the turbulence showed all the inner sea, [...] and the ground showed at the sea's bottom,/ black with sand' (XII.240–3). However, the vortical motion that dominates later accounts of whirlpools is not explicit in these descriptions of Charybdis. Instead, the whirlpool expresses its vortical motion though the narrative of Book XII as a whole. The book is structured around three accounts of Charybdis that revisit the same location but not the same experience, like a spiral movement that returns to the same radial line, albeit at a different point along it. The first account of Charybdis is Circe's description of, and instructions concerning, it; the second is Odysseus's first encounter with it, in his ship with his crew; and the third is his second encounter, after losing his ship and crew in a storm sent by Zeus. In his first encounter, reluctantly following Circe's advice to accept the loss of some men by sailing under Scylla rather than lose all men

---

[3]   The English translation of the *Odyssey* is quoted here and subsequently from *The Odyssey of Homer*, trans. Richard Lattimore (New York, 1991), and cited parenthetically by book and line.

by veering too close to Charybdis (XII.109–10), Odysseus loses to Scylla the predicted six men (XII.244–59), despite an attempt to guard against her (XII.228–31). However, when he is forced a second time into the proximity of Scylla and Charybdis, and it is his own life that is at stake, Odysseus finally discovers 'some way for me to escape away from the deadly Charybdis' (XII.113), which he had sought from, and been denied by, Circe (XII.116–26). After a long night of being carried back to Scylla and Charybdis on his destroyed ship's keel, lashed to its mast, this time he grabs the fig tree overhanging Charybdis. This permits his makeshift raft to be sucked into Charybdis, and he waits from dawn until dinnertime for Charybdis 'to vomit/ the keel and mast back up again' (XII.431–41).

Immediately after this third account of Charybdis, Odysseus tells his Phaeacian audience that he arrived, ten days later, at Calypso's island of Ogygia, and excuses himself from repeating the events he had related yesterday because 'It is hateful to me/ to tell a story over again, when it has been well told' (XII.452–3). Thus Book XII and, with it, the entirety of Odysseus's autobiographical tale in Books IX–XII, conclude with a condemnation of repetition. Such mere repetition is to be distinguished from, and indeed contrasted by, the vortical progression set out by Circe that governs Book XII.[4] Even Odysseus's lashing his ship's keel to its mast (XII.424) was the second time his mast had saved him in the book. It had already done so, when Odysseus ordered his crew to lash him to the mast in order to facilitate his hearing of the Sirens' song. The episode of the Sirens also participates in the book's motif of recapitulation in another way. The knowledge that they offer to Odysseus is specifically the matter of the other Homeric epic:

For no one has ever sailed past this place in his black ship
Until he has listened to the honey-sweet voice that issues
From our lips; then goes on, well pleased, knowing more than ever
He did; for we know everything that the Argives and Trojans
Did and suffered in wide Troy through the gods' despite. (XII.186–90)

From this metafictional detail Burkhardt Wolf concludes that '[t]he *Odyssey* therefore is a recursion of the *Iliad*, and the latter epic is said to have arisen from artistic inspiration allegorized here in the form of the sirens, their

---

[4]   See Burkhardt Wolf, 'Muses of Cartography: Charting Odysseus from Homer to Joyce', trans. E. A. Beeson in *Literature and Cartography: Theories, Histories, Genres*, ed. Anders Engberg-Pederson, (Cambridge, MA, 2017), 143–72, p. 168, n. 23.

singing, and their promise of supreme knowledge'.[5] In turn, recursions of
the *Odyssey* in later texts revisit the elements above – the journey to the
dead, the siren song, the whirlpool, the mast, and even the act of lashing –
by rearranging them into innovative combinations that produce new meanings and enrich past ones.

The most recognisable reappearances of these elements might be in
the Roman poets, who connect both Scylla and Charybdis to Hades. The
Aeneid begins with a whirlpool that takes Orontes. In contrast to his predecessor, Virgil accentuates its vortical motion: 'ast illam ter fluctus ibidem/
torquet agens circum et rapidus vorat aequore vertex' ('but the ship is
thrice on the same spot whirled round and round by the wave and engulfed
in the sea's devouring eddy') (*Aen.* I.116–17).[6] Then, before remaking
the *Odyssey*'s *nekyia* as a *katabasis* to the underworld in the *Aeneid*, Virgil
has the prophet Helenus supplement a Circean warning about Scylla and
Charybdis with the improved advice to avoid them altogether by sailing
around Sicily rather than attempting to thread the needle between them
(III.420–32). Helenus describes the whirlpool in the terms of an abyss,
chasm, or underworld: 'atque imo barathri ter gurgite vastos/ sorbet in
abruptum fluctus rursusque sub auras/ erigit alternos, et sidera verberat
unda' ('and, at the bottom of her seething chasm thrice she sucks the vast
waves into the abyss, and again casts them upwards, lashing the stars with
spray') (III.421–3). The only other time Virgil uses 'barathrum' in the
Aeneid is in a simile describing an opening to the underworld:

> non secus ac si qua penitus vi terra dehiscens
> infernas reseret sedes et regna recludat
> pallida, dis invisa, superque immane barathrum
> cernatur, trepident immisso lumine Manes.

> (even as though beneath some force, the earth, gaping open deep below,
> should unlock the infernal abodes and disclose the pallid realms abhorred of
> the gods, and from above the vast abyss be descried, and the ghosts tremble at
> the inrushing light.) (VIII.243–6)

---

[5]   Wolf, 'Muses of Cartography', p. 149.
[6]   The text and prose translation of the *Aeneid* are quoted here and subsequently
from Virgil, *Eclogues – Georgics – Aeneid I–VI*, trans. H. R. Fairclough, rev. edn
(Cambridge, MA, 1935), or Virgil, *Aeneid VII–XII – The Minor Poems*, trans. H.
R. Fairclough, rev. edn (Cambridge, MA, 1934), and cited parenthetically by book
and line.

Thus, by using 'barathrum' only in connection with them, Virgil semanti-cally associates Charybdis with the underworld. Ovid does not dwell on Charybdis, but he does link Scylla to the underworld. In the *Metamorphoses*, after an overblown allusion to them in Medea's humorous profession of love for Jason (*Met*. VII.62–5), Scylla and Charybdis are reintroduced (XIII.730–4) to make Scylla the audience of Galatea's tale of Polyphemus. This, in turn, sets up Scylla's own origin story (XIII.898–968, XIV.1–74). Enraged that the human Scylla has ignored his overtures, the merman Glaucus demands that Circe make Scylla share his passion. Instead, Circe punishes her. The next time Scylla wades in her favourite pool, she reaches into the water and feels dogs where her loins should be.[7] Ovid's comparison of these dogs to the jaws of the hellhound Cerberus ('Cerbereos rictus', XIV.65) confers an infernal aspect to Scylla, one that John Milton will exploit in his personifica-tion of Sin in *Paradise Lost* (1667), where he both repeats Ovid's allusion to 'Cerberean mouths' (*PL* II.655) and compares Sin to Scylla (II.660).[8]

Homer, Virgil, and Ovid all feature prominently in Dante's Christian *Commedia*: their works influence Dante (indirectly in the case of Homer, where Dante relies on Latin authors for his knowledge of the text) and they themselves figure as historical poets who count Dante among their number (*Inf*. IV.79–102). Dante honours Homer as 'l'altissimo poeta' (IV.80) and the 'poeta sovrano' (IV.88), and the *Inferno* may be the most revisionist treatment of Odyssean motifs until James Joyce.[9] The con-centric tiers of Dante's subterranean hell resemble the funnel shape of Charybdis. Dante makes the connection explicit. In Canto VII, he draws a topographical and choreographical analogy between Charybdis and the movements of the avaricious in the fourth circle: 'Come fa l'onda là sovra Chariddi,/ che si frange con quella in cui s'intoppa,/ così convien che qui la gente riddi' ('As does the wave, there over Charybdis, breaking itself against the wave it meets, so must the folk here dance their round', VII.22–4). Four circles lower, in an inversion of *Odyssey* XI, the shade of

---

[7]   The word for pool, 'gurges' (*Met*. XIV.51), is used in other texts to denote a whirlpool, though not here. The text and English translation of the *Metamorphoses* are quoted here and subsequently from Ovid, *Metamorphoses*, trans. Frank Justus Miller, vol. 2 (Cambridge, M. A., 1916), and cited parenthetically by book and line.
[8]   The text of *Paradise Lost* quoted here and subsequently is from John Milton, *Paradise Lost*, ed. Alastair Fowler, 2nd edn (Harlow, 1998), and cited parenthetically by book and line.
[9]   The text and prose translation of the *Inferno* are quoted here and subsequently from Dante Alighieri, *Inferno 1: Italian Text and Translation*, vol. 1, part 1, of *The Divine Comedy*, trans. and ed. Charles S. Singleton, Bollingen Series 80 (Princeton, 1989), and cited parenthetically by canto and line.

Odysseus (now identified by the Latin form of his name, Ulixes) is visited by the living Dante. The tale told of Ulysses's final voyage revisits the substance of the Sirens and Charybdis episodes of *Odyssey* XII. Ulysses recounts his eventual seduction by the siren promise of gaining experience of the world – 'l'ardore/ ch'i' ebbi a divenir del mondo esperto' ('the longing that I had to gain experience of the world', *Inf.* XXVI.97–8) – and how he, in turn, tempts his crew with experience beyond human limits: 'non vogliate negar l'esperïenza/ di retro al sol, del mondo sanza gente' ('choose not to deny experience, following the sun, of the world that has no people', XXVI.116–17). Passing the Pillars of Hercules which Ulysses characterises as warning signs to prevent human passage ('dov' Ercule segnò li suoi riguardi/ acció che l'uom più oltre non si metta', 'where Hercules set up his markers, that men should not pass beyond', XXVI.108–9), the crew reach the southern hemisphere. On the approach to the island of Mount Purgatory, they are beset by a whirlwind ('un turbo', XXVI.137). Revolving with the sea three times like Virgil's Orontes, Dante's Ulysses recalls how he and his crew were taken under:

> Tre volte il fé girar con tue l'acque;
> a la quarta levar la poppa in suso
> e la prora ire in giù, com' altrui piacque,
> infin che 'l mar fu sovra noi richiuso.

> (Three times it whirled her round with all the waters, and the fourth time it lifted the stern aloft and plunged the prow below, as pleased Another, till the sea closed over us.) (XXVI.139–42)

In parallel to his metaphorical succumbing to the Sirens' offer of global knowledge ('Over all the generous earth we know everything that happens', *Od.* XII.191), Ulysses now succumbs to Charybdis, in a metaphorical third encounter with the whirlpool. The 'Another' who sinks Ulysses' ship at his pleasure is not just One other than Ulysses, but also One other than Poseidon, the god who first thwarted Odysseus's progress on the seas. Ulysses's final odyssey ends where his first began, in defiance to (yet another) divine will. This vortical conclusion to Ulysses's life, to his posthumous autobiographical tale, and to Canto XXVI will prove extremely influential. In the nineteenth century alone, it is imitated by Edgar Allan Poe, Herman Melville, and Jules Verne. The hell to which the whirlpool drags Ulysses is itself shaped like a whirlpool writ large, formed through the turbulent displacement of earth rather than that of water. For Dante, both the antipodean whirlpool and the subterranean hell are Charybdian vortices.

Poe's Whirlpools

For Edgar Allan Poe, creativity is combinatorial. One of his repeated axioms is that '[a]ll novel conceptions are merely unusual combinations'.[10] In contradiction of Coleridge's claim (derived from Jean Paul Richter) that 'Fancy combines, Imagination creates', Poe insists that '[t]he fancy as nearly creates as the imagination'.[11] Elsewhere he elaborates on this: Poesy is a response, however unsatisfactory, 'to a natural and irrepressible demand', composed first of 'the thirst for supernal BEAUTY' and second of 'the attempt to satisfy this thirst by *novel* combinations among those forms of beauty which already exist – or by novel combinations *of those combinations which our predecessors, toiling in chase of the same phantom, have already set in order*'.[12] We have already seen examples of novel combinations by Virgil, Ovid, and Dante of the elements of *Odyssey* XII. One of Poe's novel achievements is his combination of two adjacent but previously discrete elements in the *Odyssey*: the Sirens and Charybdis. Dante had brought them closer together. Now, Poe unifies them into a single harrowing image.

One of the most common motifs in Poe's stories is 'the recurrence of the *spiral* or *vortex*', elements that occur always 'at the same terminal point in their respective narratives'.[13] Poe's whirlwinds convey objects vertically: 'the whirlwind of chaotic fire' in 'Metzengerstein' (1832) consumes the horseman as he ascends a staircase, and the whirlwind in 'The Fall of the House of Usher' (1839) accompanies the descent of the mansion into the tarn.[14] Poe's whirlpools likewise facilitate descents (and in one case, both

[10]   Edgar A. Poe, 'Review of "Alciphron, a Poem"', *Burton's Gentleman's Magazine* 6.1 (January 1840), 53–56, p. 53. Poe's paraphrases of himself omit the categorical 'All', see [Edgar Allen Poe] 'American Prose Writers. No. 2. N. P. Willis', *The Broadway Journal* 1.3 (18 January 1845), 37–8, p. 37; partially reproduced by Poe in a footnote in Edgar A. Poe, 'The Literati of New York City', *Godey's Lady's Book* 32.5 (May 1846), 194–201, p. 197 (itself reprinted in 32.6 [June 1846], 289–96, p. 292). For an elaboration of this 'combinatory aesthetic', see Meredith L. McGill, *American Literature and the Culture of Reprinting, 1834–1853* (Philadelphia, 2003), p. 170.
[11]   Poe, 'Review of "Alciphron, a Poem"', p. 53.
[12]   Edgar Allan Poe, 'Review of *Ballads and Other Poems*', *Graham's Magazine* 20.4 (April 1842), 248–51, p. 249 (emphasis in original).
[13]   Richard Wilbur, 'The House of Poe', in Robert Hillyer, Richard Wilbur, and Cleanth Brooks, *Anniversary Lectures, 1959* (Washington, 1959), 21–38, pp. 22–3 (emphasis in original).
[14]   Edgar A. Poe, 'Metzengerstein', *Southern Literary Messenger* 2.2 (January 1836), 97–100, p. 100; and Edgar A. Poe, 'The Fall of the House of Usher', *Burton's Gentleman's Magazine* 5.3 (September 1839), 145–52, pp. 151 and 152.

a descent and an ascent). But unlike his whirlwinds, which the fleeing narrators observe from a distance, Poe's whirlpools are experienced by their narrators from within.

Poe's 'MS. Found in a Bottle' (1833) ends in a whirlpool, and the primary subject of 'A Descent into the Maelstrom' (1841) is a whirlpool. The first half of 'MS. Found' is a conventional first-person report of a nautical voyage, beginning with the narrator's lengthy assurance of his 'habits of rigid thought' and his 'deficiency of imagination'.[15] Just past the story's midpoint, he is flung from his ship onto another ship populated by a *Flying Dutchmen*-like crew, and his narration becomes fragmentary, with increasing numbers of evocations of the macabre and supernatural. The ship, headed for the southern pole, reaches a realm of ice and is caught in a whirlpool. The text breaks off amid a description of 'plunging madly within the grasp of the whirlpool' and 'going down'.[16] The narrator's dedication to recording his experience even while circling 'round and round the borders, of a gigantic amphitheater' might seem incredible, but he had already concocted a plan: '[a]t the last moment I will enclose the MS. in a bottle and cast it within the sea'.[17] The existence of the manuscript implies that the narrator must have succeeded. 'A Descent', by contrast, begins with the narrator and a local fisherman high on a cliff overlooking the Norwegian whirlpool between the Lofoten islands. The first third is composed of the narrator's eye-witness impressions, supplemented by lengthy quotations of natural histories. The next two-thirds consist entirely of the fisherman's account of his personal experience of the whirlpool three years earlier. The fisherman loses two brothers and despairs. Yet this despair of survival provides the clarity of mind that enables him, paradoxically, to concoct a scientific survival plan. It succeeds, and the tale ends without returning to the framing device of the first narrator.

The differences between these two tales are many and have been discussed often. The protagonist of the first story perishes; that of the second survives. The first features many supernatural elements; the second is superficially more 'realistic', and frequently categorised as one of Poe's tales of 'ratiocination'. Such observations are not misleading, but it is worth drawing attention to the many ways, beyond a reuse of the whirlpool device, in which Poe revisits and repurposes for 'A Descent' the motifs of 'MS. Found'. Some parallels

---

[15]   Edgar A. Poe, 'MS. Found in a Bottle', *Baltimore Saturday Visiter* 3.38 (19 October 1833), 1, cols 1–5, col. 1. This text appears entirely on the front page of a broadsheet newspaper, so it is cited hereafter by column.

[16]   Poe, 'MS. Found', col. 5.

[17]   Poe, 'MS. Found', cols 5 and 4.

between the two texts are broad. Both 'MS. Found' and 'A Descent' may be divided into two distinct sections, and both are influenced, in various respects, by Coleridge's *Rime of the Ancient Mariner*. But there are many specific points of similarity. Each text invokes hell both by direct reference to it and by allusion to Dante. 'MS. Found' employs oxymoron twice to do so: the narrator describes becoming 'dizzy with the velocity of our descent into some watery hell' and the ship 'rolling every moment her top-gallant yardarms into the most appaling [sic] hell of water, which it can enter into the mind of man to imagine'.[18] Similarly, the first narrator of 'A Descent' identifies the Maelstrom with one of the classical rivers of the underworld when he looks 'down from this pinnacle upon the howling Phlegethon below'.[19] Both texts also allude to Dante's notorious inscription over the gate to hell: 'LASCIATE OGNE SPERANZA, VOI CH'INTRATE' ('ABANDON EVERY HOPE, YOU WHO ENTER') (*Inf.* III.9). The narrator of 'MS. Found' admits that 'I could not help feeling the utter hopelessness of hope itself, and prepared myself gloomily for that death which I thought nothing could defer beyond an hour' and the fisherman in 'A Descent' recollects, '"To be sure," I thought, "we shall get there just about the slack – there is some little hope in that" – but in the next moment I cursed myself for being so great a fool as to dream of hope at all'.[20] Finally, caught within the whirlpool, the fisherman recalls '[h]aving made up my mind to hope no more'.[21] Both stories associate chaos with foam, though in contradictory ways: 'MS. Found' refers to 'a chaos of foamless water', while the fisherman in 'A Descent' describes his brother's boat plummeting 'into the chaos of foam below'.[22] The infernal nature of the whirlpool is also connoted by Poe's use of 'abyss', twice in 'MS. Found' and seven times, all in reference to the whirlpool, in 'A Descent'. As if he were Dante describing his and Virgil's descent through the funnel of hell, the fisherman remarks that '[o]ur progress downward, at each revolution, was very perceptible, but slow'.[23]

Both stories also invoke the sublime. 'MS. Found' asserts the sublime in a description of the ghost ship: '[f]or a moment of intense terror she paused upon the giddy pinnacle, as if in contemplation of her own sublimity, then

---

[18]   Poe, 'MS. Found', cols 3 and 4.

[19]   Edgar A. Poe, 'A Descent into the Maelstrom', *Graham's Magazine* 18.5 (May 1841), 235–41, p. 236. Phlegethon also features in the Christian hells of Dante (*Inf.* XII.46–54, XII.100–39, XIV.76–84, and XIV.121–35) and Milton (*PL* II.580–1).

[20]   Poe, 'MS. Found', col. 3; Poe, 'A Descent', p. 238.

[21]   Poe, 'A Descent', p. 239.

[22]   Poe, 'MS. Found', col. 5; Poe, 'A Descent', p. 240.

[23]   Poe, 'A Descent', p. 240.

trembled and tottered, and, came down'.[24] But 'A Descent' conveys more successfully the sensations of becoming encompassed, as it were, by the sublime.[25] The fisherman claims:

> I began to reflect how magnificent a thing it was to die in such a manner, and how foolish it was in me to think of so paltry a consideration as my own individual life, in view of so wonderful a manifestation of God's power. I do believe that I blushed with shame when this idea crossed my mind.[26]

He also reflects that '[n]ever shall I forget the sensations of awe, horror, and admiration with which I gazed about me' and that '[t]he general burst of terrific grandeur was all that I beheld'.[27] Pressing against the edges of human contemplation, the narrators of both stories are also led to remark on the limits of time and space. In 'MS. Found' the narrator despairs that '[w]e are surely doomed to hover continually upon the brink of Eternity, without taking a final plunge into the abyss' and, later, that 'about a league on either side of us, may be seen, indistinctly and at intervals, stupendous ramparts of ice, towering away into the desolate sky, and looking like the walls of the universe'.[28] These bounds of human experience are also mentioned by the fisherman in 'A Descent', who relates that 'I could make out nothing distinctly, on account of a thick mist in which everything there was enveloped, and over which there hung a magnificent rainbow, like that narrow and tottering bridge which Mussulmen say is the only pathway between Time and Eternity'.[29] This comparison of the rainbow to a marker between time and eternity makes it a counterpart to the Pillars of Hercules. But this bridge, called as-Sirāt in Islam, is associated with hell. In the words of George Sale, whose 1734 translation of the Qur'an was reprinted into the nineteenth century, the bridge 'is laid over the midst of hell' and, while the good will cross it without obstacle, the wicked will from it 'fall down headlong into hell, which is gaping beneath them'.[30] Likewise in 'A Descent', the whirlpool gapes beneath the rainbow, and into it the fisherman's boat initially 'rushed

---

[24]   Poe, 'MS. Found', col. 3.

[25]   Poe, 'MS. Found', col. 3.

[26]   Poe, 'A Descent', p. 239.

[27]   Poe, 'A Descent', p. 239.

[28]   Poe, 'MS. Found', cols 4 and 5.

[29]   Poe, 'A Descent', p. 240.

[30]   George Sale, trans., *The Koran; Commonly Called the Alcoran of Mohammed: Translated from the Original Arabic. With Explanatory Notes, Taken from the Most Approved Commentators. To which is Prefixed a Preliminary Discourse*, 2 vols (London, 1821), vol. 1, pp. 120–1.

headlong into the abyss' and later, bearing only his brother, 'plunged head-long, at once and forever, into the chaos of foam below'.[31] The brother's will to live is what dooms him, as he clings desperately to the boat that descends to the centre of the whirlpool. Like Dante's Lucifer who by incessantly flap-ping his wings, in order to escape hell, keeps frozen the lake that imprisons him (*Inf.* XXXIV.50–2), the brother's desire to escape the funnel is what keeps him trapped in it. By contrast, the fisherman's abandonment of the hope to save his own life is what permits the mental lucidity that enables him to save his life after all.[32]

Closely linked to the boundaries of human experience in both stories is the arousal of intense curiosity, tantamount to fascination with the prospect of gaining new knowledge. In 'MS. Found', the narrator describes the acute effects within him of this siren song, in terms similar to those of Dante's Ulysses:

[t]o conceive the horror of my sensations is, I presume, utterly impossi-ble—yet a curiosity to penetrate the mysteries of these awful regions pre-dominates even over my despair, and will reconcile me to the most hideous aspect of death. It is evident that we are hurrying onwards to some excit-ing knowledge—some never-to-be-imparted secret, whose attainment is destruction.[33]

In 'A Descent', even as he revolves within the whirlpool, the fisherman's curiosity is fixed on the nature of the whirlpool itself. To employ the terms of another Poe text, this fascination seems driven by the 'imp of the perverse':

[a]fter a little while I became possessed with the keenest curiosity about the whirl itself. I positively felt a *wish* to explore its depths, even at the sacrifice I was going to make; and my principal grief was that I should never be able to tell my old companions on shore about the mysteries I should see. These, no doubt, were singular fancies to occupy a man's mind in such extremity.[34]

---

[31]   Poe, 'A Descent', pp. 239 and 240.

[32]   This dialectic is explored in terms of Poe's *Eureka* in Richard D. Finholt, 'The Vision at the Brink of the Abyss: "A Descent into the Maelstrom" in the Light of Poe's Cosmology', *The Georgia Review* 27.3 (Fall 1973), 356–66.

[33]   Poe, 'MS. Found', col. 5.

[34]   Poe, 'A Descent', p. 239 (emphasis in original). See Edgar A. Poe, 'The Imp of the Perverse', *Graham's Magazine* 28.1 (July 1845), 1–3.

Furthermore, the fisherman relates a counterintuitive interest in theoretical questions, however mechanical, about his situation within the whirlpool's funnel:

> I have already described the unnatural curiosity which had taken the place of my original terrors. It appeared to grow upon me as I drew nearer and nearer to my dreadful doom. I now began to watch, with a strange interest, the numerous things that floated in our company. I *must* have been delirious—for I even sought *amusement* in speculating upon the relative velocities of their several descents toward the foam below.[35]

The speculative calculations enjoyed by the fisherman, which lead to his devising a successful method of escaping the whirlpool, might tempt us to categorise 'A Descent' with Poe's other tales of 'ratiocination'. What this classification risks misrepresenting is the story's suggestion that the character's clarity of mind results from the fisherman's contemplation of the sublime, enabled by his abandonment of concern for his life. The metaphysical aspect of the narrator's insight is suggested by five references to the depth-plumbing moonlight, among them that 'the rays of the full moon, from that circular rift amid the clouds which I have already described, streamed in a flood of golden glory along the black walls, and far away down into the inmost recesses of the abyss', and that '[t]he rays of the moon seemed to search the very bottom of the profound gulf'.[36] As if by rays of insight, the fisherman's preternatural lucidity enables him to envision a survival scheme.

The fisherman's particular method of escape from the Maelstrom in 'A Descent' unites into a single memorable episode previously disparate Odyssean motifs. Comparisons to the *Odyssey* are drawn early in the fisherman's narrative, when both masts break and he laments 'the main-mast taking with it my youngest brother, who had lashed himself to it for safety'.[37] Unlike Odysseus' precaution against the Sirens, the mast provides no protection for one of the fisherman's two brothers. After the boat, with the fisherman and his other brother still aboard, enters the whirlpool and revolves within its funnel, the fisherman notices that 'at every revolution, we passed something like a barrel, or else the yard or the mast of a vessel'.[38] An equivalence is thus drawn between cylindrical cask barrels and masts. As if recapitulating his younger brother's Odyssean tactic in

---

[35]   Poe, 'A Descent', p. 240 (emphasis in original).
[36]   Poe, 'A Descent', pp. 239 and 239–40.
[37]   Poe, 'A Descent', p. 238.
[38]   Poe, 'A Descent', p. 240.

order to rehabilitate it, the fisherman recalls that 'I resolved to lash myself securely to the water cask upon which I now held, to cut it loose from the counter, and to throw myself with it into the water'.[39] He signals his plan to his remaining brother, who refuses to let go of the ring-bolt at the base of the foremast, 'so, with a bitter struggle, I resigned him to his fate, fastened myself to the cask by means of the lashings which secured it to the counter, and precipitated myself with it into the sea, without another moment's hesitation'.[40] His strategy is successful: the buoyancy of the cask barrel keeps him high enough within the whirlpool until it subsides. It is a remarkable example of Poe's 'novel combination' of elements that a predecessor has 'already set in order': surviving Charybdis by means of Odysseus's anti-Siren technique of lashing oneself to a cylindrical object linked expressly in the text to masts.[41] Moreover, association of the Maelstrom with Charybdis is not only metaphorical: two of the authorities the first narrator cites by name in 'A Descent', Athanasius Kircher and Jonas Ramus, had identified the Norwegian whirlpool as the historical Charybdis.[42]

One of the most obvious differences between 'MS. Found' and 'A Descent' (that the narrator of the former perishes in a whirlpool while the fisherman in the latter survives one) risks obscuring the close connection between their endings. Although the narrator of 'MS. Found' evidently does not survive, his manuscript does. It survives the whirlpool by being secured in a buoyant object. The fisherman of 'A Descent' likewise survives by securing himself to a buoyant object. The bottle and cask are not only both cylindrical in shape but their intended functions, before being repurposed at sea, differ only in quantitative terms. The fisherman survives by becoming, so to speak, a manuscript affixed to a large bottle. The fisherman is himself the text, recounting his tale orally, like Coleridge's Ancient Mariner, to the primary narrator. His transformation is not only internal but external, having become unrecognisable and ghostly:

Those who drew me on board were my old mates and daily companions – but they knew me no more than they would have known a traveller from the spirit-land. My hair had been raven-black the day before, and now it is

[39]   Poe, 'A Descent', p. 240.

[40]   Poe, 'A Descent', p. 240.

[41]   Poe, 'Review of *Ballads and Other Poems*', p. 249.

[42]   Poe, 'A Descent', pp. 236–7; see Athanasius Kircher, *Mundus Subterraneus* (Amsterdam, 1664), pp. 146–7, and Jonas Ramus, *Ulysses et Otinus Unus & idem* (Copenhagen, 1702), pp. 125–46.

white as you see. They say too that the whole expression of my countenance had changed.[43]

The cask that preserves this fisherman-text-spirit resurfaces ten years later as a casket in *Moby-Dick* (1851). A search aboard the *Pequod* to replace the life-buoy with a suitable 'cask' leads Queequeg to nominate his coffin.[44] This prompts Starbuck to note the oxymoron: 'A life-buoy of a coffin!'[45] A few pages later, Ahab examines the literary motif more closely: 'A life-buoy of a coffin! Does it go further? Can it be that in some spiritual sense the coffin is, after all, but an immortality-preserver?'[46] Foreshadowing the novel's conclusion, Ahab had already associated the Maelstrom with hell in his famous pledge: 'Aye, aye! and I'll chase him round Good Hope, and round the Horn, and round the Norway Maelstrom, and round perdition's flames before I give him up'.[47] In the final chapter, when the *Pequod* does succumb to a whirlpool, the alignment between whirlpool and hell, and between the ship and Satan, is clarified:

> so the bird of heaven, with archangelic shrieks, and his imperial beak thrust upwards, and his whole captive form folded in the flag of Ahab, went down with his ship, which, like Satan, would not sink to hell till she had dragged a living part of heaven along with her, and helmeted herself with it.[48]

In the end, Ahab descends to the depths by lashing himself to the whale inadvertently by his harpoon's rope, while Ishmael is saved by the life-buoy-coffin that resurfaces one last time:

> now, liberated by reason of its cunning spring, and, owing to its great buoyancy, rising with great force, the coffin life-buoy shot lengthwise from the sea, fell over, and floated by my side. Buoyed up by that coffin, for almost one whole day and night, I floated on a soft and dirgelike main.[49]

---

[43]   Poe, 'A Descent', p. 241.
[44]   Herman Melville, *Moby-Dick* (New York, 1851), p. 579.
[45]   Melville, *Moby-Dick*, p. 579.
[46]   Melville, *Moby-Dick*, p. 583.
[47]   Melville, *Moby-Dick*, p. 180. Milton, to whom Melville alludes many times in *Moby-Dick*, compares the jostling elements Satan encounters in Chaos, shortly after departing Hell on his cosmic voyage to Eden (*PL* II.1019–20), to the Homeric whirlpool.
[48]   Melville, *Moby-Dick*, p. 634.
[49]   Melville, *Moby-Dick*, p. 635.

Thus, Melville takes the subtext of Poe's cask and makes it text. Its symbolic significance is reflected on by both the narrator and other characters, while also embellishing the Dantean tradition of whirlpools as an image of, and portal to, hell.

Poe's Whirlpools in Science Fiction and Science

The French translations of Poe of the 1840s and 1850s were beloved of Jules Verne, who was inspired to write his only work of criticism about 'Edgar Poe and his Works' (1864). Across sixteen large pages in the magazine *Musée des familles: Lectures de soir*, Verne seeks to introduce readers to Poe by surveying a range of Poe's tales. Even though Verne spares only seventeen words on 'MS. Found in a Bottle' and eight on 'A Descent', the latter's Maelstrom is featured as the subject of one of the six illustrations accompanying the article.[50] In contrast to the passing attention to 'MS. Found' and 'A Descent', Verne devotes four pages to *Aventures d'Arthur Gordon Pym*, Charles Baudelaire's 1858 French translation of Poe's 1838 novel, *The Narrative of Arthur Gordon Pym*. Written in a style meant to entertain the reader with Poe's story, however truncated, Verne's blow-by-blow summary is the first time Verne would retrace *Pym*'s course. The lengthiness of Verne's paraphrase evinces his fascination not just with the plot but with its ambiguous ending:

[a]nd now we rushed into the embraces of the cataract, where a chasm threw itself open to receive us. But there arose in our pathway a shrouded human figure, very far larger in its proportions than any dweller among men. And the hue of the skin of the figure was of the perfect whiteness of the snow.[51]

Echoing the claim made in the novel's concluding 'Note' that Pym's manuscript is incomplete, Verne quotes the last three paragraphs of Pym's narration.[52] He then remarks: '[e]t la récit est interrompu de la sorte. Qui le reprendra jamais? un plus audacieux que moi et plus hardi à s'avancer dans le domaine des choses impossibles' ('and that's how the narrative breaks off.

---

[50]   Jules Verne, 'Edgard Poe et ses œuvres', *Musée des familles: Lectures de soir* 30.7 (April 1864), 193–208, pp. 204 and 205.

[51]   Edgar Alan Poe, *The Narrative of Arthur Gordon Pym* (New York, 1838), p. 198.

[52]   Edgar Poe, *Aventures d'Arthur Gordon Pym*, trans. Charles Baudelaire (Paris, 1858), p. 274. In Baudelaire's edition, the 'Note' is assigned a chapter number and name, 'Conjectures', both of which weaken its pretence as an editorial paratext.

Who will ever take it up again? Somebody more daring than I am, some-body bolder at pushing on into the realm of things impossible').[53] Over thirty years later Verne answered his own challenge: he wrote a novel in which a reader of Poe's *Pym* discovers that Pym was a historical person and decides to search for him, using a heavily annotated copy of Poe's novel as his guide. Published periodically in 1897 as *Le Sphinx des glaces*, and translated poorly into English with substantial abridgements in 1898 as *An Antarctic Mystery*, Verne's novel 'works almost like a palimpsest on Poe's work'.[54]

In this second major engagement with *Pym*, Verne's characters not only encounter the characters and locations of Poe's novel, they also recapitulate Verne's prior engagement with *Pym*: the entirety of the fifth chapter com-prises Verne's narrator's paraphrase of Poe's novel, roughly twice the length of Verne's epitome in 1864. It includes more analysis, from the narrator's point of view, than Verne's 'Edgard Poe et ses œuvres' did, and the narra-tor even quotes, anonymously, Baudelaire's since-famous 'Notes nouvelles sur Edgar Poe', originally published as a preface to his second volume of translations of Poe's tales.[55] Like the chapter in which it is quoted, and like Verne's own effort at literary criticism, Baudelaire's preface is yet another form of recirculating Poe's texts. This instance goes so far as to repeat Poe's ideas from 'The Poetic Principle' as if they were Baudelaire's, but that is not the case with Verne's narrator's quotation of Baudelaire.[56] Verne acknowl-edges the source as 'le plus original de ses critiques' and we may presume that the most pertinent reason Baudelaire is not credited by name is that his preface was published in 1857, while Verne's story is set in 1839. To identify the source of the quotation would have exposed the anachro-nism. This chronological slippage is a microcosm of Poe's *The Journal of Julius Rodman* (1840), a travelogue inspired by and substantially imitat-

---

[53]   Jules Verne, 'Edgard Poe', p. 207. Translation is from Jules Verne, 'Appendix 2: Verne on Pym', in *The Sphinx of the Ice Realm: The First Complete English Translation*, trans. and ed. Frederick Paul Walter (Albany, 2012), 377–84, p. 384.

[54]   David Seed, 'Breaking the Bounds: The Rhetoric of Limits in the Works of Edgar Allan Poe, His Contemporaries and Adaptors', in *Anticipations: Essays on Early Science Fiction and Its Precursors*, ed. David Seed (Liverpool, 1995), 75–97, p. 88.

[55]   Jules Verne, 'Le Sphinx des glaces', ch. 5, *Magasin d'éducation et de recreation* (2nd series) 5.52 (1897), 105–115, p. 114, quoting Charles Baudelaire, 'Notes nou-velles sur Edgar Poe', in Edgar Poe, *Nouvelles histoires extraordinaries*, trans. Charles Baudelaire (Paris, 1857), v–xxiv, pp. xv–xvi.

[56]   Lois Boe Hyslop and Francis E. Hyslop Jnr, eds, *Baudelaire as Literary Critic* (University Park, PA, 1964), p. 114.

ing Lewis and Clark's *History of the Expedition* (1814) and Washington Irving's *Astoria* (1836). By setting the Journal in 1791–92, Poe's Rodman can appear to have anticipated Poe's sources, which are seen by the fictional editor of the Journal not as predecessors but as subsequent validators of Rodman's accounts.[57] Reflecting the relationship between Poe's text and its sources, Poe's narrator is dominated by anxiety that he has been preceded in his expedition: 'I could not help being aware that *some* civilized footsteps, although few, had preceded me in my journey—that *some* eyes before mine own had been enraptured with the scenes around me.'[58] Rodman must qualify his rivals as 'civilized' predecessors because his obsession with being able, one day, to experience a previously unseen scene depends on discounting indigenous experiences, without whose testimony, paradoxically, he would not have an image of his goal: '[b]ut I was anxious to *go on*—to get, if possible, beyond the extreme bounds of civilization—to gaze, if I could, upon those gigantic mountains of which the existence had been made known to us only by the vague accounts of the Indians.'[59] The spectacle of a gigantic mountain beyond the bounds of civilisation returns us, once again, to the last sighting by Dante's Ulysses, who shared Rodman's 'burning love ... *of the unknown*'.[60] Rodman's discrediting of indigenous predecessors in order to maintain the illusion that virginal territory could somewhere exist for him is an anachronistic endeavour. Rewriting the past, denying one's sources, or pre-dating the present are different methods for pretending priority, recapitulation in denial about its derivative nature.

By contrast, in *Le Sphinx*, as in many of his novels, Verne constantly foregrounds his predecessors. Verne had assured his publisher that familiarity with Poe's novel would not be necessary, so he devotes a chapter titled 'Le roman d'Edgar Poë' to paraphrasing *Pym*.[61] Verne's narrator concludes his summary of Poe's novel by quoting Pym's final lines, as Verne had done before. He then remarks: '[t]el est ce bizarre roman, enfanté par le génie ultra-humain du plus grand poète du Nouveau Monde. C'est ainsi qu'il se termine ... ou plutôt qi'il ne se termine pas' ('and there you have the peculiar novel created by the superhuman genius of the New World's greatest

---

[57]   See Seed, 'Breaking the Bounds', 85–8.

[58]   Edgar A. Poe, 'The Journal of Julius Rodman', ch. 5, *Burton's Gentleman's Magazine* 4.5 (May 1840), 206–10, p. 208 (emphasis in original).

[59]   Poe, 'Journal', p. 208 (emphasis in original).

[60]   Poe, 'Journal', pp. 207–8 (emphasis in original).

[61]   Verne, 'Le Sphinx', ch. 5, p. 105. See Jean Jules-Verne, *Jules Verne: A Biography*, trans. Roger Greaves (New York, 1976), p. 193.

poet. This is how it ends ... or rather doesn't end').[62] Having informed the reader about his predecessors' experiences by reprising the narrator's first encounters with them through *Pym*, the narrator can proceed to recount his second encounters with his predecessors. When he finally reaches the huge figure that perplexed Pym and his readers, he discovers that it 'n'était qu'un aimant colossal' ('was simply a colossal lodestone') 'd'une force d'attraction prodigieuse!' ('with prodigious attracting power!').[63] By revealing the giant figure to be a large rock, howsoever magnetic, Verne seems to have, in part, synthesised the conclusion of *Pym* with that of 'MS. Found', whose concluding note added in 1850 describes Mercator's map on which the north pole is 'represented by a black rock, towering to a pro-digious height' within the Polar Gulf.[64]

While *Le Sphinx* is certainly Verne's most extensive continuation of *Pym*'s ending, it was not the first. *Vingt mille lieues sous les mers* (*Twenty Thousand Leagues Under the Seas*) (1869–70) was the first novel in which Verne wrote a new ending for *Pym*. Verne's narrator Aronnax refers to Poe by name twice in the novel, but the first time is not in his capac-ity as a poet or storyteller. Poe's first credential in *Vingt mille lieues* is as an exceptional swimmer. After relating his fall overboard from the *Abraham Lincoln*, Aronnax admits to the reader that he is a good swimmer but no match for Byron or Poe, 'qui furent des maîtres' ('who are both masters').[65] Presumably, Aronnax alludes to Byron's four-mile swim across the Hellespont in 1810 to demonstrate that it was possible for Leander to have accomplished the same feat. Twenty-five years later, in response to a comparison drawn between Byron's and his own reputation for swim-ming, Poe dismissed it with the claim that '[a]ny swimmer "in the falls" in my days, would have swum the Hellespont, and thought nothing of the matter'.[66] While it is out of modesty that Aronnax rejects comparison of himself with Byron or Poe, Poe had rejected the comparison of himself to

---

[62]   Verne, 'Le Sphinx', ch. 5, p. 115. Translation from Verne, *Sphinx*, trans. Walter, p. 50.

[63]   Jules Verne, 'Le Sphinx des glaces', ch. 15 ('suite'), *Magasin d'éducation et de récréation* (2nd series) 6.71 (1897), 321–30, p. 326. Translation from Verne, *Sphinx*, trans. Walter, pp. 253, 252.

[64]   Edgar Allan Poe, 'MS. Found in a Bottle', in *The Works of the Late Edgar Allan Poe*, ed. N. P. Willis, J. R. Lowell, and R. W. Griswold, vol. 1 (1850), 150–160, p. 160.

[65]   Jules Verne, 'Vingt mille lieues sous les mers. Le tour de monde sous-marin', chs 7–8, *Magasin d'éducation et de récréation* 11.124 (1869), 97–100, p. 97. Translation from Jules Verne, *Twenty Thousand Leagues Under the Seas*, trans. William Butcher (Oxford, 1998), p. 41.

[66]   [Edgar A. Poe], 'Swimming', *Southern Literary Messenger* 1.9 (May 1835), 468.

his predecessor because '[i]t would have been a feat comparatively easy to swim twenty miles in still water'.[67] While Byron had retraced Leander's route in order to validate his mythical predecessor, Poe, like his Rodman, had discounted the value of his predecessor's act as if that of a rival. Aronnax's nod to Poe the swimmer occurs early in the novel, at the beginning of the fourth installment (chapters 7 and 8), and the next time Aronnax mentions Poe is in the novel's final installment, in the penultimate chapter. When Nemo has been navigating the North Atlantic without Aronnax knowing their bearings for two or three weeks, the latter describes his disorientation by comparison to both Poe and Pym:

> Je me sentais entraîné dans ce domaine de l'étrange où se mouvait à l'aise l'imagination surmenée d'Edgard Poë. A chaque instant, je m'attendais à voir, comme le fabuleux Gordon Pym, « *cette* figure humaine voilée, de proportion beaucoup plus vaste que celle d'aucun habitant de la terre, *jetée en travers de cette cataracte qui défend les abords du pôle!* » [emphases mine]

> (I felt myself carried off into the realm of the extra-natural, where Poe's overworked imagination moved at ease. At each moment I expected to see, like the fabulous Gordon Pym, 'a shrouded human figure, very far larger in its proportions than any dweller among men, thrown across the cataract which defends the approaches to the Pole'!)[68]

Aronnax quotes Baudelaire's translation of the penultimate sentence of Pym's narrative. But Aronnax extends the quotation by twelve words (indicated by my italics) that are not in Baudelaire's translation. A recent translator, Frederick Paul Walter, relocates the misleading inverted comma to a 'correct' position, banishing 'thrown across the cataract that guards the outskirts of the pole!' out from the quoted territory and into the realm of Verne's prose where it seems to belong.[69] But in so doing, Walter obscures Verne's impersonation of Poe via Aronnax. Verne's ventriloquism here may be regarded as intentional because, after its initial publication in

---

[67]   [Poe], 'Swimming', 468.

[68]   Jules Verne, 'Vingt mille lieues sous les mers. Le tour de monde sous-marin', chs. 22–3, *Magasin d'éducation et de récréation* 13.151 (20 June 1870), [193]–[199], p. [194] (printed as '294' but a correction on p. 225 notes that the preceding two sheets were mispaginated, so *'au lieu de:* pages 293 à 324 *lisez:* pages 193 à 224'). Italics indicate words not in Baudelaire's translation of Poe's *Pym*. Translation from Jules Verne, *Twenty Thousand Leagues*, trans. Butcher, p. 374. Butcher's translation maintains the misleading inclusion of Verne's words within inverted commas.

[69]   Jules Verne, *Amazing Journeys: Five Visionary Classics*, trans. Frederick Paul Walter (Albany, 2010), p. 534.

Magasin d'éducation et de récréation (1870), the *guillemet fermant* remains 'uncorrected' in the first single-volume edition (1871) and through, for example, the twenty-fourth printing (c. 1880).[70] It is also valid to presume that Verne knew Poe's passage well enough because, in his 1864 survey of Poe's works, Verne had quoted it with the words that do in fact follow it in Baudelaire's translation.[71]

For readers familiar with *Pym*, Aronnax's evocation of Poe's novel might set up an expectation that in this final installment the *Nautilus* would ultimately emerge, if not near the south pole, then in the southern hemisphere, which might in turn underline a parallel with Dante's Ulysses foreshadowed by the 'Outis' meaning of Nemo's anonym. However, the *Nautilus* surfaces near the Arctic, not the Antarctic. Aronnax learns the location from the crew's exclamations of 'Maelstrom! Maelstrom!' Verne's apparent misdirection by Aronnax's allusion to the southern polar conclusion of *Pym* might lead to the expectation now of a contrast with, or differentiation from, Ulysses; instead, Aronnax reinforces the Odyssean parallel. Yet if the expected Homeric allusion would be to Charybdis, Verne surprises the reader again by having Aronnax reflect that the Maelstrom is 'justement appelé le « Nombril d l'Océan, »' ('fittingly called the "navel of the ocean"').[72] This is the same epithet by which Athena refers to Calypso's island of Ogygia, the hero's location at the outset of the *Odyssey* (I.50). Then Aronnax describes the threat of the Maelstrom in terms that seem to derive from Ramus, as quoted by Erik Pontoppidan:

> Là sont aspirés non-seulement les navires, mais les baleines, mais aussi les ours blancs des régions boréales [...] Quel fracas que celui de ces eaux brisées sur les roches aiguës du fond, là où les corps les plus durs se brisent, là où les troncs d'arbres s'usent et se font « une fourrure de poils, » selon l'expression norwegienne!

> (Not only are ships sucked in, but also whales and even polar bears from the Arctic [...] What a din from the waters broken on the sharp rocks of the bottom, where the hardest bodies break up, where tree-trunks wear them-

---

[70]   Jules Verne, *Vingt mille lieues sous les mers. Illustré 111 dessins par de Neuville* (Paris, 1871), p. 427, and Jules Verne, *Vingt mille lieues sous les mers*, 24th printing, 2nd part (Paris, [c. 1880]), p. 345.

[71]   Verne, 'Edgard Poe', p. 207, quoting Poe, *Aventures d'Arthur Gordon Pym*, trans. Baudelaire, p. 273.

[72]   Verne, 'Vingt mille lieues', chs. 22–3, pp. '297' [197]. Translation from Jules Verne, *Twenty Thousand Leagues*, trans. Butcher, p. 379.

selves out, where they produce a 'fur of hair', as the Norwegian expression has it!)[73]

Aronnax's claim that a 'fur of hair' is a Norwegian expression is probably Verne's invention, but it appears to be a rephrasing of Ramus's description of trees 'torn to such a degree as if bristles grew upon them'.[74] Besides the shredded trees, the ships, whales, bears, and sharp rocks are all in Ramus's *Norriges Beskrivelse* (1735), and quoted by Pontoppidan. Even though, elsewhere in the novel, Aronnax mentions Pontoppidan twice, by name, as a source for stories about mysterious sea monsters and the giant squid, it is likely that Verne found the details for his description of the Maelstrom in Poe's 'A Descent'. The elements mentioned above are all included in Poe's quotation of Ramus from the *Encyclopedia Britannica* (1797), whose unacknowledged source is *The Natural History of Norway* (1755), the English translation of Pontoppidan's Danish *Norges Naturlige Historie* (1752).[75] Beyond those commonplaces, Verne's emphasis on the sound of the whirlpool is inspired directly by Poe. The specific words Aronnax chooses to describe the noise are borrowed from the French translation of 'A Descent'. Verne punctuates the beginning of three sentences in a row with different terms to convey the clamour: '[e]t quel *bruit* autour de notre frêle canot! Quels *mugissements* que l'écho répétait à une distance de plusieurs milles! Quel *fracas* que celui de ces eaux [...]' [emphases mine] ('[w]hat a noise around our frail boat! What moanings echoed from miles around! What a din from the waters [...]').[76] All three of these words, *bruit, mugissements,* and *fracas,* occur in the same paragraph in the first French translation of 'A Descent':

> mon attention fut éveillée par un *bruit* puissant, et qui grossissait à chaque minute, *bruit* pareil aux *mugissements* d'un immense troupeau de buffles épars sur quelque prairie américaine. [...] Mais c'était surtout entre la côte et Moskoe que la masse des eaux tumultueuses se ruait à grand *fracas.* [emphases mine]

[73]   Verne, 'Vingt mille lieues', chs. 22–3, pp. '297' [197] and '298' [198]. Translation from Jules Verne, *Twenty Thousand Leagues*, trans. Butcher, p. 379.

[74]   Erich Pontoppidan, *The Natural History of Norway* (London, 1755), p. 79, translating Erich Pontoppidan, *Norges Naturlige Historie* (Copenhagen, 1752), p. 126, quoting Jonas Ramus, *Norriges Beskrivelse* (Copenhagen, 1735), p. 234.

[75]   For the first recognition that *Britannica* lifted from Pontoppidan, see Edmund Clarence Stedman and George Edwards Woodberry, eds, *The Works of Edgar Allan Poe*, vol. 4 (Chicago, 1894), pp. 290–1.

[76]   Jules Verne, 'Vingt mille lieues', chs. 22–3, pp. '298' [198]. Translation from Jules Verne, *Twenty Thousand Leagues*, trans. Butcher, p. 379.

(I became aware of a loud and gradually increasing sound, like the moaning of a vast herd of buffaloes upon an American prairie; ... it was between Moskoe and the coast that the main uproar held its sway.)[77]

Besides descriptive detail, Verne also borrows plot elements from 'A Descent'. In *Vingt mille lieues*, after becoming caught in the whirlpool, the dinghy carrying Aronnax, Conseil, and Ned Land detaches from the *Nautilus*. As in Poe's story (though the hydrological explanations differ), the smaller craft escapes while the larger craft is taken under. In terms of its shape, however, the *Nautilus* has more in common with Poe's cylindrical cask than with his smack, and Aronnax has hope it might have survived the whirlpool. If so, Aronnax does not condemn Nemo. He hopes instead for his redemption, and remarks that '[s]i sa destinée est étrange, elle est sublime aussi' ('if his destiny is strange, it is also sublime').[78] In the final chapter of *Vingt mille lieues*, Aronnax asks, '[m]e croira-t-on? Je ne sais. Peu importe, après tout' ('[w]ill I be believed? I do not know, but that is not important').[79] Although a generic commonplace for fantastic narratives, Aronnax's words echo the final lines of 'A Descent': 'I told them my story – they did not believe it. I now tell it to *you* – and you will put no more faith in it than did the merry fishermen of Lofoden.'[80]

Nemo's descent into the Maelstrom was a harbinger of Poe's influence on science fiction. That influence is now known well and retold often, but it enters a phase of new imaginative reach a century after Verne's appropriation. In 1965, Arthur C. Clarke published 'Maelstrom II', a short story in which an astronaut must abandon his spacecraft at the apogee of its doomed arc from, and back to, the surface of the moon. During his ordeal, the astronaut remembers Poe's fisherman and reflects on his situation's relevance to his own circumstances: '[h]e, too, was trapped in a maelstrom, being whirled down to his doom; he, too, hoped to escape by abandoning his vessel. Though the forces involved were totally different, the parallel was striking.'[81] Clarke not only adapted Poe's tale as a science fiction story but also drew a direct analogy between Poe's whirlpool and a phenomenon

---

[77]   Edgar Poe, 'Une descente au maelstrom', trans. O. N., *Revue britannique* (6th ser.) 5 (September 1846), 182–203, p. 185. Poe, 'A Descent', pp. 235–6.

[78]   Verne, 'Vingt mille lieues', chs. 22–3, pp. '299' [199]. Translation from Jules Verne, *Twenty Thousand Leagues*, trans. Butcher, p. 381.

[79]   Verne, 'Vingt mille lieues', chs. 22–3, pp. '299' [199]. Translation from Jules Verne, *Twenty Thousand Leagues*, trans. Butcher, p. 380.

[80]   Poe, 'A Descent', p. 241.

[81]   Arthur C. Clarke, 'Maelstrom II', *Playboy* 12.4 (April 1965), 84–6, 90, 178, and 180, p. 90.

specific to outer space. When the contemporary resurgence of research and public interest in black holes would assign that particular phenomenon as the heir to, and the dominant tenor for, the meanings previously ascribed to the whirlpool in science and science fiction, an enduring cultural association would be forged.

Walt Disney's adaptation of *20,000 Leagues Under the Sea* (1954), directed by Richard Fleisher, does not retain the whirlpool conclusion of Verne's novel. Instead, the film's special-effects set-piece is the battle with the giant squid; in the film's denouement, the *Nautilus* strikes a reef, floods, and sinks. Twenty-five years later, however, the film would inspire another Disney film that not only revisits Verne's Maelstrom and Dante's hell but makes their novel combination the film's focus. The most expensive Disney production at the time, and the first Disney film rated PG, Gary Nelson's *The Black Hole* (1979) is a post-*Star Wars* attempt to retell *20,000 Leagues* in space, with hints of *The Flying Dutchman* and Joseph Conrad's *Heart of Darkness* (1899). Despite its inferiority to both *20,000 Leagues* and *Star Wars*, it has many individual elements that recommend it: the production design, the character design of an evil robot, the memorable score by John Barry, and above all the visual impact of the *USS Cygnus*, a flying Eiffel Tower lit up like the Crystal Palace by night. Lost twenty years before, the *Cygnus* (named, presumably, after the first black hole to be tentatively identified) is discovered orbiting a black hole by a passel of astronauts aboard the *Palomino* including Ernest Borgnine, Joseph Bottoms, Robert Forster, Yvette Mimieux, Anthony Perkins, and a knock-off R2-D2 with a voice like C-3PO.[82] Viewing a holographic image of the funnel-shaped black hole, Borgnine's character calls it 'straight out of Dante's *Inferno*', and Bottoms' character remarks that 'Every time I see one of those things I expect to spot some guy in red with horns and a pitchfork'. Both on the holographic image, and when viewed through the ship's windows, the black hole is first depicted as a funnel of blue swirls; over the course of the film the blues change increasingly to reds. Once aboard the *Cygnus*, the astronauts find a crew of robots captained by the single human survivor of the mission, Dr. Hans Reinhardt (played by Maximillian Schell). His first mate is a frightening robot who is red in colour, with a horned visor and buzzsaw hands in lieu of a pitchfork. This robot is named Maximilian, like the actor playing Reinhardt, also clothed in red, and presumably represents Reinhardt's shadow self.

---

[82]   Cygnus X-1 was also the subject of a bet between Stephen Hawking and Kip Thorne, made in December 1974 and conceded by Hawking in June 1990, that it did contain a black hole. See Marcia Bartusiak, *Black Hole* (New Haven, 2015), p. 156.

Their mirroring, and Maximillian's murder of Perkins's character against Reinhardt's orders, evokes the relationship between Dr. Morbius and his id monster in *Forbidden Planet* (1956).

Reinhardt is obsessed with the black hole and has invented an anti-gravity bubble to protect his ship while he studies it. His plan is to travel through the black hole or, as the admiring scientist played by Perkins phrases it, to 'literally voyage into the mind of God'. The visiting astronauts discover that the crew of masked androids are in fact the human crew, now lobotomised, whom Reinhard had claimed left the ship voluntarily. The astronauts escape the *Cygnus* in a probe ship before Reinhard pilots the *Cygnus* into the vortex, but both vessels are sucked into the black hole. Unable to escape the gravitational influence of Clarke and Stanley Kubrick, a half-hearted imitation of the stargate sequence from *2001: A Space Odyssey* (1968) ensues, to portray the 'descent'. At the bottom of the black hole, Reinhardt arrives in hell. He fuses with his robotic shadow self, Maximilian, and appears to become trapped within the robot, as they survey a panoramic landscape of hell that recalls Harry Lachman's *Dante's Inferno* (1935). These images are then replaced by a crystalline cathedral nave through which a flying, angelic if not Beatrician, figure leads the astronauts' probe out of the black hole and back to regular space. The film ends abruptly, having relied on visual storytelling without any exposition or dialogue for its final ten minutes. *The Black Hole* thus synthesises the whirlpool that pulls down Captain Nemo with Dante's funnel-shaped abyss, together with a third image of the effects of a black hole according to general relativity. The black hole's warping of space and time for those pulled into it is represented by the stretching and warping of the film frames during the 'descent' sequence. Besides reflecting astrophysicists' claims of what would happen to someone who enters a black hole, it also parallels Dante's confusion at hell's lowest point, where directionality and vertical orientation become relative. Nearly ten years later, Stephen Hawking quoted the *Inferno* in his own description of the effects on astronauts, like those in the movie, who might fall into a black hole:

> [o]ne could well say of the event horizon what the poet Dante said of the entrance to Hell: 'All hope abandon, ye who enter here.' Anything or anyone who falls through the event horizon will soon reach the region of infinite density and the end of time.[83]

---

[83]   Stephen Hawking, *A Brief History of Time: From the Big Bang to Black Holes* (Toronto, 1988), p. 89.

Naturally, Hawking's point is scientific rather than poetic. It is no criticism of his literary aside that Gary Nelson's film is perhaps a degree truer to Dante's vision, however inelegant its execution. By providing his inadvertent pilgrims with a route out of the bottom of hell, not by turning around but by continuing forward, through a thirty-second *Paradiso*, before emerging to see once more the stars, Nelson pays off the promise made by Borgnine in the film's first scene that we are looking at something out of Dante.

A year before Hawking's *A Brief History of Time* (1988), Jean-Pierre Luminet had published his own book on *Les Trous Noirs* (1987). Many of his chapters and subsections are accompanied by epigraphs. The last section of his ninth chapter, 'The far horizon', about 'The inverted world' of the black hole interior, bears the same inscription from the *Inferno* that Hawking quotes: 'All hope abandon, ye who enter here.'[84] Luminet also doubles down on the commonplace analogy between black holes and whirlpools by quoting not one but two stories by Poe and mentioning Verne in passing. He takes for his eleventh chapter the title 'A descent into the maelstrom' and appends an epigraph from Poe's tale: 'I became possessed with the keenest curiosity about the whirl itself. I positively felt a wish to explore its depths, even at the sacrifice I was going to make; and my principal grief was that I should never be able to tell my old companions on shore about the mysteries I should see.'[85] The third section he titles 'The cosmic maelstrom', and he takes his epigraph from the last sentences of 'Manuscript found in a bottle': '[b]ut little time will be left to me to ponder upon my destiny! The circles rapidly grow small—we are plunging madly within the grasp of the whirlpool—and amid a roaring and bellowing thundering of ocean and of tempest, the ship is quivering—oh! God!—and ... is going down!'[86] Luminet then explains the scientific purpose of these literary embellishments:

> [t]here is a profound analogy between a rotating black hole and the familiar phenomenon of a vortex, whether it be the swirling water which goes down a plug hole when a bath is emptied, or the giant whirlpools produced by sea currents, such as the legendary maelstrom off the coast of Norway (described by Edgar Allen [sic] Poe in his *Tales of the Grotesque and Arabesque*), or even the Corrievreckan in the Scottish Hebrides mentioned by Jules Verne in his book *The Green Ray*.[87]

---

[84]   Jean-Pierre Luminet, *Black Holes*, trans. Alison Bullough and Andrew King (Cambridge, 1992), p. 134.

[85]   Luminet, *Black Holes*, p. 147.

[86]   Luminet, *Black Holes*, p. 150.

[87]   Luminet, *Black Holes*, p. 150.

A footnote to this last remark then adds: '[a]lso it should not be forgotten that at the end of *Twenty Thousand Leagues under the Sea*, Jules Verne caused the submarine *Nautilus* to disappear into one of these marine abysses.'[88] The fact that the whirlpool analogy to black holes endures in scientific texts of both the popular and technical variety, as well as in science fiction texts, speaks to its resonance as a theoretical, visual, and cultural metaphor. Science fiction texts that have continued to associate black holes with hell, such as *Event Horizon* (1997) and *Doctor Who* ('The Impossible Planet' and 'The Satan Pit', 2006), are indebted to the history of their cultural predecessors, whirlpools, and the long association of whirlpools with hell. These three elements – hell, whirlpool, and black hole – together form an epitome of the cosmographical range of the terrifying sublime, from subterranean cavities to the surface of the globe to the heights of stars.

Works Cited

2001: A Space Odyssey (1968), dir. Stanley Kubrick

20,000 Leagues Under The Sea (1954), dir. Richard Fleischer

Alighieri, Dante, *Inferno 1: Italian Text and Translation*, vol. 1, part 1, of *The Divine Comedy*, trans. and ed. Charles S. Singleton, Bollingen Series 80 (Princeton, 1989)

Bartusiak, Marcia, *Black Hole* (New Haven, 2015)

Baudelaire, Charles, 'Notes nouvelles sur Edgar Poe', in Edgar Poe, *Nouvelles histoires extraordinaires*, trans. Charles Baudelaire (Paris, 1857), v–xxiv

'Breakthrough Discovery in Astronomy: First Ever Image of a Black Hole', posted by European Commission, 10 April 2017, https://www.youtube.com/watch?v=Dr20f19czeE

The Black Hole (1979), dir. Gary Nelson

Clarke, Arthur C., 'Maelstrom II', *Playboy* 12.4 (April 1965), 84–6, 90, 178, and 180

Clery, Daniel, 'For the First Time, You Can See What a Black Hole Looks Like', *Science*, 10 April 2019, https://www.sciencemag.org/news/2019/04/black-hole

Conrad, Joseph, *Heart of Darkness*, in Hynes, Samuel, ed., *The Complete Short Fiction of Joseph Conrad* 4 vols (1992–3); vol. 3, *The Tales* (London, 1992), 1–86.

Crane, Leah, 'First Ever Real Image of a Black Hole Revealed',

---

88   Luminet, *Black Holes*, p. 150, n. 4.

New Scientist, 10 April 2019, https://www.newscientist.com/article/2199330-first-ever-real-image-of-a-black-hole-revealed

Dante's Inferno (1935), dir. Harry Lachman

Doctor Who, 'The Impossible Planet' (2006), dir. James Strong

Doctor Who, 'The Satan Pit' (2006), dir. James Strong

Event Horizon (1997), dir. Paul W. S. Anderson

Finholt, Richard D., 'The Vision at the Brink of the Abyss: "A Descent into the Maelstrom" in the Light of Poe's Cosmology', *The Georgia Review* 27.3 (Fall 1973), 356–66

Hawking, Stephen, *A Brief History of Time: From the Big Bang to Black Holes* (Toronto, 1988)

Homer, *The Odyssey of Homer*, trans. Richard Lattimore (New York, 1991)

Hyslop, Lois Boe, and Francis E. Hyslop Jnr, eds, *Baudelaire as Literary Critic* (University Park, PA, 1964)

Jules-Verne, Jean, *Jules Verne: A Biography*, trans. Roger Greaves (New York, 1976)

Kircher, Athanasius, *Mundus Subterraneus* (Amsterdam, 1664)

Luminet, Jean-Pierre, *Black Holes*, trans. Alison Bullough and Andrew King (Cambridge, 1992)

McGill, Meredith L., *American Literature and the Culture of Reprinting, 1834–1853* (Philadelphia, 2003)

Melville, Herman, *Moby-Dick* (New York, 1851)

Minahen, Charles D., *Vortex/t: The Poetics of Turbulence* (University Park, PA, 1992)

Milton, John, *Paradise Lost*, ed. Alastair Fowler, 2nd edn (Harlow, 1998)

Ovid, *Metamorphoses*, trans. Frank Justus Miller, 2 vols (Cambridge, MA, 1916)

Poe, Edgar A., 'American Prose Writers. No. 2. N. P. Willis', *The Broadway Journal* 1.3 (18 January 1845), 33–48

–––––, *Aventures d'Arthur Gordon Pym*, trans. Charles Baudelaire (Paris, 1858)

–––––, 'Une descente au maelstrom', trans. O. N., *Revue britannique* (6th ser.) 5 (September 1846), 182–203

–––––, 'A Descent into the Maelstrom', *Graham's Magazine* 18.5 (May 1841), 235–41

–––––, 'The Fall of the House of Usher', *Burton's Gentleman's Magazine* 5.3 (September 1839), 145–52

–––––, 'The Imp of the Perverse', *Graham's Magazine* 28.1 (July 1845), 1–3

–––––, 'The Journal of Julius Rodman', ch. 5, *Burton's Gentleman's Magazine* 4.5 (May 1840), 206–10

–––––, 'The Literati of New York City', *Godey's Lady's Book* 32.5 (May

1846), 194–201

—————, 'Metzengerstein', *Southern Literary Messenger* 2.2 (January 1836), 97–100

—————, 'MS. Found in a Bottle', *Baltimore Saturday Visiter* 3.38 (19 October 1833), 1, columns 1–5

[—————], *The Narrative of Arthur Gordon Pym* (New York, 1838)

—————, 'Review of "Alciphron, a Poem"', *Burton's Gentleman's Magazine* 6.1 (January 1840), 53–56

—————, 'Review of *Ballads and Other Poems*', *Graham's Magazine* 20.4 (April 1842), 248–51

[—————], 'Swimming', *Southern Literary Messenger* 1.9 (May 1835), 468

Pontoppidan, Erich, *The Natural History of Norway* (London, 1755)

—————, *Norges Naturlige Historie* (Copenhagen, 1752)

Ramus, Jonas, *Norriges Beskrivelse* (Copenhagen, 1735)

—————, *Ulysses et Otinus Unus & idem* (Copenhagen, 1702)

Sale, George, trans., *The Koran; Commonly Called the Alcoran of Mohammed: Translated from the Original Arabic. With Explanatory Notes, Taken from the Most Approved Commentators. To which is Prefixed a Preliminary Discourse*, 2 vols (London, 1821)

Seed, David, 'Breaking the Bounds: The Rhetoric of Limits in the Works of Edgar Allan Poe, His Contemporaries and Adaptors', in *Anticipations: Essays on Early Science Fiction and Its Precursors*, ed. David Seed (Liverpool, 1995), 75–97

Star Wars (1977), dir. George Lucas

Stedman, Edmund Clarence, and George Edwards Woodberry, eds, *The Works of Edgar Allan Poe*, vol. 4 (Chicago, 1894)

Verne, Jules, *Amazing Journeys: Five Visionary Classics*, trans. Frederick Paul Walter (Albany, 2010)

—————, 'Appendix 2: Verne on Pym', in *The Sphinx of the Ice Realm: The First Complete English Translation*, trans. and ed. Frederick Paul Walter (Albany, 2012), 377–84

—————, 'Edgard Poe et ses œuvres', *Musée des familles: Lectures de soir* 30.7 (April 1864), 193–208

—————, 'Le Sphinx des glaces', ch. 5, *Magasin d'éducation et de recreation* (2nd series) 5.52 (1897), 105–15

—————, *The Sphinx of the Ice Realm: The First Complete English Translation*, trans. and ed. Frederick Paul Walter (Albany, 2012)

—————, *Twenty Thousand Leagues Under the Seas*, trans. William Butcher (Oxford, 1998)

—————, 'Vingt mille lieues sous les mers. Le tour de monde sous-marin', chs 7–8, *Magasin d'éducation et de récréation* 11.124 (1869), 97–100

–––––, 'Vingt mille lieues sous les mers. Le tour de monde sous-marin', chs 22–23, *Magasin d'éducation et de récréation* 13.151 (20 June 1870), '293' [193]–'299' [199]

–––––, *Vingt mille lieues sous les mers. Illustré 111 dessins par de Neuville* (Paris, 1871)

–––––, *Vingt mille lieues sous les mers*, 24th printing, 2nd part (Paris, [c.1880])

Virgil, *Aeneid VII–XII – The Minor Poems*, trans. H. R. Fairclough, rev. edn (Cambridge, MA, 1934)

Virgil, *Eclogues – Georgics – Aeneid I–VI*, trans. H. R. Fairclough, rev. edn (Cambridge, MA, 1935)

Wilbur, Richard, 'The House of Poe', in Robert Hillyer, Richard Wilbur, and Cleanth Brooks, *Anniversary Lectures, 1959* (Washington, 1959), 21–38

Wolf, Burkhardt, 'Muses of Cartography: Charting Odysseus from Homer to Joyce', trans. E. A. Beeson, *Literature and Cartography: Theories, Histories, Genres*, ed. Anders Engberg-Pederson (Cambridge, MA, 2017), 143–72

The Song of Orpheus

MARGARET KEAN INTERVIEWS DAVID ALMOND

A Song for Ella Grey (2014) won the Guardian Children's Fiction Award 2015. Claire is in love with her best friend, Ella Grey, but Ella has fallen passionately in love with Orpheus. When tragedy strikes, Claire agrees to help Orpheus break through the gates that bar entry to the Ouseburn river to begin his descent into the dark in an attempt to bring Ella back from Death. This is Claire's story.

MK In your reworking of the Orpheus myth in *A Song for Ella Grey* (2014) you locate the entrance to Hades in post-industrial Newcastle. You set most of your stories in the North-East, and often employ motifs of descent. There are plots that tumble us down a mineshaft or ask us to find the courage to cross the threshold of a dark tunnel mouth or to navigate a tidal river. What is the importance of place for your storytelling?

DA I started to do it first in a collection of stories that became *Counting Stars* (2000). I began deliberately to use the landscape of Tyneside and of Felling, and it was a place that was filled with memories for me. The stories were a way of dealing with some tragic instances in my own life: a couple of deaths. For the first time, I found a way to write stories that could cope with those things without just saying, "Oh, wasn't it terrible". It brought some kind of composure to my personal experiences to craft them into stories, and this involved deliberately using the landscape, the streets and the fields and the river and the sea. That became the imaginary geography in which all these stories could take place. I had tried to do it before. I had written about Northumberland, but once I began to use deeply personal experience, that's when the landscape opened up again. I could see it anew as an undiscovered place that I could explore, and plunder, and search through, and find out things about myself, and also find some kind of common experience. At that point the landscape began to take on some kind of mythic character for me.

MK Is your phrase 'imaginative geography' a reflection of the way that you take us through those journeys?

DA These weren't just stories about me, they were stories about my sisters, my brother, my parents, and, beyond that, they were a broader sharing of a communal experience. If I was going to write about this place, these characters, then I had a kind of responsibility to be sure that the people who lived inside that landscape would be able to read and share the stories. But there is something about the strange dynamism of writing for a small group of people whom I love and know and have experiences with that can reach out to the broader community.

MK The protagonists in your stories often need to discover more about the past to better understand and inhabit their own present. Does this model how knowledge can be passed forward to the next generation?

DA I never planned to write for young people or for children. It was only when I began to write *Skellig* [1998, Whitbread Children's Book of the Year and awarded the Carnegie Medal] that I realised, "Oh! This is a book for young people". And these really mysterious things began to happen: things that I seemed to have nothing to do with it. The characters that I was writing about would start to take these dangerous journeys and go into places of darkness. My job was to follow them, and the process of writing itself became a journey.

MK Returning to some of the early personal experiences that you were mentioning (the death of your sister, for example) was presumably difficult?

DA Yes, but I was going into those experiences with language, with the ability to write stories. You don't go into those places totally exposed, you go in with these tools and toys that allow exploration. So when I was writing *Counting Stars*, I was aware that I was going into what were for me very dangerous areas. Areas which could have just released horrors. But because I was going in there with language and with storytelling, it was a way of controlling those situations. I went in, brought out a story, and shared the story with the world. *Ella Grey* is a culmination of that process. I had begun to realise what I was doing, and I thought it is time to tell this story: the Orpheus story.

MK So the Orpheus myth is something that you have thought about for a long time?

DA I used to be a primary school teacher, and Orpheus was one of the stories I told to children on council estates in Gateshead. They loved it. We did it as a dramatisation in an assembly once, a Georgie Orpheus: he's lost his wife, and he wants her back. The kids all got it because everyone has experience of some kind of loss or grief. It has a kind of elemental power.

Maybe also, the Orpheus story was one of my routes out of Catholicism: to see that a journey to hell didn't have to involve getting stuck down there. A journey to the underworld could be a positive journey. You went down and came out with something so powerful that it could change the world, and you were changed in the process. So, it was a personal recreation of my Catholicism, my becoming Orpheus.

MK To become Orphic, in the sense of acknowledging the recreative power of both singer and song, is at the core of *Ella Grey*. The active verb 'I sing' becomes intensely important as the story reaches its climax, where Orpheus is in the underworld. The narration pays a great deal of attention to who is singing, but also to the nature of song and how it can alter and transfer allegiance, how it can come to belong to more than one voice or generation.

DA The notion of song has become more and more important to me over the years. Now, I'm writing poetry, and recently I've done work with musicians. I worked with Kathryn Tickell, a Northumbrian pipe player and composer, on a touring piece built around my short story, *The Dam* (2018), about the building of the Kielder Dam in Northumberland [a 1980s engineering project which involved flooding the Kielder Valley]. The story is all about song and the continuity of music, despite the apparent destruction. One of the things we did on stage was the 'I sing' passage from *A Song for Ella Grey*. We performed it as spoken word with music: "I sing", "I sing", "I sing", "I sang".

MK The passage is a strikingly affirmative piece of prose poetry within the novel, which celebrates life and the natural world. It must have made for a remarkable live performance.

DA My writing all these years has been about voice, about singing out, about bringing something back that is beautiful, so to be on a stage and to present it to a live audience felt important. Writing is never just something on the page. It's something that lifts off the page, then goes into people's ears, and into their minds, and into their memories, and into their futures. Once you have entranced the audience with music – which is what you are trying to do with language in a book – they just open themselves to you. I have a great sense that this will help me in my future writing: to know what people want. They positively want to be moved, to be made to laugh and to cry.

MK *Ella Grey* is the narration of a new story, which insists on the immediate, conscious vitality of young adults in springtime, but it beats in time with rhythms that stretch far back in terms of a cultural inheritance.

DA I wrote it when my own daughter was about fifteen. I saw her in these friendship groups, and I saw the wonderful connections that they made between each other. It had to be a story about love, about growing up, about discovering their sexuality, and who they were, and what they were going to be. It is also a story of coming up against the whole idea of loss, love and loss: the discovery that love and loss are so deeply connected. Finding how to write it was a matter of knowing who the narrator was. As soon as I found out who the narrator was, the story took its own path. When something needed to happen, there was a kind of inevitability about it: "Oh, then that's how this happens!" And it was strange because obviously you know the story. You know what is going to happen. You think, "Oh gosh, she is going to die *again*. He is going to go down there *again*". But it had a beautiful rhythm and momentum to it once I found Claire's voice. Clare had to tell the story, and right from the start she is telling you: "I know how this ends up, you know how this ends up. This is it, this is how it happens". Initially I thought Ella would tell the story, Eurydice would tell the story. But then I realised she can't. Once the story begins, she's lost, so she can't tell you anything. And, of course, Orpheus couldn't tell the story, except for his section. So it had to be someone who loved Ella: Claire is our representative in loving Ella, and in telling this story that has been told since the beginning of time. It is as if Claire is saying: "you all know this story, you all know how it is going to end up. Oh no! It is my turn to tell it. I don't want to tell it but I am going to tell you it". Once Claire started to tell the story, she became aware of things I, as a storyteller, might be aware of: the cracks in the pavement that lead down to the underworld, an awareness of the coalmines underneath our feet.

MK In an earlier novel, *My Name is Mina* (2010), you have the main character work out that, if she wants to tell the story of her own journey to the underworld, she will have to use the third person. Are you building on that insight when, in *Ella Grey*, you provide a narrative that allows both the first and the third person to be involved in retelling the Orpheus myth?

DA I was really aware when I was writing Mina that she kind of represented me: she went on these journeys and came back and told me. The writer's journey is about going into the places of darkness and finding ways to get there through different characters, through different kinds of masks, so the characters tell you their stories. There was a sense when I was writing *Ella Grey* of putting on a series of masks, and one of the masks was Claire. The part of the story that couldn't be told by Claire was the Orphic journey: she hadn't been there. But she could find a way of telling it by doing that writer-y thing of leaping out of self and psyche. I got closer and closer to the moment when Orpheus has to go down. And I thought "how is he going to do that?", and then I thought of masks: Claire has to put on a mask and become Orpheus. She finds a different kind of articulation, a different way of speaking, of singing, because she had to stay at the gates while Orpheus goes down.

MK You don't flinch from the violence of the myth: the Maenads still tear Orpheus apart, limb from limb. You simply include this and let them state their case. Does their channelling of such an intense emotive reaction warn your readers that one baffling potential aspect of love is as something that is going to be destructive?

DA Whenever I have used violence, it is not totally destructive. Orpheus is scattered and eaten by dogs and crows and seagulls, but the song is heard. Flannery O'Conner said that she found that acts of violence could bring her characters into a state in which they could receive grace. A very dark notion, so I am not saying that I am doing that, but there is something about violence that can produce a more benign result. It is a very Catholic notion that pain can put you in a position that means you can receive grace. And it is a part of Catholicism which I detest. But it seems to make the writing the death of Orpheus in the way that I did just have to be there.

MK I'd like to turn to a different aspect of the reading experience with this book, which is so beautifully designed and illustrated. One of its most striking elements is the reversal of the reading norm for the journey to Hades: black pages with white typeface provide the way to progress through the darkness. In your acceptance speech for the Hans Christian Andersen Prize [2010], and again at the start of *Ella Grey*, you identified the dynamic of storytelling as leading towards the light. You have said before that stories are told at night-time because it is dark; story being what children need to overcome their fears and to help them to grow.

Perhaps in *Ella Grey*, this notion is realised in a Hades story told in white lettering on intensely dark pages?

DA I take care with how my stories look on the computer screen as I am writing, careful of the line lengths and white space. The black pages were the designer's idea. It gives great elegance to the retelling, and is a collaboration between the writer, illustrator, editor, and publisher.

MK Hell can be experienced in ways which are not cognitive, and to hold open your novel at the Hades section is, to me, a starting point for an immersive experience. The experience is comprehended visually, to pull me in and down. Yet the layout used, the fonts and the graphics, the shaping of movement in the type on the page, 'dis'locates me just enough to see typography as a tool with which to explore the experience of Hell.

DA A sense of the page itself is becoming more interesting to me, of the page as a doorway, an entrance point. We are not on the page, we are in the page. I recently read an amazing book, *The Mind in the Cave* [by David Lewis-Williams, 2002], about cave painting. He suggests that the artists did not paint onto walls, but saw the wall itself as a thing which they went through, through the act of drawing. The act of making those marks was a way of accessing something that was just on the other side of the wall.

MK When Ella touches Orpheus's shoulder, he can't help but turn. It is the 'gentlest of touches', but to respond is to cause her final demise. As readers, we desire to be with the page, to access fully what it can show us, but by holding on to this experience we know we have to accept the loss of Ella.

DA The Orphic story is a way of recreating what has been lost. I think that is what stories are. Every time a story is told, something that is told in the story is recreated again, so we don't lose these things. One of the purposes of storytelling is to sing the world into existence. I love the sense that if you do something beautifully enough, the world will respond, and will grow, and will be reformed. *A Song for Ella Grey* is about going down into the underworld, but you bring the story back again. At the heart of this is something so beautiful, that the world just says: "Yes! I will rise".

Works Cited

Almond, David, *A Song for Ella Grey*, illus. Karen Radford (London, 2014)

-----, *Counting Stars* (London, 2000)

-----, *The Dam*, illus. Levi Pinfold (London, 2018)

-----, *My Name is Mina* (London, 2010)

-----, *Skellig* (London, 1998)

Lewis-Williams, David, *The Mind in the Cave: Consciousness and the Origins of Art* (London, 2002)

Index